"Dave writes with obvious respect for writers. He goes deep into the heart and head with advice that leads to success. A first-class book."
—Lucille S. deView, syndicated columnist
and writing coach for major newspapers

"Provides not only the nuts and bolts, but also the power tools. I learned to write from Dave's books."
—Donna Davidson, author of award-winning novels
Elizabeth's Gift and *Lord Kingsford's Quest*

"A wonderfully helpful guide for anyone who wants to start writing— and keep writing."
—Stedman Mays, agent, Scribblers House LLC Literary Agency

"A must-have book for writers who want to turn their hobby into a real business. Dave provides tips, tools, and rules of writer etiquette which will make your queries stand out from the hundreds of others that cross an editor's desk each week. Don't miss this investment in your career."
—Shelly Mellott, Editor-in-Chief, *scr(i)pt* magazine

"Dave, what you have said about business writing is right on target. The pay can be very good, indeed. In fact, I've averaged $80-$100 an hour, and I'm hardly a superstar."
—Jim Fisher, copywriter and author of the upcoming book
Personal Ad Magic

To Bill Hathoot
Keep Writing
David R. Trottier

WRITE FROM THE HEART and SELL WHAT YOU WRITE

Dave Trottier mentors you at every step of the writing and selling process through practical advice, useful worksheets, and insightful writing activities.

Learn what you *must* know to succeed in these areas: Novels and nonfiction books • Writing for children • Articles and columns for magazines and newspapers • Business writing and copywriting • Self-publishing and e-publishing • Direct mail, PR, newsletters, technical writing • Ghosting, résumés, speeches, grant proposals • Movies, TV, radio, stage, and interactive • Video/DVD scripts for business • Humor, greeting cards, fillers, and games • Writing for non-profits, causes, education, and government • And more

The Freelance Writer's Bible also includes specific guidance:

- Set up your writing business for almost nothing
- Double your writing income
- Create a writing mission statement
- Get off to a fast and profitable start
- Turn personal and writing blocks into steppingstones
- Learn how to get writing assignments and enjoy a competitive edge
- Discover the great paradox of creativity
- Get paid before you write
- Convert the writing process into a great writing adventure
- Learn the seven secrets to great query letters
- Become a writing entrepreneur and build your empire
- Stay focused with a master plan and weekly action plans
- And much, much more

— Everything you need under one cover —

The Freelance Writer's Bible

Your Guide

to a Profitable

Writing Career

Within One Year

BY DAVID TROTTIER

SILMAN-JAMES PRESS ✳ LOS ANGELES

William C. Heidemann, "Sweet William Cottage" story, © 2005 William C. Heidemann
Kerry Cox, "Bed of Lies" query letter, © 1993, 2005 Kerry Cox with permission of *Hollywood Scriptwriter.*
J. D. Taylor, excerpt from his essay "Apples and Oranges," © 2005 J. D. Taylor
Excerpts from *2004 Writer's Market* copyright © 2003 edited by Kathryn S. Brogan and Robert Lee Brewer. Used with kind permission of Writer's Digest Books, an imprint of F+W Publications, Inc. Visit your local bookseller or call 800 754-2912.
Denis Waitley, excerpt from his audio program *The Psychology of Winning,* © 1995, 2005 Denis Waitley.
Jim "Bongo" Anderson, excerpts from his essay "Where To Ski?" © 2005 James Anderson.

First edition
10 9 8 7 6 5 4 3 2 1

Library of Congress Cataloging-in-Publication Data

Trottier, David.
The freelance writer's bible : your guide to a profitable writing career within one year / by David Trottier.-- 1st ed.
p. cm.
Includes index.
ISBN 1-879505-85-1
1. Authorship. 2. Authorship--Vocational guidance. I. Title.
PN147.T76 2006
808'.02--dc22
2005030142

Cover design by Heidi Frieder

Printed in the United States of America.

Silman-James Press

1181 Angelo Drive
Beverly Hills, CA 90210

*Dedicated to the developing writer
and to students and clients
who have inspired me with their dedication and creative vision.*

Acknowledgments

I thank Gwen Feldman and Jim Fox, my publishers, for their efforts in making this work better. I am particularly grateful to Greg Alt, Terri Jadick, and Lucille S. deView for reading the manuscript before publication. The following individuals also offered helpful suggestions, encouragement, or information: Jeff Stowell, Don Moriarty, Dan Viets, Robert Olague, Veronica Viers, David R. Smith, Connie Snape-Norton, Don Miles, and my wonderful wife, Marsha Sawyer-Trottier.

Contents

Book I – Discover your creative vision

What to expect from your writer's journey *3*

I write; therefore, I am *5*
> *Writing commitment for the next 30 days – Your safe harbor – Your legacy – A letter to your child – What the world needs now is . . . – Ten values – Inventory of past creative experiences – Values priorities*

The possible dream *14*
> *What you want from writing, Part 1 – What you want from writing, Part 2 – Three categories of writing opportunities – If I were a rich man – Your writing attitudes and values – What do you read? – Five adjectives*

Your creative vision and your writing mission *20*
> *Preparing for your quest – Your writing mission statement*

Book II – Write with freedom and confidence

What stops you from writing? *27*
> *My first writing assignment – Fears, blocks, and barriers – Hurdling barriers and breaking through blocks: Your own mini-movie, starring you – Your inner kingdom*

Alchemy: Converting blocks into steppingstones *35*
> *1. Procrastination or scribaphobia (fear of writing) – 2. Perfectionism – 3. Comparing yourself to Hemingway – 4. Museheimer's Disease – 5. Fear of not being as good as you had hoped – 6. Fear of wasting time – 7. Exaggerating fears and problems – 8. Fear of failure*

and self-doubt – 9. Fear of success – 10. Negative self-talk – 11. Anger – 12. Anxiety – 13. Lack of creativity, skills, ability, etc. – Character/Craft Worksheet: Talents and Skills You Possess – 14. Self-defeating attitudes – 15. Chronic Ambivalence Syndrome – 16. Stuckitis – 17. Not enough time – Time log – Time tally – Time evaluation – My schedule for my writing business

Creativity 52
Relaxing into the Alpha Writer State – Your brain is a two-piston writing machine – What is creativity? – A hippaglobium activity – The great paradox

The Writing Process 63
1. Generate ideas – 2. Set project parameters – Create a writing project – 3. Write the first draft – 4. Revise for content – 5. Polish for publication – Write a brief narrative

Book III — Sell to 17 key writing markets

Setting up your writing business for little or no money 87

Fee Guidelines for Freelance Copywriters 92

1. Copywriting 93
How to attract clients — How to get paid — The types of assignments you'll get

2. Public relations writing 106

3. Writing for causes, education, and government 110

4. Scripts for business and education 112
How to find work — Writing the business video/DVD script — Getting paid

5. Technical writing 117

6. Your ghostwriting and editorial service 118

How to multiply your profits 122

7. Articles for magazines *123*
    The article writing process — Manuscript submission guidelines for articles, stories, and other short works — Rights you can offer — Double your income, double your fun

How to write a query letter *128*
    Query tips – e-queries – Sample queries

8. Newspaper articles and columns *136*

9. Short fiction and poetry *140*

10. Greeting cards and humor *142*

11. Movies, TV, and stage *145*

12. Nonfiction books *150*
    Getting published – If you write with another writer

Sample book proposal *154*

13. Novels *162*
    Getting published – The two golden keys to success

How to find an agent *166*

14. Writing for children and teenagers *168*

15. Self-publishing books, reports, newsletters, and other media *172*
    Marketing to a specific market segment — Writing franchises and subscription newsletters — Marketing to the general public

16. E-publishing and the Internet *185*
    e-zines – Web writing – e-books

17. Teaching, consulting, and self-promotion *188*
    Who you are – Build your website and publish your e-zine – Teach, speak, and promote

Book IV — Create your strategic marketing plan

Making dreams come true *195*
> *Your power cycle – Making time your ally*

Your strategic marketing plan *199*
> *Set goals for the next 12 months – Marking your progress with milestones – Assets, resources, and contacts – Meeting challenges – Putting proven marketing principles into action – Clarifying your purpose, audience, and strategy – The features and benefits of your written work – Project plan*

Your action plan *219*
> *Weekly Action Plan – Keep records – Queries & Submissions Log – Meetings, E-mail & Telephone Log*

A writing career within one year *225*
> *Sample Strategic Marketing Plan #1*

How to make $100,000 a year *234*
> *Sample Strategic Marketing Plan #2*

Support and resources *242*
> *Websites, publications, and books – Grants, awards, and contests – Colonies and conferences – Writers' groups and organizations*

A personal challenge *248*

Index of writing opportunities *249*

General index *252*

DISCOVER YOUR CREATIVE VISION

BOOK I

What to expect from your writer's journey

One night, shortly before a great man died, he stood with a friend by the window. The two gazed out at a stormy night together. The rain pelted his windowpane. He turned to his friend and said, "When I was a boy, I'd stare out the window on nights like tonight and I'd dream about the man I wanted to be. And I can only hope that I've become that man."

Today, at this moment, you are gazing through a foggy window and dreaming about the writer you want to be. I am that friend standing next to you who is going to help you see clearly through the window to your career so that one day you can say, "I've become the writer I dreamed I would be."

To that end, I am your mentor, and today we begin a journey together.

Bear in mind that writing is not for sissies and that markets are competitive. But you can succeed. And if you are willing, you will succeed. It won't be easy, but the world is waiting for the next great writer to appear. My central desire is to keep you writing. That is why I'm sharing my secrets with you.

In fact, I am calling you to join me on a great adventure. You may have written thousands of pages before this moment and enjoyed success, or you may have written very little. Regardless of your current situation, you begin a new writer's journey today.

Think of this book as a compass, especially prepared to help you on your journey into the extraordinary world of the professional writer. There will be tests and obstacles as you develop your discipline, skills, and knowledge. On this quest, you will also attract allies and discover other helps. At some point, you will enter the innermost cave of your deepest fears and blocks, and will emerge reborn.

In the end, you will seize the treasure and receive your reward—the fulfillment of your writing dream.

The journey described above is called the *hero's journey*, based on Joseph Campbell's book *The Hero with a Thousand Faces*. This hero's journey has been popularized in many movies, most notably *Star Wars*. Think of this "Bible" as both your light saber that separates truth from error and your sure guide to the Ways of the Writing Force.

The Freelance Writer's Bible contains four books:

Book I: Discover your creative vision and channel your passion. With this book, you will *find* your dream. Through a series of insightful exercises, you will learn more about yourself as a person and as a writer. You will envision your quest and learn how to keep writing. At the end of this book, you will create your writer's mission statement.

Book II: Write with freedom and confidence. With this book, you will *write* your dream. Expect to tap the font of your "inner voice that knows," develop your creativity, and become a whole-brained writer. You will also develop your skills, and learn how to apply the alchemy of writing to refine your work into gold.

Book III: Sell to 17 key writing markets. With this book, you will *sell* your dream. Here, the focus is on selling what you write, whether it's the great American novel or the next Lexus brochure. You will learn the ins and outs—the realities—of virtually every commercial and traditional writing market under the sun. Expect to understand precisely what to do to sell your work to a particular market.

Book IV: Create your strategic marketing plan. The worksheets and principles of this book put everything together into a laser-sharp, individualized plan just for you. At the end you'll find resources, an index of writing opportunities, and a complete general index.

Read the "Bible" with a pen in your hand. When you get an idea, jot it down. When something strikes you as "right," write down its application for you. When you find yourself saying, "I should try that," mark it, or jot it down in your writer's journal.

I suggest you read the "Bible" through from beginning to end. It is designed as a workbook with many useful activities, applications, and worksheets. However, you can also use it as a reference work, choosing just those things that you feel you need. If you are only interested in the markets, then Book III, the largest of the four books, is where you should go. Updates to the "Bible" will appear at www. keepwriting.com.

As your mentor, my goal is to get you started on a path that will lead you to a full-time writing career within one year. However, you can also use it to create a part-time career or a five-year master plan. Use it as a guide to set and achieve any personal writing goal you have. I also want to give you specific guidance on how to make money as a writer. Most importantly, I want to touch your writer's soul and help you become the complete writer you were meant to be.

Let's begin right now.

I write; therefore, I am

Writers write. You are a writer if you write. Say that right now. Out loud: *I am a writer!* Don't ever be afraid to say you're a writer. When someone asks you about what you do, say *I am a writer.* Affirm that deeply. It feels good, doesn't it? That's because writing is an absolutely worthwhile and rewarding use of your time. Don't let family members and friends tell you it's a waste of time. For my money, it's the best therapy I never paid for.

Keep writing.

The more your write, the more you become aware of the magic that is inside you. Keep writing and be glad you are a writer. It exercises the mind and frees the spirit. It's a wholly worthwhile use of your time.

Now let's get down to brass tacks.

How much time are you willing to put into your writing over the next month? Four hours a day? Four hours a week? Every Tuesday night from 8-10 p.m. and every Saturday from 8-12 a.m.? Sit down for a moment and make a commitment to yourself. You may include in that figure the time you spend with the "Bible." How many hours will you devote to writing during the next 30 days? You can express this as hours per week or hours per day, but write down your commitment before continuing.

Writing commitment for the next 30 days

During the next 30 days, how many hours (per week or per day) are you willing to commit to your writing?

_____

_____

In Book IV, we will return to this issue, and you will set many additional goals. As a writer, it is important to develop discipline. Discipline is the ability to do what you know you should do when you don't feel like doing it.

The firstborn child of discipline is persistence. In nearly two decades of teaching and consulting with writers, I can tell you that persistence is more important than talent. I have seen too many talented writers drop out and too many mediocre or semi-talented writers succeed because they developed discipline and persevered. According to Richard Bach, author of *Jonathan Livingston Seagull*, "The professional is the amateur who didn't quit."

Regardless of your level of talent, you can become the next great writer, if you are willing. In fact, the next great writer is already within you. It is up to you to set him or her free. A wise friend once asked me to recall a moment in my life in which I was absolutely wonderful in every way. It wasn't easy, but I recalled a day when I was creative, loving, and seemingly at the top of my game in every area. It was as if the highest ideals that I held inside had found expression. He then said, "That wonderful you is the real you. The rest is an aberration." What's true of me is true of you, for that which is most personal is most universal. The next great writer is within you ready to emerge.

Your safe harbor

This first exercise will prepare you for all other exercises in this book. After you have read this paragraph, close your eyes. Imagine a place that is completely serene—an imaginary or real place where you would like to be. This can be a place in nature or a place with another person, a hero, or even a Higher Power. It needs to be a place where you feel completely *safe* and completely *relaxed*. Most writers conjure up an imaginary lake, stream, seashore, or mountain. They feel the breeze; they hear the birds; they *experience* their safe harbor.

In the space below, describe your safe harbor.

My backyard on a warm summer day. The birds are chirping. The hummingbirds buzzing as the wife tends to her garden. I've got a cold beer in my hand and the stereo is playing up tempo as the breeze rustles the trees

Retreating to your safe harbor is a mental device that will calm your *thinking mind* and summon your *subconscious mind* to bring forth insights and push them into consciousness. The truths of your soul and the source of your creativity are inside you; they just need a way to reveal themselves.

In many of the exercises, I will ask you to *freewrite*. Freewriting means just that—writing freely without constraints. It also means to keep writing; in other words, keep your pen moving or your keyboard clicking. If you have a moment where nothing is coming, just doodle. Don't stop writing until you *feel* you are done. Freewriting is more of a feeling and intuitive process than it is a thinking one. Just write whatever pops into your head, regardless of how bizarre it may seem. Your subconscious is pushing information into consciousness.

Of course, a lot of what you write will be nonsense, but you'll get a feeling when the good stuff comes. Trust the process. Consider reading the chapter on creativity (in Book II) before continuing on.

◆ ◆ ◆ ◆ ◆

Let's go inside for a moment. Let's go deep, and meet that exceptional writer within you. Even if you are an established writer, the next segment of our journey will be beneficial to you. *To know who you are as a writer, you must know who you are.*

What follows are three exercises designed to help you become better acquainted with yourself.

Your legacy

Assume you will die 20-30 years from now. (Imagine this even if you are 80 years old.) What do you want people to say at your funeral? What do you want to be remembered for? And who do you want to remember you? What will be your greatest accomplishments before you die? I suggest you write this eulogy as a freewriting exercise; that is, write the rough draft without stopping to think. Write for about 10-15 minutes. Hold on to the eulogy; we will come back to it later.

_____

_____

_____

_____

_____

_____

_____

_____

_____

_____

_____

_____

_____

_____

_____

_____

_____

A letter to your child

In this exercise, assume that you have a young child (even if you don't).
Let's suppose that, for whatever reason, you will never be able to see that
child again. However, you can give that child your last words of advice in a
letter. You have 10-15 minutes to flesh out the letter. What will you say?

What the world needs now is . . .

According to the song, what the world needs now is love, sweet love. What else does it need, in your opinion? Be as specific as you can, and name at least five things.

1. _____

2. _____

3. _____

4. _____

5. _____

The above three exercises are designed to reveal your *values*, your highest ideals, those principles or beliefs that are most important to you, that bring you personal fulfillment or make you happy. Your responses should reveal a great deal to you about what you hold close to your heart. For example, in the "What the world needs now is" exercise, did you choose political needs, spiritual needs, relationship needs, or other types of needs?

In the next exercise, you will list your top ten values, what you care about most. Here's a list of common values to get you thinking. This list is by no means all-inclusive. Add other values as they occur to you.

Making money	Adventure	Health
Independence	Time with family	Accountability
Financial independence	Trust	Positive communication
Living it up	Leadership	Public service
Individual service to others	God, religion	Doing what is right
Being efficient	Perfection	Enjoying nature
Organization	Everything in its place	Recognition
Possessions	Knowledge, wisdom	Honesty, morality
Cheerfulness	Discipline	Creative self-expression

Collaboration	Competition	Excellence
Emotional expression	Taking risks	Sharing
Challenging work	Relaxation	Political involvement
Sports	Friendship	High position
Forgiveness	Revenge	Getting along with others
Education	Self-improvement	Exercise, fitness

Ten values

Using the above three exercises as source material, list your ten most important values. Be honest! The truer you are to yourself, the better your chance to maximize your potential.

1. _____
2. _____
3. _____
4. _____
5. _____
6. _____
7. _____
8. _____
9. _____
10. _____

Now that we have peered into the future and touched on the present, let's look into the past. Keep in mind that everything you reveal in these exercises will become material for some future writing project.

Inventory of past creative experiences

What was the most creative period in your life? Or what do you consider to be your most creative accomplishment? It can be an event, a writing project, a project of some other kind, a personal moment, or an accomplishment at your place of work or even as a child. Look for a time when your creativity most influenced what you did.

_____

_____

_____

_____

_____

_____

_____

What was the most productive period in your life? Describe a time when you accomplished a great deal, whether in your writing, or in your work, or in some other area? This "productive period" can be thought of in terms of weeks, months, or years.

_____

_____

_____

_____

_____

_____

_____

When were you so involved with something that you lost track of time? When have you felt the most passion? When were you the most excited? You can list more than one instance.

_____

_____

_____

_____

_____

_____

_____

What was your greatest inner battle? What was the issue? What was the outcome? And what did you learn from the battle?

_____

_____

_____

_____

_____

Of what accomplishment are you most proud?

_____

_____

_____

_____

What was your bravest moment? What was your weakest moment?

_____

_____

_____

_____

_____

Values priorities

Drawing from your list of ten values and from the above inventory, make any adjustments to your list of ten values. From that list, choose your top five values and prioritize them from 1 to 5.

1. _____

2. _____

3. _____

4. _____

5. _____

The things that you value are likely to be the things about which you are most passionate, the things about which you want to write. Let's clarify your vision by learning more about your inner writer.

The possible dream

In some of your happiest daydreams, you have seen yourself as a fulfilled writer, and perhaps even a rich writer. Of course, these were just daydreams, passing wishes that may have seemed unattainable. But what if those impossible daydreams became possible dreams? That's the objective of the next series of exercises.

What you want from writing, Part 1

Why do you want to write? What do you hope to gain from the experience? What benefits do you expect to enjoy or are currently enjoying? Take 10-20 minutes to brainstorm a list of all of the positives you can think of.

_____

_____

_____

_____

_____

_____

What you want from writing, Part 2

I'm sure your list from Part 1 includes some of the following: money, recognition, communicating something valuable to others, self-discovery, healing, inspiration, self-expression, fame, fulfillment, feeling creative, and independence. Now, look at your list of benefits, and choose your top five. List more than five if you'd like, but they should be in priority order. Also, be sure to make your choices in light of your values.

1. _____

2. _____

3. _____

4. _____

5. _____

Three categories of writing opportunities

Book III contains the necessary marketing information to succeed in 17 different areas of writing. These 17 can be placed in one of three categories: commercial writing, traditional writing, and entrepreneurial writing.

Commercial writing is anything you write for a business or institution. As a general rule, it is the best money for the effort and the risk. There is less competition in this area, making it "easier" to make a good living. In fact, many business writers and copywriters make six figures a year. There is a high demand, and there is no spec writing (writing on the "speculation" that you will sell your work after you write it) after you have established yourself. It is the rational choice if you want to make a reasonably steady income as a writer.

The downside is that you do not own the copyright to your work, you are seldom given a byline, and the client determines the general content and nature of the project. However, it *is* creative writing. Don't let anyone tell you differently.

Traditional writing is what we normally think of as writing: novels, magazine articles, stories, screenplays, and so on. The average income of a traditional writer is less than that of a commercial writer. However, there are traditional writers who are millionaires. There is an opportunity for fame and fortune, but the odds are longer.

On the other hand, you are more likely to make a lasting contribution to others in this area of writing. There is more opportunity for recognition, and your byline is seen by everyone who reads your material. Traditional writers enjoy following their creative instincts and usually prefer an unstructured work environment.

Entrepreneurial writing includes self-publishing and other forms of self-promotion. This type of writing requires a larger financial investment on your part, but the rewards can be significant. Although all writers must also be marketers, this area requires more business acumen and "hustle" than the others. If you are decisive, self-reliant, and able to get other people excited about your ideas, then this area might be worth looking at.

Which of the following types of writing appeals to you the most: commercial, traditional, or entrepreneurial?

_____

Does this choice closely align with your top choices in the "What do you want from writing, Part 2" exercise?

_____

_____

If I were a rich man

If you were a billionaire with unlimited time on your hands, what would you write? If money were no object, what would you enjoy writing the most? List up to ten possible writing projects. These could range from a detective novel to a video script for a particular company. Perhaps you want to write a travel article about Casablanca or a book about the value of recycling. Maybe you want to write grants for poorly funded schools. If you cannot think of specific writing projects at this point, go through the list of the 17 writing areas, and choose those that are most appealing to you.

_____

_____

_____

_____

_____

_____

_____

_____

_____

_____

Thus far, you have identified what you want from writing and the kinds of writing that are attractive to you. Now, let's look at your beliefs and attitudes about writing.

Your writing attitudes and values

There are many reasons to write, and writing can have many purposes. Below, you will find a list of preferences about writing. Put these in priority order, with #1 being the highest priority. Don't rush this exercise. Relax and have fun.

_____ I like to express my feelings and ideas. I enjoy that creative feeling.

_____ I like to empower people with useful information.

_____ I like to persuade people to take some action or to think differently.

_____ I like to inspire people.

_____ I like to entertain people.

_____ I like to make people laugh.

_____ I like to help people develop their abilities.

_____ I love words and enjoy crafting readable sentences and paragraphs.

_____ I like to shock people, and turn them around to a new point-of-view or way of thinking.

_____ I like to tell stories.

_____ I like seeing my name in print.

_____ I like to write whether or not I sell anything.

_____ Writing should be uplifting or have some high purpose.

_____ Writing should communicate some kind of message.

_____ Writing does not need to have a purpose.

_____ Writing is like any other career in that its primary purpose is to make money.

_____ _____

_____ _____

_____ _____

_____ _____

_____ _____

The priorities you list above should tell you a lot about your *writing soul*. For example, if you love words and enjoy crafting readable sentences, then you might do very well as a commercial writer. If you like to make people laugh, maybe you're the next Dave Barry, or maybe the next great screenwriter, or maybe a greeting-card writer. If you like to inform people or persuade them, perhaps journalism or writing non-fiction books is your ticket. If money is the primary objective, then you will likely choose those writing areas that can make you the most money. If your passion is to inspire others, then that suggests a desire to write for others more than yourself.

Most people enjoy writing the same types of material that they enjoy reading.

What do you read?

What do you read? List recent titles or types of books, magazines, or other materials that you choose to read in your free time.

_____

_____

_____

_____

_____

Five Adjectives

Write down five or more adjectives that describe you as a writer, and five that describe your writing. For example, one of my students describes herself as deep and perceptive, and she sees her writing as funny and accessible.

You as a writer   **Your writing**

_____   _____

_____   _____

_____   _____

_____   _____

_____   _____

Your creative vision and your writing mission

All of the previous exercises have led you to this point. Now it's time to put everything together into your mission statement. Your writing mission statement should consist of a few sentences that clearly describe the yearnings of your writing soul. What were you born to write? What kind of writer and person were you born to be? As you review your responses to these exercises, you will likely see recurring themes and patterns.

Here are your guidelines for creating a mission statement:

1. Write in affirmative, present-tense statements. For example: *I write with richly detailed prose that is clear and visual.* Of course, that may not be completely true at the present, but if you sense that potential within you, write it out as if it exists right now, at this moment in time. In reality, it does.

Keep in mind that you are creating the possible dream, not the impossible dream. There's a big difference between a fantasy . . . and the possible dream that you inwardly sense is true for you. You have many talents and abilities that are part of your nature, some of which have not fully emerged. These will suggest a vision to you of how things will be.

2. Do not write in future tense. Instead of *I will write popular romance novels,* write *I am a popular romance novelist.* The seed within you contains the plant. Your passion and practice is what makes it root, grow, and bloom.

3. Do not use negative statements of any kind. Instead of *I am not a procrastinator,* write *I am a disciplined writer who starts and completes projects on time.*

Here is the mission statement one of my clients wrote after she completed the exercises in Book I.

I am a teacher and communicator. I have a way of explaining things so that they are easily understood. I create worthwhile writings that elevate, enlarge, enlighten, or entertain. I value responsibility (the ability to respond), discipline (accepting the work of growth), enthusiasm, and positive self-expression. I love seeing people grow and enjoy encouraging that process.

I have a penchant for light humor and clear explanations that makes my writing more accessible to others. I continually develop my craft and expect to get paid for those skills.

Since I am well-organized and outgoing, I relish the marketing side of writing. I don't mind doing commercial writing and greeting cards if doing so eventually sets me free to write those things that I am most passionate about—children's books (helping children grow and learn) and how-to books for adults (helping them grow and learn). Words are things, and I enjoy finding the right word, regardless of the writing project.

Notice that the above mission statement contains no goals, just affirmations about writing values and the writer's place in the world. The above is also written in first person. Each statement states a truth about that person. Your mission exists right now in this moment of time. So affirm things in present-tense "I" statements.

Your mission statement can be as long or as brief as you wish. It should be personal to you. Think of it as an expression of your creative vision and passion.

Preparing for your quest

Review your responses to all of the previous exercises. As you do, take notes in the space below or on a separate piece of paper. This should be deeply personal. You'll eventually use these notes in creating the final draft of your mission statement.

_____

_____

_____

_____

_____

_____

_____

_____

_____

_____

_____

_____

_____

_____

_____

_____

_____

_____

_____

_____

_____

Your writing mission statement

Write the final draft of your mission statement here.

_____

_____

_____

_____

_____

_____

_____

_____

_____

_____

_____

_____

_____

_____

_____

_____

_____

_____

_____

How do you feel? I'm sure you're feeling pretty good about yourself. You have selected some specific writing projects that have stirred your passion and you have a writing mission. Now, keep writing as you take the next step.

WRITE WITH FREEDOM AND CONFIDENCE

BOOK II

What stops you from writing?

Fear. And doubt.

That's what I had plenty of when I started my writing career, and yet I found a way to get started. This is my story.

My first writing assignment

I was a marketing executive for a mid-sized firm in the mid-eighties. And I was sick of it. I wanted to write and teach, but had not really tried my hand at either. However, I had written a lot of marketing materials, so I felt that was a logical place to start.

One day, I came across an impressive eight-page brochure that was beautiful in every respect except one—it contained tons of typos.

Battling my fears, I drove straight to the company's headquarters. I sauntered past the receptionist and, before she could stop me, I was on the elevator. When I glanced back through the closing elevator door, I saw her tethered to her desk by telephone wires and waving madly at me to come back and sign in. I smiled innocently and waved back as the elevator doors closed.

The corner office on the top floor was my destination. If my instincts were correct, this would be the president's office. They were, and it was. I nodded at his secretary and slipped into his office before she could ask, "Who the heck are you?"

Seeing that I had penetrated his domain, the president assumed I had an appointment. I introduced myself and handed him his brochure. "A beautiful job, sir. I wanted to personally congratulate you. It certainly impressed me." He nodded, and a self-satisfied grin spread across his face. I had learned in my executive years to always open with a positive, and then to absolve the decision-maker of all guilt for the negative. Thus, I continued, "I'm sure you didn't have an opportunity to look at the final draft, because if you had, you would have spotted these typos."

"Typos?" he asked, looking suddenly faint.

That's when I knew *he* had done the writing. I had to be careful now. "Even with something as formidable as this, the typos add an unprofessional aspect to an otherwise brilliant piece. If you'd like, I'd be happy to edit your other collateral at a reduced rate, so you can put your time to more important things."

"Yeah, too bad I didn't see this before it was printed." He was hoping for more ego-massaging. I complied.

"Your people should always get a final okay from you, sir. That's why I came directly to you." The deal was cinched.

I look back at this experience and shiver. Where did I get the guts to do this? How did I find my Warrior energy? I'll explain with an illustration I first heard from Denis Waitley in a motivational presentation entitled *The Psychology of Winning*.

Suppose I lay a plank of wood on the ground. The plank is about 12 inches wide and 100 feet long. On one end, I place a $100 bill. Now, suppose I offer you the $100 if you can walk the plank without falling off. No problem, right? That's because the desire for success is greater than your fear of failure.

But now suppose that plank lies between the rooftops of two ten-story buildings. Now fear has entered the equation and you won't walk the plank. That's how some aspects of writing can seem. The fear of failure looms bigger than the potential reward.

However, what if your baby is in the other building and the building is on fire? That's when you defy your fear to get to your baby. You walk the plank and go through the fire. That's courage.

That baby on the other side is your writing career. In my case, when my passion (or desire) became stronger than my fear, then my writing business began to grow.

In Book I, we focused on positives, on your desires and your writing dream. In this chapter, we will deal with the common negatives that ravage the careers of most writers. To deal with these, you must first name them. The exercises in this chapter are some of the most important in this book.

Fears, blocks, and barriers

What stops you from writing? What keeps you from succeeding as a writer? What are your fears? What is your deepest fear? What obstacles must you overcome? In this, as in all exercises, honesty is the best policy. You must admit to the problems in order to resolve them. Brainstorm for about 10-20 minutes.

_____

_____

_____

_____

_____

_____

_____

_____

_____

_____

_____

_____

_____

_____

_____

From the list above, name your five biggest fears and barriers that block your writing.

1. _____

2. _____

3. _____

4. _____

5. _____

Among the fears, blocks, and barriers that you have chosen, you'll find some of these: procrastination, perfectionism, comparing yourself to Hemingway, fear of not being as good as you had hoped, fear of wasting time, self-doubt, fear of failure, fear of success, negative self-talk, anger, general anxiety, lack of creativity, lack of ability, lack of time, not knowing where to start, and general stuckitis. We are going to deal with all of these and more a little later. First, let's dip into our inner fountain of knowledge for some insights.

Hurdling barriers and breaking through blocks: Your own mini-movie, starring you

Go to your safe harbor (as described in Book I). Choose your biggest barrier, the fear that you can't seem to overcome, the seemingly immovable block. Personify it. In other words, give it a personality, character traits, and an attitude so that it can communicate with you. For example, what would procrastination look like if it were a human, or a monster, or an object?

Once you have done that, interact with this antagonist. Have a conversation with it. Create a mini-movie with action and dialogue. Freewrite until you receive some insight or resolution. It's okay to cry. I have seen many students, male and female, do just that.

One student (we'll call her Debra) saw procrastination as her roommate. Here's a condensed version of the imagined conversation. My comments appear in brackets.

Debra: It's time to write.

Procrastination: Do it tomorrow.

Debra: What was that?

Procrastination: Do it tomorrow. That *is* your modus operandi—your habit.

Debra: It is?

Procrastination: Sure.

Debra: Not this time.

Procrastination: Is there anything in the fridge?

Debra: You're trying to derail me.

Procrastination: Nonsense. You do that on your own. [That is the insight.]

Debra: I do?

Procrastination: Sure.

Debra: Not this time. (Debra grabs a baseball bat.)

Procrastination: What's on TV?

Debra: There's a show about a woman who kills her roommate.

Procrastination (seeing the club and suddenly fearful): Her roommate?

Debra: I think it's time for you to move out.

Procrastination: I'll move out tomorrow.

Debra: You'll move out right now. (And she chases Procrastination out the door.) [That was an important part of the insight—she needed to start right now.]

Another student imagined his block as a twenty-foot high, two-foot thick wall. He couldn't break through it. He tried a sledgehammer, a jackhammer, and a tank. The wall would laugh at him each time. Nothing worked. This was one tough block, so he decided to jump over it, *Matrix*-style. The wall stopped laughing. When he shared this with me, I looked him in the eye and said (in the voice of Morpheus from *The Matrix*), "You are the one. You are the next great writer."

In my early days, I had a block about making money as a writer. So I imagined money as a beautiful woman standing in some public room. Summoning my Warrior energy, I soon found the courage to enter the room and approach her. Here's a condensed version of a conversation that I had with my block.

Money: What are *you* doing here?

Trottier: I want you. I need you—

Money: Snap out of it—you're crazy.

Trottier: No, I'm not. Uhh . . . we should be together.

Money (laughing): You're not good enough for me.

[This was the insight. I believed I wasn't good enough (as a writer and as a person) to make money. Somehow I had gotten the message that I was not worthy of success.]

Trottier (confidently): I used to believe that, but now I know we were meant to be together.

Money (looking surprised, then smiling): So . . . what took ya so long?

(Trottier steps forward and embraces her.)

◆ ◆ ◆ ◆ ◆

Imagine your primary fear, barrier, or block as a person, creature, or object. (You can try this with as many blocks as you'd like, but I suggest that you only confront one at a time.) Now create a mini-movie. Interact and/or converse with your fear, barrier, or block until you receive some insight or resolution. This should take about five to ten minutes, but let it go longer if it needs to.

Your inner kingdom

According to Carl Jung (in *Archetypes and the Collective Unconscious*), there is such a thing as a collective unconscious, and certain archetypes are common to all of us, regardless of race or nationality. The names that I prefer for the four most prominent of these archetypal characters are the King, the Magician, the Warrior, and the Lover. All four of these live inside of you, but need nurturing.

The King creates the quest (Book I and Book IV). The Magician conjures the strategy or plan (Book IV). The Warrior serves the King through purposeful action (Book II and Book IV). The Lover gives counsel along the way (Books I-IV.) You will naturally develop all four of these as you continue your journey.

I opened this chapter with a story of how I got started in the writing business. Fortunately, I was able to summon my Warrior and charge into that building and seize the treasure (get that first writing assignment). In Book I, you focused on desire and the benefits of writing. Nourish your vision and desire so that it becomes larger than your fears and barriers, and you will free the inner writer.

I recall a writer (we'll call her Veronica) who interacted with her fear by creating her own mini-movie. I sensed that she had had some kind of catharsis, so I asked her about her experience. Veronica said that she realized that her block was her mother who used to tell her as a child that she could not do anything right. I asked her what she told her mother, and she said, "I didn't tell her anything. I simply sent her away. I stopped listening."

I said, "In reality, she's already been gone for a long time, hasn't she?" Veronica nodded, and I said, "But you've kept her alive in your head by telling yourself that you can't write."

She realized that I was right. When she silently berated herself, she used her mother's words. She put herself down just as her mother had done years before. Once Veronica fully comprehended that fact, she understood that she had the power to stop talking to herself like her mother used to talk to her. She was in the heat of an alchemical melt.

I said, "What you need now is a Lover." What I meant by that was she needed to develop the Lover within her and encourage herself. She needed to replace the negative self-talk with positive self-talk.

I mentioned earlier that during your hero's journey, you might enter the innermost cave and experience a death and rebirth. That's what Veronica had done, and now she was healing the deep wounds of the past.

The Warrior, though wounded, should enter the forest at its darkest point. What is your darkest fear? That's where you need to go. Enter the forest there, and go through your fear. When you do, a lot of confusion will dissipate and rays of sunlight will light your path. And you will discover that your deep wounds are healing.

Alchemy: Converting blocks into steppingstones

Alchemy is the word we use to describe the transformation (or transmutation) of lead into gold. In terms of writing, it is converting blocks into steppingstones, turning negatives into positives.

Alchemy happens in three stages. The first is the accumulation of information, realizations, and thought. The second stage is incubation—the contents are placed under pressure or allowed to ferment. This is called the melt. The third stage is the intuitive explosion, "Ah ha! Eureka! I've found it!"

Blocks are the best thing that can happen to you. If the pressure of your desire is strong enough, your blocks will melt away and be replaced with a golden pathway. Let your passion move you through all of your blocks.

What follows is a list of 17 blocks that most of us experience. These do not appear in any particular order.

1. Procrastination or scribaphobia (fear of writing)

This is characterized by a conscious or unconscious avoidance of writing. If you find yourself volunteering to shovel the snow rather than write, then you probably have this block. This block will become a steppingstone for at least two reasons: 1) You have the opportunity to uncover and face the specific fear that is holding you back, and 2) you can reverse this right now this second.

Make a commitment to start writing beginning today or tonight. Write something every day, even if it is only for 15 minutes. Make the commitment right now. (This is in addition to the writing commitment you made in Book I.)

Now, set the "Bible" aside and begin writing something you've wanted to write, or return to something that you have stopped writing. Write for at least 30 minutes before returning.

◆ ◆ ◆ ◆ ◆

Now, why are you afraid to write? What is the resistance? Why do you procrastinate? The reason could be any of the blocks listed below. Often, there is an underlying fear of not being equal to the task. Realize that you will grow as you continue to write and learn, but you must write in order to grow. It's one of the truths of life.

Whatever the reasons, identify these fears about writing and courageously face them and eliminate them, one by one. Rally your Warrior and charge through your fears. Build your passion to write and focus on the benefits of writing and your mission or quest. You will find your fears shrinking until they are in total remission.

Have a definite writing schedule. Force yourself to write. Invariably, the first three pages will be crap, but once they are written, the creative juices will begin to flow. Write something every day, even if it is just 15 minutes in your writer's journal or notebook before you go to bed. Some writers visualize one friendly person, perhaps a friend or a composite of the envisioned readership, and write for that one person.

An athlete seldom jumps into a major workout or a game without first doing warm-ups to work out the kinks, stretch the muscles, and prepare the body for optimal performance. Writing is no different. Try a few reps of letter-writing to warm up, or a few laps with your writer's journal, or even the obligatory three pages of crap already mentioned. Once your mind is warm, it can more easily perform.

2. Perfectionism

Your work does not need to be perfect, it just needs to be written.

Even the great ones make errors. Yes, I have found nitpicky errors even in classics. Perfection is a terrible goal because you can never achieve it.

The result is disillusionment and despair, followed by new unrealistic goals that cannot be achieved, followed by more despair. It's a vicious circle, a downward spiral.

Most of us have a bit of perfectionism in us because it is so much a part of our culture. If you are a perfectionist, perhaps you feel that you are not acceptable or worthy unless you are perfect. That might be the result of having received a lot of criticism in your childhood. Turn this block into a steppingstone by accepting your imperfections. I am not talking about indulging yourself, but about accepting errors and mistakes along the way. You do not have to be perfect to be admired, loved, and accepted. It might take a little time to reach that ideal, so don't be a perfectionist about letting go of your perfectionism. *The real goal is not perfection, but excellence*—striving to be the best writer (and person) you can be.

I've seen writers absolutely paralyzed because their work cannot be perfect right from the start. If you've ever learned a language, you know that you must make a certain amount of mistakes before you can speak well enough to communicate. Keep writing and watch your ability to communicate improve.

3. Comparing yourself to Hemingway

You are right—you will never be Ernest Hemingway. But then realize that Hemingway could never be you. You have your own place in the universe, so stop comparing yourself to others.

4. Museheimer's Disease

This is refusing to write until your Muse arrives. It's an excuse to procrastinate. Don't fall for the false belief that there is a Muse assigned specifically to you who will come down from Mount Parnassus and whisper in your ear, "Write this."

This pernicious disease is sometimes manifested by the notion that you must be in a natural setting with absolute quiet except for tweeting birds in order to write. This block easily becomes a steppingstone when you realize two things: 1) Your Muse is already inside you, identified earlier as your Lover, and 2) You can be in a natural setting any time you'd like—just visualize your "safe haven."

To get in the mood, play some music, read what you wrote the day before, or create some ritual to precede your writing session. Visualize yourself standing in front of a swimming pool. Now dive in.

The truth is, writing is work, and professional writers write because they have to write. As Jack London put it, "You can't wait for inspiration. You have to go after it with a club." That club is your keyboard, your pen.

5. Fear of not being as good as you had hoped

As writers, we all have expectations and hopes. Sometimes these expectations are too high. I would like to be a great writer, but I have learned over the years that I am a good writer who has learned his craft, but I am not a great writer. However, as I learned to write, I found that I had other writing gifts and talents that I never would have realized if I hadn't written.

Whether you become as wonderful a writer as in your fondest dreams or whether you don't is irrelevant. This I do know, and this is the steppingstone:

As you keep writing, you will save your writing soul and find your place in the universe.

Have faith in the process. E. B. White said that "writing itself is an act of faith." So listen to your "inner voice," your writer's soul, and don't let expectations and fears paralyze you. You cannot be the writer you want to be all at once with the first strokes of your pen. You must start down the path.

Also, take care that your expectations aren't too low. Goals should make you stretch, but not so much that you snap a ligament.

6. Fear of wasting time

As you contemplate becoming a writer, are you worried that you are going to make a fool out of yourself? Are you afraid that your family and friends are going to laugh behind your back? Are you worried that you are wasting your time? Do you silently wonder, "Can I really do this?"

In life, there are risks. You must make the decision to write or not to write, but once your foot is in the arena, you must fight until you are victorious. Victory is becoming the writer you were meant to become.

If you enjoy writing, then write. As mentioned earlier, it is an absolutely useful practice. It is therapeutic and cleansing, and it sharpens your mind. Your ability to communicate with the written word is a plus in the workplace, even if you don't become a professional writer. And the joy of creating something that is of value to you is one of life's most sublime experiences.

Convert this block into a steppingstone by earning the respect of yourself and the support of your family. If you are diligent in your writing, eventually they will realize that writing is important to you. Solicit their support. Doing that will bring you a warm feeling of having asserted yourself as a writer.

(Also, please review what I wrote about Block #5 above.)

7. Exaggerating fears and problems

FEAR is an acronym that stands for False Evidence Appearing Real. Many of our fears about writing are blown out of proportion, and some are even unfounded. It is easy to get focused on our fears and problems; when we do, they become larger than they really are.

I have a client (we'll call him Brandon) who was afraid to send his work out because it might be rejected. I asked him, "What would a rejection mean?" Brandon said, "That it's the end of my writing career." I told him that I have kept every rejection notice that I have ever received. I have more than a hundred. And I make my living as a writer; obviously, my career is still intact.

I asked him what else a rejection meant. He said, "It means that the piece is worthless."

I replied, "No, it doesn't. It means that your piece does not currently meet the needs of one overworked editor. It's not a value judgment."

If you focus on your fear, you give your fear power over you. (See also Blocks #8 and #10 below.) If you see your writing as an extension of yourself, then any criticism of your writing becomes a criticism of yourself.

Transmute this block into a steppingstone by choosing to see your exaggerated fear as a reminder that you need to focus on your passion and desire. Also, *reframe* criticism as feedback; that is, choose to see criticism as feedback because that's really all it is. Some feedback is helpful, and some is not, but it is seldom intended as a personal attack. If you feel yourself getting *defensive*, change your viewpoint of the feedback, or you may become *offensive* and hurt your career.

8. Fear of failure and self-doubt

Some of the greatest writers, artists, and composers have doubted themselves and their ability. The list includes Hemingway and Beethoven. Stephen King nearly gave up his career before it began until his wife rescued his first few pages of *Carrie* from the trash receptacle. Self-doubt is nothing to be alarmed about. Just keep writing and your confidence will eventually return. Write through your block.

If you find yourself unable to finish a work or, if finished, unable to send it out to be read by others, then you likely have an overblown fear of failure (see #7 above) or a fear of success (see #9 below). In most cases, the path to success is strewn with failure. This is the crucible where the alchemical melt takes place. This could be an innermost cave where your writing soul is reborn. Failure and rejection is part of the process, part of the writer's journey.

Naturally, you will want to minimize rejection and failure, but, at the same time, you will want to accept them as part of the developing process. Learn from your mistakes and rejections, and then let them go. Don't take them personally for that is not their intent.

9. Fear of success

This is usually fear of the unknown. It is human nature to be comfortable with the status quo and uncomfortable with change. We tend to resist change. Statistics show that abused women who divorce their wife-beating husbands have a tendency to marry another wife-beater. If you are accustomed to a certain level of success or failure, then a change from that status quo may initially seem threatening. Apply alchemy by accepting the "pressure" of possible change.

Sometimes we hang onto fears and that "hanging on" becomes a block. This is another way to resist change. Think of your fear as a huge garbage can that you insist on carrying around everywhere you go. Isn't it about time to dump the garbage? Liberate yourself!

10. Negative self-talk

Over the past several years, I have been working on a book for writers and children. I have sensed that the book needs to mature, so I have not tried to finish it yet. I don't want to force the process. However, I'd like to share an idea that runs through the book.

The story is about a boy who has a dream (as all writers do), but whenever he gets close to that dream, he hears the father-voice in one ear say, "You can't do it," and the mother-voice in the other ear say, "And it's all your fault." Too many of us have these voices buzzing around our heads. (Recall Veronica's experience with her mother's voice in her mini-movie on page 34.)

We often retain the negative impressions of childhood with us and repeat them to ourselves in the form of negative self-talk. I saw a study the other day that reports that negative self-talk outnumbers positive self-talk by nine times in the average person.

Convert the negative self-talk to sensible, positive self-talk. For example, instead of, "You stupid idiot, you never get it right," call yourself by name and say, "Self, you made a mistake on this one. Keep an eye out for this type of thing in the future. Otherwise, you're doing fine." And then look for opportunities to compliment yourself. Don't worry—you won't get a big head if you are realistic.

In addition, reward yourself for your accomplishments. Find ways to pat yourself on the back. Take yourself and a loved one to dinner to celebrate a productive writing month. Mark off milestones on a wall like a growth chart. Keep a journal of gold nuggets—things you are learning—or a book in which you record your successes. The key is to give yourself as much positive reinforcement as you would want to give some other important person in your life.

The Writer's Golden Rule is *Nurture yourself as you would nurture others*. If, by chance, you are mean to other people, then go on to #11.

11. Anger

Anger, simply put, is pain from the past. Someone, or a lot of people, hurt you in the past. That hurt did not age well. It fermented into anger. Now, when someone else says or does something that reminds you of that past hurt (either consciously or subconsciously), you feel anger. It's best to deal with anger in a constructive way because anger eventually turns inward, and depression is the result.

One way to deal with hurt and anger is to write it out. I do a lot of consulting with writers, and I know in advance that a writer's first script or novel is likely to be autobiographical or contain autobiographical information. Sometimes these first scripts or novels are quite good; often they are not. But all of them are therapeutic to the writer, and they help clear the creative pipes.

Write about your hurts and anger, even if it is only in a journal. Some years ago, a study showed that college students who kept journals had 50% fewer colds than those who did not. Writing is good for you; it strengthens your immune system and heals your emotions. The ultimate alchemy is converting anger into salable material that benefits, entertains, or informs others. I imagine author John Steinbeck working out some of his anger about the working conditions of Depression-era migrant workers in his book, *The Grapes of Wrath*.

Incidentally, can anger or any other emotion be managed in a productive way, and even controlled? Do events cause emotions? The answer to the first question is "yes," and the second is "no." Even though it "feels" like an event or a particular word causes the anger, it is your evaluative thinking that actually causes the anger.

For example, you will likely react differently to an employee who calls you a jerk than to an employer who calls you a jerk. Why? The answer is obvious. If the event caused the emotion, then your reaction would be the same in both cases. The truth is that there is some very quick evaluative thinking that goes on before you react. The good news is that *you* are in control, not your emotions.

If you'd rather feel calm instead of angry when confronted with something negative, I suggest that you first examine the belief system or evaluative thinking that produces the anger. Then replace it with a new way to look at the negative stimulus. For example, I used to have a temper, but I decided that rather than taking something personally, I wanted to "win" by remaining calm. Let the other guy lose his cool. The new evaluative thinking became "I win if I stay in control." After some experience with this, I learned to *listen* to the other person's meaning behind his offensive words and became more helpful than competitive. Do I ever get mad? Of course. But not like I used to.

Why do I raise this issue? Because it means that if you have negative emotions about writing or certain aspects of writing (such as having your work rejected), you can choose to view those negative things differently and feel a more productive emotion. Naturally, this is not quite as simple as I've made it sound, but the principle is correct. It's the essence of alchemy—converting the negative into positive, transmuting the lead that holds you down into gold that ennobles you.

12. Anxiety

Anxiety is pain in the future. Worry is how we can experience future pain in advance. Sometimes it is hard not to worry. I only see this as an issue when the anxiety has you wound so tightly that you can't write. In that case, give up the worry and relax. Go to your safe harbor or meditate before a writing session.

13. Lack of creativity, skills, ability, etc.

These are excuses to block your progress. Stop making excuses.

As you shall see in a later chapter, you have a creative side. And skills can be learned. There's nothing you can do about your natural ability except to develop what's there. And you develop it by writing and learning.

It is important to build on your strengths. What gifts do you bring to the writing table? Much of Book I is concerned with these issues. What skills do you lack? What must you do to claim them?

Character/Craft Worksheet—
Talents and Skills You Possess

Using this worksheet, identify your gifts and skills in two categories. The first is "Character." That refers to traits and character-based abilities such as persistence, discipline, ability to see rejection as a positive, and so on. "Craft" refers to both your native writing talents and the skills you have developed. These might include sense of humor, clear and readable prose, clever dialogue, excellent writing mechanics (grammar and punctuation), and so on.

Character	Craft
_____	_____
_____	_____

_____   _____
_____   _____
_____   _____
_____   _____
_____   _____
_____   _____

Areas for Improvement

_____   _____
_____   _____
_____   _____
_____   _____

14. Self-defeating attitudes

In nearly two decades of working with writers, I have seen three closely related attitudes that are usually fatal in terms of a writing career.

1. My work is God's work. This is the idea that whatever the writer writes while in the creative mode is holy and should not be trifled with. It feels so good to be in a creative flow that it's easy to believe that any product of that creative flow is publishable, and even sacred. However, it is likely that it is not yet ready for the eyes of others. More likely, it will need a revision.

2. My art is more valuable than mere money. In other words, capitalism taints the artistic process. A work, therefore, should not be changed to accommodate potential readers or marketing schemes. I understand this notion because, time after time, I have seen producers and publishers fail to see my creative vision and the meaning of the work of other writers. Personally, I bear the scars of many battles.

The point to be made here, however, is that you write for a reader, and sometimes the producer or publisher is right. If you are not writing for a reader, then you are writing for yourself. Such work is usually more difficult to sell than work written with a market in mind. The writing business is a business, and there will always be a tension between the artistic side and the business side. We will deal with this issue in greater detail in Book III.

3. I went through fire for this baby, and I'm not changing a word. It is easy to fall in love with our work. Certainly, we have a passion for it. That's a good thing. But we can be so close to what we have written that we become rigid and difficult to work with.

There is a writing maxim, often attributed to William Faulkner, that's both shocking and reality-based: "Sometimes you have to kill off your darlings." In my mind, he's referring to my favorite scene in a screenplay that needs to be cut because it simply doesn't work, or my favorite phrase in a brochure that needs to be excised to make the brochure flow.

Please be open to the ideas of editors, agents, and others. You don't have to accept everything they suggest, but try to understand the reasons for their suggestions. Doing so might lead you to new ideas or a better version of what you have written.

There's a fine line between what needs to be protected in a work and what needs to be revised. There are some things you should fight for. After all, you are the author. Nevertheless, be open to the thoughts of others throughout the writing process right up to publishing day.

On the other hand, a negative or defeatist attitude towards your work is also counter-productive. If you don't believe it, who else will?

15. Chronic Ambivalence Syndrome

This is not knowing what to write, where to start, or what to write next; and it is closely related to #4 and #16. There are many ways that this block can become a steppingstone. In many cases, you do not need to know what to do next—just keep writing and trust the process. Realize that you cannot have a perfect knowledge of how the piece is going to read when you are finished. In other words, you are not in control; give up control to your instincts and the process.

If you cannot decide what to write, then the activities in Book I should be of some help in choosing a project. In addition, we will discuss 17 ways to get ideas later in this book. Meanwhile, not choosing a writing project is a form of procrastination or the symptom of some fear. Let's be honest, you know deep down inside what you'd like to write. Just do it.

Sometimes you need to explore. Sometimes that exploration should take the form of an outline, or the revision of one you have already written. It is difficult to write something from scratch or start with a blank page; outlining helps you organize your thoughts before the actual writing begins. Remember, you don't need to write the entire novel today, just a few pages.

There may be times when you will need to drop the project momentarily and read something or attend a seminar or chop some wood. Many writers benefit from belonging to a writers' group. (For more about that, see the "Support and resources" section of Book IV.)

16. Stuckitis

Think of this as an advanced case of Chronic Ambivalence Syndrome (#15), where you have lapsed into a *stuckitic coma*. Being stuck is one of the great blessings of being a writer because it naturally leads you into the alchemical process.

The first thing to do when you are stuck is to draw up all of your mental and analytical powers to solve the writing problem. The next step is to relax, wait, and concentrate on something else—badminton, pottery, the sunset. This is the incubation phase. It may last for several seconds, several minutes, several hours, several days, or even longer. It is followed by an *involuntary benign stroke*, an inspiration that usually strikes during a shower, at bedtime, or at some other calm moment.

The fourth step is a conscious evaluation or analysis of this offering from the subconscious. The beautiful thing about being stuck is it means that your conscious mind (your left brain) has done all that it can do, and that now the assignment has been turned over to the subconscious mind.

To help prevent future problems of being stuck, heed Ernest Hemingway's advice to end a session in the middle of something. Stop a writing session in the middle of a chapter, a section, or a paragraph. Have an idea where you are going next so that you can pick up tomorrow where you left off today. That helps some writers maintain a flow to their writing.

Realize that writer's block is an occupational hazard that every writer faces. When encountering any block, don't panic or catastrophize it. Just say, "Oh, this is normal. It's supposed to happen. No biggie, I'll just work through it." Relax.

Finally, trust yourself, trust the creative process within you, and trust the writing tools in your possession. Believe that everything is going to work out fine. Most of all, take the pressure off. Make writing fun, and you'll have fun writing.

17. Not enough time

This is a huge issue. How much time should you devote to this enterprise? In terms of money, one thing is certain—don't let go with one hand until the other hand is full. You need to keep your job until you are making enough money through your writing before you can quit that job. Sometimes arrangements can be made with loved ones to facilitate this transition. Of course, you may only desire a part-time writing career. Regardless of your career objectives, the key to resolving this issue is to create a writing schedule. That process begins with a time log.

Time Log

Keep track of where you spend your time for one week. For the times that you are at your regular employment, just write "Work." Otherwise, be specific about where you spend your time. For example, if it takes you 30 minutes to drive to work, then note that.

	Sun	Mon	Tue	Wed	Thu	Fri	Sat
1 a.m.							
2							
3							
4							
5							
6							
7							
8							
9							
10							
11							
Noon							
1							
2							
3							
4							
5							
6							
7							
8							
9							
10							
11							
Midnight							

Time Tally (Hours per week)

Sleep _____

Actual time working at your job _____

Breaks and lunch (at work) _____

Other meals _____

Personal hygiene _____

Time spent in cars, trains, buses, and planes _____

Quality time with loved ones* _____

Writing _____

Maintenance of house and grounds _____

Church/service/spiritual activities _____

Television and Internet _____

Other recreation, including restaurants _____

Education and reading _____

Other: _____ _____

Other: _____ _____

*Quality time does not include watching TV and movies with your family, but time spent in face-to-face discussions, working together on a project, and productive activities or play where there is significant interaction with loved ones.

Time evaluation

What is the biggest surprise in the above tally? _____

_____

How much time do you spend with the TV and computers? _____

_____

Television is usually (but not always) a big time-waster. Generally, it requires nothing of the viewer. In fact, it takes more effort to eat than to watch most TV programs. There are notable exceptions. Even having the TV on while engaged in simple household chores can rob you of thinking or reflecting time. How much of your weekly TV, video game, and Internet fun time are you willing to apply to your writing?

How much time from your other activities are you willing to give up to write? (Keep in mind that a certain amount of recreation and relaxation [including watching TV] is necessary for a healthy life. If you keep a bow strung up for too long, it will lose its spring.)

If you are a professional writer, you can use time logs to see where your writing-business time goes: research, marketing, planning, record-keeping, reading, classes and workshops, travel, and writing.

My schedule for my writing business

A lot can be accomplished with little time. I had a student who wrote a half-hour each day for a year and completed a feature-length screen-play. If writing is important to you, then you will make time for it. When you read a riveting book, you steal 15 minutes every chance you get. Many writers do the same when they write. How much time are you willing to commit?

In Book I, you committed yourself to write for a certain number of hours during the first month. Let's re-evaluate that figure and adjust your commitment. And let's think in terms of your writing *business*. As your writing business develops, you will find yourself spending about one-half of your time writing, and one-half of your time reading, learning, and selling. Of course, the actual amounts may vary depending on the type of writing you do and how experienced you are.

With the above breakdown in mind, create a schedule for your writing business. You can express this in hours per week, or specific times each day of the week, or in any terms you wish. Most writers get the best results by actually scheduling specific time blocks. Keep in mind that four hours a day is about the maximum for actual writing time. After four hours, most writers tend to get diminishing returns.

(Note: This is a preliminary exercise that will be developed more fully in Book IV.)

_____

_____

_____

_____

_____

Creativity

Relaxing into the Alpha Writer State

Lay down on the carpet in a supine position. Place a small pillow, chiropractic pillow, or rolled-up towel under your neck, and place a pillow under your knees. Lay your arms to your sides with palms up, or place your hands gently on your stomach with palms down. Now breathe in deeply through your nose, and breathe out slowly through your mouth.

Visualize the tension in your body exiting with that exhalation. Continue breathing in this manner. As you empty your body of tension, empty your mind of thoughts. Have no expectations. Just be aware of your breathing. After ten breaths, let your breathing become slow and natural. Now go to your safe harbor. Hopefully, being an Alpha Writer, you are now in the Alpha State.

Your safe harbor is a place that is completely serene—an imaginary or real place where you would like to be. You described your safe harbor in Book I. Your safe harbor is a creative place. And certainly a relaxed mind is better able to create than a mind that is tense. Paradoxically, being relaxed is an active state; it is not the same as being tired. Be both relaxed and alert. This is the aim of many meditative techniques. And since you are now in a relaxed state, why not meditate on your mission statement, or simply discard all thoughts and be open to impressions?

Reducing stress will be helpful to your writing career. In a nutshell, stress is caused by two things: 1) the perception of losing control, and 2) the perception of the importance of the event. The cure is obvious—change the perception. Keep things in perspective. Disappointments are disappointments; they are not the end of the world. Only the end of the world is the end of the world. I've seen students undergo nervous breakdowns over a grade for a class; five years hence, the class (and likely the grade) will be forgotten.

Come to terms with the past. Learn from it. Deal with your anger. Choose not to take things personally. Be primarily concerned with the important things you have to accomplish today. Don't be unduly concerned about the future. Live in the present.

Exercise. Take a hike. Practice yoga. Go bowling and knock those pins down. Walk and reflect. Meditate. Improve your diet. Use humor. Have fun. Don't take things too seriously. Improve your self-talk. In your internal dialogue, be firm with yourself but kind and encouraging.

Finally, get support. Talk to loved ones about your stressors. And write about them. After all, you are the next great writer.

Your brain is a two-piston writing machine

Our Western Society is built on the scientific method, and most of our formal education is focused on methods that train the conscious side of the student. Less value is attached to the intuitive, subconscious side. Conversely, many writing books and courses only emphasize the "inner writer," the subconscious side. The truth is that both sides of your nature need to work in harmony. These two sides correspond to the two sides of your brain.

The left hemisphere is what we might call the conscious side. The right hemisphere is the subconscious side. The left is the analytical critic, the error-detector. The right is the creative artist. The left brain is more detached and objective than the right, which is passionate and spontaneous. The right brain composes the harmony while the left brain attends to the notes. The left brain is parental and controlled; the right is childlike and free.

Left	Right
Conscious	Subconscious
Inner critic	Creative artist
Analytical; logical; the parts	Intuitive; "feeling"; holistic
Detached, objective	Passionate, imaginative
Organizes ideas into form	Churns out ideas
Verbal	Visual
Uses explanatory language	Uses evocative language
Sequential thinker; linear	Groups things together; looks for patterns
Parental	Child-like and spontaneous

Which side takes the lead in your life? _____

_____

If it is the analytical side, then you might have a tendency to approach writing as a write-by-the-numbers project. You will want definite steps and rules. If you tend to be more intuitive, you might look for inspiration to get the creative juices flowing. Rules may seem irrelevant to you.

I encourage you to develop both sides of your writer's soul so that the two can dance in step together. Sure, one or the other may take the lead, but the two need to move in unison. Why be a half-wit when you can opt for a whole-brained, holistic approach?

Traditionally, the left-brain way of thinking was seen as masculine, and the right brain as feminine. Let's marry the two! Leonardo DaVinci certainly did. He excelled in both the arts (painting, sculpture, inventions, music composition) and the sciences (physics, anatomy, engineering, geology, and aviation). And one (such as anatomy) helped the other (such as painting).

Personally, the analytical side of my nature is stronger than my creative side. In fact, there was a time when I believed that I did not have a creative side, and I placed little value on people's intuitive "feelings" about things. I was an empiricist.

A friend told me that I had an over-trained mind, and that I should read *Zen and the Art of Motorcycle Maintenance* by Robert Pirsig. That book changed my life because it demonstrated to me the value of intuition and put rationality in its proper place. From that time forward, I began developing my right brain. Where once I needed to "see it to believe it," now I find myself needing to "believe it to see it."

That's why Book I is focused on your Dream. I want you to believe in your Dream so that you can see it. The clearer your vision, the farther you'll yearn to travel.

I know that it is possible for any writer to develop the weaker side of his or her nature. I now think of myself as a two-piston writing machine. When one piston is up, the other is down (resting). They tend to alternate. I will write the first draft from the heart, with passion. But I will need a more critical eye for the second draft. The child within me needs to be free to create without interference from the parent, but once a play session is over, I need my parent to clean up the mess. Children are creative and you are a child; at least you have a creative child within you. Affirm that.

The process works a little differently with everyone, and you will want to find what works best for you. You may not yet have discovered what works best for you, so be open to new ideas.

Your creativity is enhanced when you are in a relaxed frame of mind. How do you get yourself into a creative state? You try by not trying. That sounds very Zen and even contradictory or paradoxical, but it's actually something you do every night. How do you sleep? You try by not trying. In other words, you place yourself in a position where you can sleep, and then you simply allow sleep to come to you. What happens if you *try* to fall asleep? That's the definition of insomnia. When your left brain (or conscious side) is active, it is difficult to fall asleep. That's why the conscious brain must sometimes be tranquilized.

Have you ever been in a conversation where you were trying to think of someone's name? You say, "It's on the tip of my tongue." The harder you try to *think* of the name, the more futile your effort becomes. But the moment you turn your attention to something else, what happens? Your subconscious side pushes the name into consciousness. The name was always there in your head, but you needed to occupy the left brain with something else so the right brain could produce the name for you.

Remember the process of alchemy? It begins by loading information into your brain, by thinking hard about something you are stuck on. That's how your conscious brain signals to the subconscious to work on the problem. Later, after you have relaxed, the subconscious may push the answer into consciousness.

Imagine a basketball game. The score is tied with three seconds left. A player is fouled. If he can make the free throws, his team will win. What does the opposing coach do? He calls time out. Why? To "ice" the player. What's really happening is that the opposing coach is giving the player time to *think* about those free throws. It's an attempt to pull the player out of a creative flow and insert the critic (the left brain).

In any creative session, it is important to keep the inner critic out of the process (either relaxed or otherwise occupied) so that the creative artist can emerge uninhibited. That is why in brainstorming sessions no one is allowed to make any judgments about any ideas that are offered. "All ideas are good," the leader will say. This is an attempt to keep the parent out of the sandbox and encourage the child to come out and play. Of course, after the session is over, the parent will be invited back to make sense of the child's creative offerings.

Thus, think of your parent, your inner critic, as your partner. Often, your inner critic is trying to protect you in some way. If you had overly critical parents, make sure your inner critic does not speak with their voices. Give that parental left brain a loving and nurturing voice.

What is creativity?

Creativity is *not* to manufacture something completely new out of nothing. There is no such thing as a *creation ex nihilo*. Creativity is a new twist on an old idea. It is to see what everyone else sees, but to see it in a little different light or a slightly different way. In alchemical terms, it converts the habitual into the original.

In the night sky, we see millions of stars. Many have been arbitrarily connected into what we call constellations. What if you were to take the same stars, but draw the imaginary lines differently and create a new constellation? That would be creative.

Below are the stars associated with the constellation Virgo, The Virgin (extracted from www.dibonsmith.com/stars.htm and www.astro.wisc. edu/~dolan/constellations/).

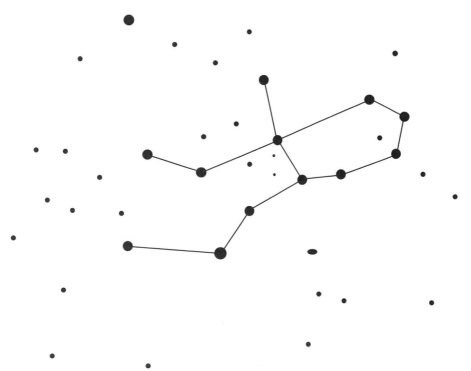

Virgo, The Virgin

57

Take a few minutes now to create a new constellation. Here are those same stars again. Use any of the stars you wish.

When the idea of creating new constellations first occurred to me, I gazed at Orion, The Hunter and tried to convert him into a TV set. I failed. A hunter he remains.

Once I realized I was forcing the process, I relaxed and returned to Virgo, The Virgin. I used my analytical nature to draw up some original sketches, but also let some intuitive ideas bubble up. Eventually, I saw Boris, The Bug crawling across the night sky upside down, his feet on the surface of the sky itself. For a view of Boris, The Bug, see the next page.

Those of you who were born under the astrological sign of Virgo can now say you are a Boris at parties. You'll be an instant hit. Isn't being creative fun?

You might think I cheated in my creation of Boris, The Bug, because I used curved lines. Who says lines must be straight? That's conventional thinking. Creativity is the ability to see things a little bit differently

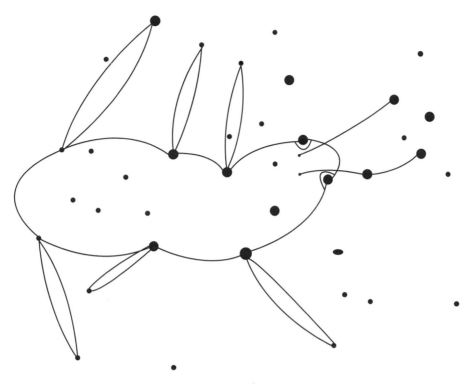

Boris, The Bug

from the norm, to view situations, people, and things in a new light. That's how analogies are born. And who says I can only draw one line between two stars? As you can see, in some cases, I drew two lines between stars. Creativity often involves a shift in perception or a leap from the "logical" to the intuitive.

In your head are numberless modules of knowledge. Think of these as stars of knowledge. You have drawn these into constellations to make sense of them and have filed them away. Creativity is making new constellations, new connections, from the same knowledge or information. Creativity searches for new relationships.

Johann Gutenberg did not create the printing press with movable type out of nothing. He was already familiar with the coin punch and the wine press. Putting these two together in a new way resulted in one of the greatest inventions in history. (The Chinese had movable type centuries earlier, but Europeans of that time did not know it.)

I just saw a PBS special on John Lennon that demonstrated how some of Lennon's work was influenced by black American artists. In other words, Lennon would hear something he liked and he would choose to view it in an innovative way; it then became a starting point or inspiration for a Beatles' song.

Imagine a scene early in the morning in some large city. Here's one description of that scene: *Garbage trucks roam vacant streets*. That's the conventional way of "seeing" that scene, but what does the "creative eye" see? *Garbage trucks roam vacant streets like mechanical monsters foraging for food*. That sentence, or something like it, might add a little more interest to the description of the scene, whether in a nonfictional or fictional piece.

My wife teases me because I am constantly trying to find new routes to the same old locations. I tell her I'm in constant search for the best routes and that I want to get off "the beaten path." In one instance, this practice may have saved my life. I was driving in the left lane of a three-lane boulevard when a guy in the middle lane pulled out a gun and eyed me angrily. Was he just "having fun," or had I cut him off earlier? I didn't know. I only knew I wanted to get out of there.

I remembered that there was an old narrow alley up ahead that I had once tried. I sped up and passed a semi that was in the middle lane, but the armed man was right behind me. I swerved in front of the truck and then into the far right lane. I slowed down quickly so that the truck was now between me and the armed man. Instantly, I turned down the old alley. From the armed man's view, I simply disappeared. On the way home, I counted my lucky stars that I knew where that alley was and could find a creative solution to my problem.

Get off the beaten path and try different routes through your mind; it may save your creative life. Look for new relationships. Shift your perception. Ask questions, including the "what if" question. Exercise your analytical, thinking side; that will inspire your creative, intuitive side. Choose to see things from a unconventional point-of-view or with a "creative eye." One of the many reasons the film *ET* was so successful is that it was mostly shot from a camera height of about three feet; in other words, we watched that film from the viewpoint of a child, not an adult. I often advise fiction writers and screenwriters (as a pre-writing activity) to write character sketches based on the viewpoint of the other characters. How does Jim see Sally? How does Mary see Sally? How does Sally see Sally? And, of course, how does the writer (you) see Sally?

A hippaglobium activity

What is a *hippaglobium*? Is it a philosophical idea? Is it an animal? Is it a medical condition? On a separate sheet of paper, draw a hippaglobium or describe it. Rely on your imagination. Have fun. Don't let the fear of failure or the fear of looking stupid infringe upon the process. Your creativity will be more abundant in a "yes" environment than in a "no" environment.

The great paradox

We have established the importance of freeing the creative mind, of releasing the inner writer. I have stated that the right brain works best when the left brain—the rule-maker—is otherwise occupied or relaxed. Thus, it only stands to reason that writers will be most creative when no constraints or restrictions are placed on their writing. Right?

Wrong.

Constraints cultivate creativity.

What is disagreeable to the artist is intrusion from the inner critic, but outside parameters are just the challenge the right brain relishes. Restrictions are inspiring. Let me give an example from the movies.

Psycho is considered one of the greatest horror films of all time, and yet there are only two acts of violence in the entire movie. Alfred Hitchcock and screenwriter Joseph Stefano were not allowed to show nudity, nor could they show a knife actually penetrating a body. Gore was not allowed. In the famous shower scene, the nudity is implied, and the knife is juxtaposed to the body, but never seen entering the body.

The Hershey's cocoa swirling down the drain was terrifying. In a word, Hitchcock and Stefano were forced to be *creative* in how events unfolded. Today, there are no or few restrictions to horror, and what do we get? Blood and guts, with little creativity. The art has not advanced.

It is possible to be creative without restrictions. There are plenty of examples. But that's not the point. The point is that constraints are helpful to the writer. I emphasize this principle because most developing writers are blocked (and sometimes angered) by the thought of restrictions. This is a conscious reaction; your subconscious mind loves it. This "block" is a veritable steppingstone to better writing.

Much of the great music of the past was commissioned. Even rock music, hip-hop, and rap adhere to some form or format. Everything artistic has two components—form and content. The creativity comes in how the writer crafts the content within the restrictions of that form. Yes, and sometimes the writer transcends that form.

The most restrictive writing form is the sonnet. Yet, some of world's best poetry comes in sonnet form. I remember the pain and joy of writing a poem in *iambic pentameter*. My college creative-writing teacher assigned me to write something worthy of the great poet-writer William Wordsworth. It took me 14 hours to write 14 lines, but I'm a better writer for it. In addition, three magazines paid me to publish it. And even though it wasn't actually worthy of Wordsworth, it was terrific for Trottier.

Michelangelo saw himself as, first and foremost, a sculptor. When Pope Julius II commissioned him to decorate the Sistine Chapel with frescoes, he was not initially interested or inspired. And yet, the result is considered one of the great works of art.

Don't be afraid of constraints, parameters, restrictions, and writing assignments. Embrace them. Of course, if no restrictions are imposed, then that's fine, too. But keep in mind that to turn lead into gold, you must first accumulate thoughts, ideas, information, and constraints. It is both the pressure of these *parameters* and the pressure of your *passion* that create the heat that causes the melt that transforms the problem into a solution. Thus, what begins as a left-brain activity culminates in a right-brain explosion—the solution bursts, bubbles, or flows into consciousness.

You can see the importance of the two sides of your nature working together. Constraints are a blessing. Approach the keyboard boldly in a happy, relaxed state of mind. Relish the writer's journey and trust the process.

The writing process

There are five general steps in the writing process:

1. Generate ideas

2. Set project parameters

3. Create the first draft

4. Revise for content

5. Polish for publication

Some of these steps may overlap.

Which of these five steps do you believe takes the most time? Which do you believe takes the least? How much time do professional writers spend on each step?

Although percentages can vary widely, depending on the writer and the type of material to be written, the following figures are reasonably accurate. Let's call these estimates:

Generating ideas and setting project parameters—30%

Creating the first draft—10%

Revising for content—45%

Polishing for publication—15%

Any surprises?

Let's discuss what goes into the creation and completion of a professionally written work.

1. Generate ideas

For some writers, ideas come easily. For others, it's the most difficult part. Whether you are searching for starter ideas or for ideas at any point in the writing process, here are 17 techniques to help make you productive.

1. Read. Science-fiction writer Ray Bradbury gives this advice: "If you stuff yourself full of poems, essays, plays, stories, novels, films, comic strips, magazines, music, you automatically explode every morning like Old Faithful." Writers not only write, they read. Read the kinds of material that you want to emulate.

2. Go to your safe harbor, meditate, or find a way to relax. In that state, suggest to yourself that you are open to knowing more about your creative center.

3. Brainstorm. Remember, all ideas are good ones until the brainstorming session is over. Have fun.

4. Freewrite. Sit down at a keyboard or with a pad of paper and start writing. Go to your safe harbor or otherwise relax your mind. With this technique, you try by not trying. You simply remain open with no expectation. Write whatever comes into your head, no matter how off-the-wall. Keep writing for ten minutes. Just let whatever is inside you gush out. Do not evaluate it or correct the spelling as you go. Doing that would invite your critical mode into the process. Stay in the creative mode by keeping the pen moving or the keyboard clicking—the physical act of typing or writing will keep the left brain occupied. If your mind suddenly blanks, just doodle with your pen or type, "More ideas are on their way."

There does not need to be any logical flow to what you are writing. If you can't seem to get started, just write, "I need an idea. Ideas are coming." And then keep writing. Continue until you get a feeling that you are on the right track or that you've hit a vein of gold. You'll have a sense, either sudden or gradual, of what you want to write about. As you can see, this is an intuitive process.

Another use of freewriting is when you already have an idea of something (such as a scene, section, chapter, etc.), but want to develop it. Just start writing about that idea and freewrite for ten or fifteen minutes. Some writers freewrite the entire first draft.

5. Blow creative bubbles. The rules for this are similar to those for freewriting. The main difference is that this technique is more visual. Some people think of it as *mind-mapping* or *clustering*.

Get a clean sheet of paper. In the middle of the page, jot down your writing problem, topic, idea, or concept. Draw a circle around it, making a bubble. Since this is a free-association exercise, it does not matter what word or words you start with. You could even write, "Idea generation" or, "Go."

Now brainstorm, using free-association. Whatever bubbles up in your mind, jot it down, circle it, and connect it to its parent. (Or simply make a list.) Go with any ideas that float by, regardless of how bizarre or strange they may seem. The connections do not need to be logical. Keep your hand moving. If you have a moment when no idea comes, don't panic—just doodle on a corner of the page until it does. Within about five or ten minutes, you'll have a feeling of what you're supposed to do. An insight will come, the solution will be revealed, or a new idea will leap into your mind. This may be very subtle or explosive. If nothing happens, just stay relaxed. Do not try to force the process.

Below, you will see the result of a brief session of my own.

Out of thin air, I chose the word "silvery" with which to start. You'll see that some of my responses seem logical and some seem completely unrelated to their parent. My first response was "moon," which led to "a star is born," and, surprisingly, "Boris, The Bug," my new favorite constellation. At the end of the exercise, I was converting lemons into lemonade. In a way, that is related to alchemy, a topic that has been heavy on my mind as I have worked on this book. However, I did not write "alchemy" in response to lemonade, but in response to "being positive." That's when I got the feeling I had *arrived*.

At that moment, I noticed three related ideas: being positive, being born, and striving for the light. It didn't take much of a jump to see how to make these ideas parallel: negative to positive, death to birth, darkness to light. This suggests an article or essay on the spirituality of self-improvement.

If I wished, I could conduct another session, using "spirituality of self-improvement" as my starting point. Blowing creative bubbles is a versatile tool that can be used in many different ways.

6. Rely on the Inspiration Cycle: Input, Incubation, Inspiration, Evaluation. After a few hours or days jamming your brain, relax and tell yourself you need a breakthrough. Then incubate. In other words, wait for the alchemical explosion. Eat. Swim with dolphins. Dance with wolves. Photograph cactus flowers. Take showers and naps. The inspiration may take a couple of minutes, a couple of hours, a couple of days, or even longer. But it comes soon enough. Now you're flying. You may continue to sail for some time. But don't stop when the flow stops. Evaluate what you've written (your Inner Critic has been waiting for just this moment) as a means to bring on the next cycle of inspiration.

7. Reflect on your past. Your past and your accumulated knowledge is research that has already been done. It's all inside you (or in your journal). You can draw from this well of experience. Write what you care about, what you have a passion for. Review the results of the previous exercises you have done.

Use the energy of pet peeves and gripes. Writing what you feel strongly about will help you keep going when the going gets tough. And keep in mind that the process of writing one piece will generate ideas for others.

8. Carry a small tape recorder or notepad. This sends a signal to the subconscious: "Wake up and get me some ideas." Carry it with you wherever you go. Place it by your bedstand at night. You will get many ideas by carrying around a recorder or notepad. Don't leave home without it.

9. Journalize. Anytime you write, you stimulate the subconscious to generate even more ideas. Consider keeping a *traditional journal*—the chronicles of your life. Another type of journal worth considering is a *learning journal*—an accumulation of things you've learned along the way. Many writers keep a *writer's journal*—a collection of ideas, descriptions, observations, scraps of conversations, and other scribblings. Transfer to your writer's journal what you collect using the notepad and tape recorder mentioned in #8 above.

10. Be an observer of people, life, and issues. Visit public places and observe. Go to a party. Hang out at an airport. Be aware of what is around you, and what is happening within you.

11. Stimulate the senses. Some writers prefer quiet and the lack of stimulation. Most writers, however, find simple ways to stimulate their senses. Engage in physical activity—gardening, chopping wood, shoveling snow, fishing, tripping to the desert, dancing, kneading clay, walking, driving, tinkering with the car. Physical activity not only relaxes you, but it stimulates the senses, and sensory details will stimulate your writing. It also occupies and relaxes your left brain so that the right brain can be free.

Listen to stimulating music. I like classical music and soundtracks because they stir my emotions and imagination. You, on the other hand, may prefer silence. You may find it helpful to look at a painting, sculpture, or other art object. Prepare a cup of tea and sip it slowly; be fully involved with it. Close your eyes and visualize as you write.

12. Empty your head. Sometimes you need to empty the junk inside your head in order to receive fresh creative impulses. I call this "cleaning the creative pipes." In your imagination (or in reality), sit by a river and watch it flow downstream. Imagine emptying your mind of all its junk and negativity, and watching the refuse flow down the river.

When I go fishing, I like to find a secluded spot by a creek in the mountains. I like the quiet of nature. Of course, the purpose of fishing is not to catch fish. I'm relaxing, emptying, and fishing for ideas. I have no expectations, but I carry my tape recorder with me just in case.

13. Study the areas of writing you are pursuing. Read books, attend seminars, and go to conferences. A successful automotive writer who was making more than $100,000 a year attended my seminar, *17 Ways to Make a Living as a Writer*. I asked him at the break why he attended. He said, "There's always plenty to learn."

14. Create rituals. Begin each writing session in the same manner. Acquire a ball cap and imprint or embroider the word "writer" on it. Whenever it is time to write, you can tell your loved ones, "I'm wearing my writer's cap tonight." Create opening and closing ceremonies for the Writer's Olympics, starring you! Writing should be fun, so have a good time.

Here is how my student Hanna begins every writing session. First, she removes all distractions (unplugs the telephone, shuts doors and windows). Second, she prepares a cup of herb tea. Third, as she savors the tea, she becomes aware of her senses. Fourth, she enters her safe harbor and says, "Analytical Brain, go to sleep so my Creative Brain can bring forth a masterpiece. A masterpiece needs to come forth." Then Hanna goes to her work area.

For you, that work area will probably be your desk with a computer and a keyboard. But it doesn't have to be. Mark Twain wrote in bed. Hemingway stood at a tall desk. And Dalton Trumbo, who won an Oscar with a movie script, sat in a bathtub with a plank across his lap to hold his typewriter. Whatever works for you is fine with me.

When Hanna, with her herb tea, needs her Analytical Brain, she calls for him. (She gives each side of her brain a gender.)

15. Steal. Shakespeare did. He borrowed most of his plots from other sources, including history. Screenwriters and novelists who followed him often do the same. *Romeo and Juliet* became the musical *West Side Story* and then *Titanic*. (In fact, James Cameron pitched this project as "Romeo and Juliet on the *Titanic*.") *Faust* became *Damn Yankees!*, *Rosemary's Baby*, and *Wall Street*. Borrow from fairy tales. *Cinderella* became *Pretty Woman*. Look for original twists on old ideas, regardless of what area of writing you pursue.

16. Ask "What if?" or some other question. What if my central character were a train engine instead of a child? (I am referring to *The Little Engine That Could* by Watty Piper.) What if this webpage had only four main sections instead of eight? How would this sequence play if I throw out this scene entirely? What if my demure heroine were a circus performer at night? Suppose I create a descriptive heading for each paragraph of this brochure and I tell the story of the product with those headings?

Don't be afraid to make a radical change to whatever you write or think about. You can always come back to your original notion later if you wish.

17. Confront your blocks and fears. We have already discussed this at length.

Once you have a gold mine full of ideas, you can search for nuggets, and pull out the one you like best. You will then be ready for the second step in the writing process.

2. Set project parameters

Once you have an idea, you need to define and refine it before you dive into the actual writing. Of course, some writers like to write the first draft before setting project parameters. This usually results in more time spent bringing the project to completion than would otherwise be needed. However, when you get an idea for a scene, chapter, or paragraph, write it down when it comes. The writing process should be flexible and adaptable to your nature and needs.

A writer is a communicator, and one of the key principles of written communication is the *Purpose-Audience-Strategy Principal* (the PAS Principle). Your purpose is your goal, what you want to accomplish with your writing. Your audience is the people your work is intended to reach. And your strategy is how you will reach them.

Purpose. What do you want your writing project to accomplish? Your purpose is your view of the value and nature of your writing project. Sometimes, the person or company who hires you determines your purpose in advance. It's likely that you have a general idea of your purpose already. The more specific your purpose, however, the more power it will have, and the easier it will be to write.

Bongo Anderson was a student of mine who wanted to write about skiing. (I have permission to use his name and essay.) I told Bongo that his topic was too general. I asked, "What do you want to say about skiing?" Bongo wasn't sure. I asked him several questions until he had created a purpose statement: *I want to convince Colorado skiers to ski in Utah.* His thesis became: *Skiing in Utah is more fun than skiing in Colorado because of better snow, easier access from the airport, and lower lift fees.*

Asking questions is a wonderful way to develop your writing project. Put your idea, topic, or thesis on the witness stand and pretend you are an attorney. Find out everything you can. Compare your idea to other ideas. Ask what others have said. Asking questions will not only shed new light on your writing project, but it may inspire new ideas or approaches.

What do you want to say about *your* topic? What is *your* thesis (summary of your entire project in a sentence or two)? What is your goal or objective? What do you want people to do or feel after they've read what you've written? Regardless of whether you agree with Bongo's thesis or not, you can see how much easier his essay was to write because he had defined his purpose. As he continued to clarify his project, he realized that he needed to ask himself what he meant by the vague expression "better snow." He learned the value of defining his parameters in advance.

Audience. No one sees the world the way it really is. All of us have a perception of reality that is influenced by our family, our religion, our culture, our ethnicity, our life experiences, our values, and our beliefs. We see everything through the filter of our past. Let's call this our *frame of reference.*

Your audience, which in most cases is your reader, has a frame of reference, a way of seeing the world. Your message might be *catch a fly.* From your reader's perspective, you might be referring to catching

71

a housefly, whereas you are actually referring to baseball. The point is to put some thought into how your reader might interpret your work. Even if you are appealing to a general audience, you will want to put some thought into how that audience might best understand what you want to communicate.

If you write a romance novel, your readership has certain expectations. You cannot ignore these altogether, but should take them into account when creating your strategy.

Virtually all writers have two audiences, or readers, that they must reach. The *first reader* is the decision-maker who decides to publish your work or not. Sometimes, it is the person who hired you to write. The *second reader* is the intended reader once your piece is published or produced. The most important of these is the first reader—the editor, the publisher, the agent, or the person who hired you to write. Be sure to identify what that person is looking for. Primarily, that person is looking for something that she can then sell to your second reader.

Ask yourself questions about both of these readers. What is their educational level? How are they likely to react to your topic or viewpoint? What are their biases and tendencies? What objections might they have? What do they expect in terms of tone or content?

Naturally, you don't want to compromise the integrity of your writing project. However, I suggest that, since you want to reach your readers, you will want to think about how to do so. It would be foolish to send an article to *Cosmopolitan* without having first read the magazine and "writer's guidelines."

Strategy. Your strategy derives from the needs and point-of-view of your audience. Your goal is to create a strategy that will reach your audience and accomplish your purpose.

Let's return to Bongo's essay on skiing. What should he include in his strategy? One consideration will be tone. What angle or slant will best reach the reader? Should he try to sound authoritative? Should he write a light piece with humor? Should he opt for a personal approach? Should he try to be persuasive?

Should he write in first, second, or third person? Generally speaking, first person provides a more personal tone. Second person involves the audience; it is often used for persuasion. Virtually all advertising is written in the second person. Third person gives your work a more objective feel.

Incidentally, the above explanation is written in third person, but it could have been written in second person, as follows: Write in first person for the personal touch. Use second person to involve your audience; that is why advertising is written that way. Use third person to sound objective and reasonable.

Bongo should also consider the many rhetorical strategies. For example, a *narrative* essay tells a personal story in first person. It utilizes the narrative strategy. Bongo could simply describe one wonderful day on the slopes—write it as a personal story.

The *comparison* strategy compares and contrasts two similar things on the same criteria. J. D. Taylor, a clever student of mine, wrote an essay about apples and oranges. They are similar—"both are fruits." But they are different—peeling "an orange requires the tools of a demolition expert." An apple doesn't require any peeling. "Just rub its pesticides off on your shirtsleeve, and your snack is ready to go." In Bongo's case, he could compare Utah skiing and Colorado skiing.

Other rhetorical strategies he could apply include *cause and effect, process analysis, classification,* and *argument.* Bongo could use this latter strategy to persuade people to take an action or adopt a point-of-view about skiing. He should argue his point or thesis using supporting evidence in a persuasive style. And, of course, he could use any combination of these strategies.

What form should the piece take? Should he write an article for a ski magazine? Is there enough material for a book? Maybe he should approach the topic obliquely by writing a novel or short story. Or perhaps he should just write a letter to the newspaper editor, giving his views.

Bongo should answer these questions and make his decisions with his potential readers in mind, while taking into account his particular skills.

Outline. My wife and I have contemplated driving across the country with our young children. (Aren't we brave?) There are three different approaches we could take in planning the trip.

The first is to just drive and see where the highway takes us. If we run out of money or gas, that will be part of the adventure. Naturally, it will cost more than if we had planned ahead, but it will be fun.

The second approach would be to plan a route with certain minutes allotted to each stop, with no changes or requests allowed. In this case, I would carry with me a whistle to signal when it's time to get back in the car.

The third would be to plan a route but be open to making changes to the plan.

In my mind, the third approach is the most sensible and useful.

The same is true for outlining. Outlines should not be written in stone, but they should be written. The purpose is to organize your thoughts, and to give you a map of where you are going. Naturally, the outline will change after you have begun the actual writing, but you will complete your project sooner than if you had not created an outline. I once planned social activities for the young adults in my church group. As you might guess, no activity went exactly according to my plan, but because I had a plan, it was very easy for me to adjust to new situations and unforeseen complications.

Research. Do the required research. With some projects, such as a personal essay, the only needed research is your personal experience and life. The nature of the project will determine the amount of research you need to do. When Laura Hillenbrand wrote *Seabiscuit*, she did months of research. This research filled dozens of boxes. The material was used again in creating the movie.

Some writers prefer researching after they have written the first draft. You should at least do enough research at this point in the process to determine whether you should move forward on the project or not.

A plan. A final parameter to be set is to create your plan for writing and marketing your project. We will deal with this in detail in Book IV. For now, let's take the initial steps towards the creation of a writing project.

Create a Writing Project

Using one of the 17 idea-generating methods, create an idea, premise, or concept of your writing project. If you have never tried "blowing creative bubbles" or "freewriting," then do so now.

_____

_____

_____

_____

Define the *purpose* of your writing project _____

_____

_____

_____

What do you know about your primary *reader* (the editor, publisher, person who hired you, writer's guidelines, etc.)? What is this person looking for? _____

_____

_____

What do you know about the ultimate *reader* of your work (the people who will eventually read your work)? How will they likely receive your work or react to it? _____

_____

_____

_____

What *strategies* will you employ to reach your readers and accomplish your purpose? Think in terms of tone, slant, approach, and/or style. Should you use first, second, or third person? What form should the work take (book, essay, brochure, poem, etc.)? What creative ideas do you have for this work that will make it stand apart from its competition?

_____

_____

_____

_____

_____

_____

In the space below, or on a separate piece of paper, create a thesis and an *outline*. Think of the thesis as the summary of your entire written work in a sentence or two. It is the topic plus the main point. The outline can be a long and detailed formal outline, or just three or four main points that support your thesis or central idea.

Thesis: _____

_____

_____

Outline:

Describe any *research* that you will need to do. _____

_____

_____

_____

_____

What are your goals or plans regarding the remaining steps (drafting, revising, and editing)? Create some kind of timeline or completion deadlines. These will become objectives to shoot for as your write your work.

_____

_____

_____

_____

_____

3. Write the first draft

You have written an outline. Now set it aside and write your first draft from the heart. Lose control. Don't edit as you go. Don't worry about spelling, punctuation, and grammar. Only refer to your outline occasionally, if at all. The work will evolve.

If you've ever been in a creative fever and then suddenly found yourself correcting spelling and punctuation, then you've experienced an intrusion of the inner critic. This affliction has blocked many a creative flow. Just relax and brush these intrusions aside—don't give them a second thought. Tell yourself, "I don't need to get this right. I just need to get this written. I can evaluate it later." Your first draft is very nearly a freewriting exercise.

4. Revise for content

If Step 3 is creation, then this step is recreation (pun intended). Now, the real work begins in giving your first draft shape, clarity, continuity, and unity. "Writing is rewriting," the saying goes. And the rewriting step will require both sides of your brain.

Before you revise your draft, revise your outline. That outline might be a one-page list of main points or a 12-page synopsis, depending on the project. The important thing is to re-assess where your project stands now by reviewing the earlier parameters you set.

Approach your draft with some level of emotional detachment. If you need to lay it down for a couple of weeks to let it get "cold," then do so. It's a practice I heartily recommend. Much of what you read may be unworthy. Don't be discouraged. The pearl takes a little time to develop.

Make sure you have a clear beginning, middle, and end. The beginning is the introduction or "set-up" of your work. The middle is the body. The end is the conclusion, recommendations, or resolution. The body will be, by far, the longest section in your work.

Your main task is to see if your content works. Is it truthful and accurate? Is the material well-organized? Are your main points clearly presented? Is there a logical flow to your writing? Is there plenty of support information along with examples? What works and doesn't work? When you read your draft, do you naturally stop at any point? If so, that's a red flag that something is not working.

You have an "inner voice" that knows what is and is not working. When I consult with writers, the common comment I hear is, "Dave, I kinda knew that already, but I needed you to tell me." As writers, we sometimes filter out that inner voice so that we don't have to do the hard work. We cling to the hope that maybe it will be okay as it is. Listen carefully to that silent inner voice, your writer's soul. Trust the process, even when you don't know for sure where you're headed. Sometimes you're flying blind and sometimes you have a complete vision.

I once had an uneasy feeling when reviewing a screenplay, so I began brainstorming by asking "What if" questions. One of those was, "What if my central character were a woman instead of a man?" It worked. Since then, I have not been afraid to make radical changes to my writing. Don't make the mistake of getting "too close" to early drafts. It is essential that you remain open to new inspiration and ideas until Step 5. What if you get stuck? You know by now that that's a good thing. Relax and trust the process. Some solutions come instantly and some take time.

When revising anything, if you find yourself inadvertently solving one problem by solving a different problem, then that's a green flag that you are on the right track. Things are coming together.

As you revise, you will find yourself seeing better ways to phrase things. I include some of those ways as part of the fifth and final step in the writing process.

5. Polish for publication

George Bernard Shaw, the acclaimed playwright, in writing a letter to a friend, remarked, "Please excuse the length of my letter. If I had more time, it would be shorter." It takes time to transform that lifeless string of sentences into an opus with sparkle and fizz. Some (or a lot) of that will happen naturally in the revising step.

Examine your paragraph structure and sentences. Is the central action of the sentence told with an active verb? Active voice is usually preferred over passive voice. *He decided* is better than *He came to a decision*, which is better than *It was decided by him*, which is better than *It was decided*. I wrote the first two versions in active voice and the second two in passive voice. In the fourth version, we don't even know who did the deciding.

Passive voice is a form of *to be* (is, was, were, has been, will have been, and so on). These are the weakest and most lifeless verbs in the language. Still, there are times when a passive voice is both preferred and useful. In fact, I wrote the previous sentence in passive voice.

As a general rule, sentences written in active voice carry a sense of movement and usually create more interest.

(Incidentally, I originally wrote the previous sentence [in italics above] as follows: "As a general rule, active voice is preferred because it is more interesting." When I realized I had used the verb "is" twice, I decided to revise the sentence using an active voice. The result [in italics above] is a stronger sentence.)

What is the strongest part of speech? Most of my students respond with "the adjective." I always hope they will respond with "the verb." That's because active, specific verbs and nouns form the foundation of great sentences. For example, let's examine the following sentence: *He was walking to the house.*

Some writers might convert this to active voice with the following revision: *He walked to the house.* That's an improvement, but it is still a weak sentence. How would you fix it?

Many writers add adverbs and adjectives to dress it up: *He walked slowly to the big, yellow house.* The adjectives and adverb help, but the sentence is still flat. Rather than begin with helping words (adjectives and adverbs), why not first make the verb and noun more specific and concrete? How about this? *Delbert staggered to the mansion.* Now the sentence creates a much clearer image in the reader's mind without the writer having to wax verbose.

The best way to reach any audience, including a general audience, is with specific language and details. Even a business memo will benefit from the use of specific language. If the memo says, *Employees will be excused early*, that's too general. At what time will they be excused? And which employees? On what day? Will they get paid for being gone? Let's revise the sentence to include the necessary specific information: *All full-time employees will be excused from work at noon, this Friday, November 13. They will be paid for a full day's work.*

Of the 17 writing areas we will discuss in the next book, virtually all of them will benefit from specific *sensory* detail. Sensory details help your reader see, hear, touch, smell, and even taste. They involve the reader. I have read many stories and essays from students and clients that present general descriptions. Here's an example.

He walked down the hot street barefoot until he found his thongs. When he put them on, he found a nice-looking car and decided to buy it.

With sensory detail, my student converted this general and vague description into a more specific (and more interesting) paragraph.

The barefoot teen tiptoed down the hot asphalt road until he spotted his worn thongs lying near the cement curb. With the agility of a roadrunner, he zigzagged across the street and plunked his bottom on the curb, rubbing his feet and removing tiny black asphalt fragments. Thank Heavens humans have thumbs! An involuntary sigh of relief accompanied the brief, deep massage. It was at that moment of comfort that his eyes rested on the fresh crimson paint of a restored '67 Mustang convertible. The chrome was so shiny that the glare from the sun nearly blinded him. Was it a mirage? He craned his neck for a better view of the roadster and decided right then and there to own it.

This is not great literature (and we've only included details of sight and touch), but at least the reader has a chance now of enjoying the experience.

Sometimes, general prose and the passive voice are exactly the right choice. One of the great novels of all time (*A Tale of Two Cities* by Charles Dickens) opens with *It was the best of times, it was the worst of times. . . .* So don't settle on just one stylistic tool. Abraham Maslow once remarked that "he who is good with a hammer thinks everything is a nail." Make sure you collect many different writing tools for your writer's toolbox.

Some writers feel they need to use big words to be effective writers. They should first take into consideration their readers. My general advice is to not be overly concerned about using big, impressive words. The important thing is to find the *right word*. Hemingway sets the example in this regard. He was not afraid of small words and simple sentences.

The bottom line is that you want to find your own voice and develop your own writing style(s).

Your final editing task is to check your work for typos, spelling, punctuation, and grammar. It doesn't make any sense to do this early in the process, since many paragraphs will be deleted or radically revised anyway. Do this last.

As you proofread your writing, read aloud. You will catch many more errors that way. When you read silently, your eyes and brain often see things the way they should be seen, and gloss over errors.

Write a brief narrative

Think of a singular experience from your past, either from your childhood or later. The experience should have taught you some lesson or be memorable for an important reason. (If applicable, you may use the idea created in the previous exercise.) As you recall and relive that experience (without doing any writing), identify at least one *specific* detail of each of the five senses (sight, sound, touch, smell, and taste). Do the best you can. For example, if you don't recall a detail of taste, then that's fine. If you recall four specific details of sight, then great.

_____

_____

_____

_____

_____

_____

_____

_____

In addition, identify one or two emotions that you felt and that any other people involved felt. Finally, what was the key moment in your experience? What would you say was the point, lesson, message, or theme of your experience? _____

_____

_____

In the space below or on a separate sheet of paper, and using the above details and information, write a short narrative or story describing your experience for a general reader.

_____

_____

_____

_____

_____

_____

_____

_____

_____

_____

_____

_____

_____

_____

_____

_____

_____

_____

_____

_____

_____

_____

Now that you have written a draft of your narrative, circle all of the verbs and put a rectangle around each noun. For the most part, are your verbs and nouns specific and concrete? Have you used the *right words* to recreate the experience in the mind and heart of your reader?

◆ ◆ ◆ ◆ ◆

The writing tips we have discussed in this book apply to all 17 areas of writing. Naturally, you will want to continue developing your craft in the specific areas of writing you have chosen.

In Book III, you will learn how to sell what you write. Are you ready? Let's go!

SELL TO 17 KEY WRITING MARKETS

BOOK III

Setting up your writing business for little or no money

The entirety of Book III is devoted to making money for you. The focus is on selling your work in 17 key writing areas. You can make a living in any of the 17 areas of opportunity.

Read each chapter of this book because what you learn in one area may help you in another. Once you have chosen your writing areas of interest, you will want to continue learning about those areas as you build your writing business. Before we plunge into any specific writing opportunity, however, let's first set up your writing business—legally, physically, mentally.

Setting up legally. What should you call your writing business? I suggest you simply use your name. Otherwise, you may have to file for a fictitious name or DBA (doing business as) permit with your state government. You will not need a resale license or sales-tax license unless you sell something tangible, such as books, to customers.

Business licenses are usually issued by cities. However, don't worry about getting one until you are actually making money as a business writer or entrepreneur.

Keep track of all relevant expenses and capital expenditures. These become bona fide deductions from your writing income. You can declare these even if you lose money in a given year. However, once you declare yourself to be a writer with the IRS, you must make a profit in at least *three of the first five years* you "declare yourself" a writer, so don't declare yourself until you are making some kind of writing income. How do you declare yourself? By completing a Schedule C at the end of the year as part of your income tax return.

If you are a voracious reader or have a problem with insomnia, let me recommend IRS Publications 334 and 583. These publications contain everything you could possibly want to know about taxes for small-business owners like yourself. However, you are not likely to need them. Instead, the standard 1040 package should be plenty. The main tax forms you need are the 1040 and Schedule C. You may need additional forms, but you'll be led to these by the above two forms. In addition, you'll need Form 1040-ES.

Don't panic. I'm going to help you with these. They're not as difficult as you might think. I've known space scientists and computer programmers who have breezed through them. However, I must make the following disclaimer:

> *Because the tax code changes so often, I cannot guarantee that anything I write about taxes will be completely accurate. Also, since I am not an attorney or an accountant, I am not qualified to give legal or accounting advice; anything I write in this "Bible" should not be construed as such. Always consult with an attorney or CPA for such information.*

Form 1040-ES is for estimating your taxes. It's not usually part of the regular annual tax forms you use to report your taxes. When you receive significant writing income without taxes being automatically deducted from that income, then the IRS wants you to pay your taxes in advance every quarter. This form helps you estimate those taxes so that you know what to pay. It's simple.

The Schedule C is the form you use when you earn money as an independent contractor and not as an employee. As a freelance writer, you are an independent contractor and small-business owner. You work for yourself. You should use the Schedule C to report your writing income and expenses. You will calculate your social-security tax (self-employment tax) on Schedule SE.

Let's review a list of possible expenses you may be able to deduct as a writer on your Schedule C: advertising, mileage directly related to writing, professional services (print houses, CPAs, copyright registration fees), licenses and taxes, office expenses (paper, pens, photocopies, toner, files, computer disks, and other office supplies), postage, business-related phone calls, writing publications, and membership fees. You can deduct travel if it's for writing purposes. Write down the date and the business purpose of the trip. If you drove, calculate the number of miles you traveled. You can usually deduct the cost of seminars you attend (including travel) and educational expenses that improve your writing skills; college educational expenses that lead to a degree are seldom deductible because they (in theory) give you those skills in the first place.

You may deduct an office in your home (Form 8829) if that office or space is used exclusively for writing. You'll want to read up on what the current rules are. As a general guideline, do not deduct an office in your home if you are going to move soon.

If you make capital expenditures (major purchases) for computers or office furniture for your business, for example, you may depreciate these (Form 4562).

If reading this makes you dizzy, then consider hiring an accountant or using a tax preparation service. Another alternative is tax preparation software such as TurboTax. If you hire someone to do your taxes, then all you will need to worry about is keeping track of your expenses, along with the receipts for those expenses.

Preparing your writing environment. You don't need to set up an office, although you can if you have space. Most writers simply sit down at the family computer. If you don't have a computer, buy one. Even a used PC with Microsoft® Word® (a component of the Microsoft® Office® system) or other word-processing software is infinitely better than a typewriter. You will need access to a computer printer as well. It is unlikely you will need a separate business telephone line, unless you are a commercial writer. Your chair should provide adequate lumbar support, and the lighting should not tire your eyes.

At the end of each writing day, back up any writing files that you used during that day. And "save" regularly while you are writing.

You do not need a printed letterhead. You can create your own letterhead with your computer software. Don't put "writer" or "freelance writer" on your stationery; it usually comes across as amateurish. All you need is your name, address, phone number, and e-mail address. A 24-pound stock will be more impressive than the usual 20-pound stock. As a general rule, do not use a brightly colored stock, but opt for a more professional (and thus, more conservative) color such as white, ivory, gray, and so on. Make sure any written communication is well expressed and free of errors in punctuation and grammar. Sign in blue or black ink.

Business cards are seldom necessary. If you must create one, don't include the term "writer." We'll discuss "calling cards" in the next chapter.

Be organized. Keep files of writing projects and other information. You may want a file cabinet, although a box will do. You may need a system for keeping track of clients, queries, clips (copies) of your work, finances, and so on. I keep a log of every phone call I make or receive that relates to writing. I also keep track of every query and every submission. I maintain an appointment calendar of any appointments, whether in person or by phone. I will provide examples of some of the logs that I use in Book IV.

The only outright purchase I am going to recommend is a subscription to *Writer's Digest*. If you are going to write articles, stories, books, and other traditional markets, I recommend *Writer's Market,* published annually by Writer's Digest Books. Also, consider the *Canadian Writer's Market* by Sandra B. Tooze.

Mental preparation. If you've done the exercises in the first two books, then you are ready. Think of yourself as a professional writer. You own a writing business. You are serious and committed. Try to get support from loved ones. Realize that about half of your dedicated time will be devoted to selling your work and learning about your craft. Don't be afraid to ask for writing assignments or for money. Prepare yourself to receive criticism, both positive and negative. Be close to your manuscript baby when you are nurturing her and somewhat detached when you evaluate her and sell her. Be patient and persevere.

If you have no writing credits or clips (copies of published work), write some free articles for the local newspaper, your church's newsletter, or a publication of your current employer. If you have some knowledge or skill of a particular trade or business, write an article for a trade publication. Donate your services to a non-profit organization as described in Chapter 3 of this book. Network as described in Chapter 1 of this book. In other words, get your feet wet now.

And be open-minded about business writing. After attending my seminar in Hilo, Hawaii, one student secured contracts worth $1,800 the next day. A Rhode Island woman wrote the following:

> Before your seminar, I had believed that the only "legitimate" freelance writing was the so-called traditional magazine writing. It hadn't occurred to me that commercial writing was not only legitimate but also highly profitable. Of the 17 writing opportunities we discussed, I have successfully tackled 10 during the past 9 months. I have prepared brochures, written and produced newsletters, prepared press releases and press kits, written ad copy, published magazine articles, and written business reports. . . . Business writing makes the best use of my communication skills, business experience, and education. Best of all, I am having a ball!

What follows is a general guide to what you might be paid for a variety of freelance assignments.

Fee Guidelines for Freelance Copywriters

Amounts can vary depending on your experience and reputation, the client, economic conditions, geographical region, and the specific nature of the project.

Hourly rate .... $30-$130+
Daily rate .... $400-$1,000
Per-word rate .... $1-$2
Ad (full page, print) .... $150-$550 (less for newspaper ads)
Ad, E-mail .... $35-$100 per hour
Ad, Radio .... $50-$400
Ad, Television .... $250-$600+
Annual report (large) .... $3,500-$15,000 ($600-$1,500 small)
Audio cassette script .... $20-$50 per finished minute
Brochure .... $150-$750 per page ($75-$125 per hour)
Business article .... $.75-$1 per word
Business letter .... $100 per page (more for form letters)
Business plan .... $2,000-$6,000
Case studies .... $50-$60 per hour
Catalog .... $50-$80 per page (more for direct-mail catalog)
Desktop publishing .... $30-$60 per hour
Direct-mail package (to generate leads) .... $40-$125 per hour
Direct-mail package (to generate sales)..... $50-$150 per hour
Editing and rewriting................................ $30-$100 per hour
Fund-raising campaign brochure............... $35-$75 per hour
Gags for entertainers .... $10-$40 per gag or joke
Ghostwriting .... $25-$60 per hour (more if no credit or byline)
Grant proposals .... $35-$100 per hour
Newsletter .... $200 per page
Pamphlet or booklet .... $.50-$1 per page
Press kit .... $250 per item ($500-$3,000 for the entire kit)
Press release (1-3 pages) .... $100-$400
Public relations .... $35-$125 per hour
Proofreading .... $20-$40 per hour (or $3 per page)
Research .... $25-$75 per hour
Résumé .... $250-$500
Sales letter .... $250-$800 per page
Speech (half-hour in length) .... $2,000-$4,500
Technical writing or business writing .... $40-$100 per hour
Video or DVD script .... $200-$500 per minute (or 10% of budget)
Webpage (writing only) .... $30-$70 per hour ($50-$250 per page)

POSSIBLE TERMS AND CONDITIONS

1. Revisions of copy are free; changes in concept or nature of the assignment are extra.
2. A written agreement is required for all projects.
3. Fee is payable 50% in advance with the balance due on receipt of the final revision. (Large jobs such as video scripts and business plans are payable 25% in advance, with like amounts paid at different work stages, with the final 25% paid on completion.)
4. There are no additional charges to the client.

1. Copywriting

As you might guess from the testimonials you just read and the fee chart above, this area is probably the best money for the effort. To illustrate: Recently an ad agency called me and asked me to rework a brochure. That was just over four hours' work for a quick $500. Of course, you won't make that much in your first assignment, but the potential is there. After all, there is a big demand and less competition than you will find in the traditional areas of writing. Why make pennies per word when you can make dollars per word? It's also easier to get paid.

Your basic task is to contact businesses and advertising agencies and sell them your writing skills in developing marketing collateral such as brochures, newsletters, flyers, reports, public relations materials, and other sales literature. This area also includes writing and creating ads and direct-mail materials. Writing *copy*, or content, for the above is referred to as *copywriting*. This writing area also includes creating web-pages, product sites (dedicated to selling a single product or range of products), and banners for Internet advertising.

How to attract clients

Regardless of your writing preferences, I recommend that you read carefully the following list. You will likely get new ideas on how to promote your work. If you are just starting out as a freelancer, I recommend that you first try those methods that are simple and inexpensive. These are not listed in any particular order, but the first one is key.

Build an arsenal of work samples. Make sure you get copies *in finished form* of any work that you do. You can also include any published articles in your arsenal. If you have done anything for a present or past employer, include that. Write copy for a bogus company and include that. Offer a small business a half-price deal; you'll end up writing a piece that you can show. Donate your services to a non-profit organization. Write an article for a trade magazine or small newspaper, even if it is for free. Anything that appears in print conveys the sacred truth that you are a professional writer. Use these as ammo to fire at prospective clients.

You don't need an oversized leather portfolio of dozens of items to show clients. With the Purpose-Audience-Strategy Principle in mind, focus your sights on your prospective client and create a strategy that will reach that prospect and accomplish your purpose—getting a commission. From your arsenal, select specific pieces to show to the particular client with whom you are meeting. Talk to her about her needs and what she's trying to accomplish. Let her ask you about your work or qualifications, and *then* open your arsenal and select relevant pieces for her to see.

As a support to the above, consider creating a website that showcases your work.

Build a website. Think of a website as a support to the things you are already doing. Resist the temptation to spam. However, e-zines and e-mail to established clients are a great way to stay in contact, so build an e-mail list of clients and people who contact you through the Internet. For more information on developing a website, see Chapter 17: "Teaching, consulting, and self-promotion" in this book. E-zines are explained in Chapter 16.

Publish articles and columns. Write a brief article of about 500-1,200 words for a business or trade publication, or even the local newspaper. The topic could be something like "Ten Tips for Writing Tantalizing Ads" or "Making Your Next Brochure a Winner." In other words, address a need that your writing services meet. Be sure to query the editor first. (See Chapter 7 of this book for detailed information.) Even if you are not paid for your article, think of it as free advertising. Some publications, including newspapers, will accept a free column from you if they think it is print-worthy. At the end of any column or article, include a brief blurb about you and how you can be contacted.

Once the article or column is published, make copies and use them as "calling cards." Send a copy to a potential client (and then follow up with a phone call), add it to your arsenal of work samples, or use it in connection with a direct-mail campaign.

Print a calling card and stationery. Do you need business cards? Probably not. I've usually used samples of my work as my calling cards. However, at one time, I created a card that simply said, "Dave Trottier

– precisely the person you seek." That way, I could specialize in anything. If someone needed a brochure, I could say, "That's what I do," and hand them my card. I could have just as easily handed them a brochure, flyer, article, or newsletter rather than a business card.

You can create your own letterhead on your computer. Use a conservative 24-pound paper as discussed earlier.

Develop your voice of conviction. Your number one asset is your enthusiasm. Your skills, ideas, credits, and work samples are just bait. If you can speak (in person, on the phone, or through the written word) with a voice of conviction about your services, then that will go a long way towards getting clients. You have a mission statement; you are now a missionary. Be confident, not arrogant. Be pleasantly persistent, not obnoxiously persistent.

How do you gain self-confidence? By doing. Your confidence grows over time as you continue to work. Trust the process and watch yourself grow in ability and income.

Network. There are many types of businesses you can approach. There are large corporations that often hire independent contractors because of the additional cost of retaining employees. You are that independent contractor. Naturally, many corporations will retain people in-house, but they also use advertising agencies and public-relations firms. Contact these types of companies as well.

Although advertising agencies will have employees that do most of the writing, they often farm-out jobs. You will want them to know that you are available. Virtually all advertising agencies will have an art director. This is usually the person who shepherds a given project.

There are many independent art directors who have relationships with clients and agencies. Art directors are often looking for writers to connect with because it enhances their own marketability. One of the smartest things I did when I got started was connect with Jack, The Art Director. He could not write and I could not draw. Because he knew me, he was able to tell clients and agencies that he had a writer. This increased his marketability. I, in turn, could refer business to him.

I also approached printers that sometimes received assignments they couldn't handle because of inadequate written communication skills. I told them I was a writer and would like to bring some of my business to them. In return, I would appreciate any referrals they could give me. If you approach printing companies or other related businesses, ask them if you can leave some information on the counter.

One time, an art director, a photographer, a printer, and I formed an informal team and created a superb brochure about our services. All four of us donated our services, so the brochure cost us nothing. In addition, we all had a nifty brochure or "calling card" that we could show potential clients.

An excellent source of work is small businesses and local concerns. Small businesses are often quite open to meeting potential writers. Besides approaching people at their places of business, you can call them or write them. In addition, you can try to meet them where business people gather. Your attitude at such gatherings is: "What are you working on? I'd love to be involved." Many business organizations sponsor luncheons or events; be there. Read the business section of the local newspaper for notices and information.

Ask for referrals. Any referral you can get is a huge plus. There are six general categories of people that you know:

- Business people who can hire you
- Business people who can refer you to people who can hire you
- Ordinary people who can hire you
- Ordinary people who can refer you to business people who can hire you
- Clients
- Places where you shop

In the last instance, I recall talking to the owner of a small shop about her marketing needs. The conversation eventually evolved into what I did for a living. Before the conversation was over, I had a deal.

Collect testimonials. When you get a verbal compliment from a client, ask if you can jot it down and use it. Send happy clients a letter asking for their "thoughts," "experience," or "opinion" of your services. Ask them to write it by hand on your letter and to return it in the enclosed stamped envelope. Make sure they have granted permission in writing to be quoted. If you don't get a response, don't approach them again or mention it again.

Give discounts. As a young buck, I worked as a custodian and grounds-keeper to keep myself in college. After completing an accounting class, I decided that being a bookkeeper would be more fun than cleaning toilets at four in the morning. I offered small businesses a 50% discount on my services for the first two months. After that, my fee would revert to my regular rate. I acquired two clients immediately. Consider trying this same tactic with businesses in your area. Make sure you establish up-front the length of time your discount is in effect and the fee your client will pay when that period expires.

Offer free gadgets. I am referring to pens, coffee mugs, and other premiums bearing your name and phone number. I have not tried this angle myself; I've always thought an article, newsletter, or brochure would be more useful. However, my printer recently gave me a letter-opener with his company name and phone number on it, and I call him for printing jobs because that letter-opener is right in front of me. Furthermore, an established writer making six figures as a free-lancer told me at one of my workshops that his free coffee mug was a winner.

Place a small ad. Consider classified advertising in newspapers under "writing services" or "freelance writing," and, once you are established, use trade journals such as *Advertising Age*. After all, you don't have to confine yourself to doing business in your own town or city. You can go national once you are somewhat established. Read ads of competitors and decide on how to set yourself apart from the pack. If you are having success with classified ads, consider a small display ad.

Make speeches. If you're a talker, offer to speak for free at a business-club event or luncheon. Or create a two-hour seminar on marketing for small businesses. Network after the event. The more useful your information is to listeners, the more likely they'll want to hire you. For more information on teaching, see Chapter 17 in this book.

Write a newsletter. A simple, one-page self-mailer or e-mail version (e-zine) works great. This is something that you can use as a calling card or direct-mail piece. Aim your newsletter at current clients (even if you don't have any), so prospects receiving the newsletter will assume you have a clientele. Naturally, the newsletter will contain useful and impressive information.

Create brochures and flyers. If you create your own brochure, it must look great because people will judge you by it. They will compare it to what they envision for themselves. I recommend a two-fold brochure that can fit in a standard #10 business envelope. Naturally, a brochure can be used as a calling card and be included in a direct-mail campaign.

Plan and execute a direct-mail campaign. This is an effective advertising method if done right. It can also be expensive, so don't get too elaborate. All you need is a well-written, one-page sales letter and perhaps an enclosure such as a brochure, newsletter, or relevant article written by you. If you have the bucks, consider a reply card of some kind. (Consult with the post office about the cost of business-reply cards.) Make sure your phone number and your e-mail address are on your sales letter. Invite the prospect to call you.

Address the envelope and letter to an individual. Don't send anything to "Occupant" or "Business Owner." Collect names from professional lists or just the Yellow Pages. The sales letter will include the following three sections:

- An attention-getting statement, fact, quote, or question.

- The reason the prospect needs you. Include your qualifications.

- What the prospective client should do next and how he or she will benefit.

If you don't hear from the person within 7-10 days of the mailing, call him or her. Make sure you follow up on any contact you make, regardless of how you initially made that contact.

Before you conduct a mailing, test the letter on about 5%-10% of the names you have collected.

Generate word-of-mouth advertising. Do you realize you are in control of this? You directly influence the amount of word-of-mouth advertising. If you do a great job for one client, the word will get around. Many professional freelance copywriters reach a point where they don't have to prospect for new clients.

Build a reputation. Sometimes getting very good at one specific thing pays off. However, I recommend that you get very good at several related things.

Encourage repeat business. You do that by giving your client quality work, and also by being responsible in meeting deadlines and understanding needs. Stay in touch with clients with a note, newsletter, e-mail, article, or something you think they'd like. Be considerate of production assistants, secretaries, and other people employed by your client. If the company is large, make your services available to other departments of the same company. Let the client know of other areas in which you "specialize." Don't hit too hard; use a velvet glove.

Have a plan. Regardless of the methods you choose to find work, make sure you have a clear plan and focus. When you set up a meeting, set personal goals for that meeting, but make sure the meeting itself is focused on the client or prospect. Don't be afraid to ask for the assignment or commission.

Start now. Don't wait to get started because you don't feel you have a perfect knowledge of the writing business. That "perfect knowledge," if it exists, can only come with experience. Just dive in and start swimming. Keep track of leads and have a follow-up program. Use the logs I provide in Book IV.

Continue your education. Pick up brochures and literature everywhere you go. Study the good stuff and the bad stuff. Read books in the field. When you work with other professionals, such as printers and art directors, quiz them about what they do. Learn the jargon of the industry.

How to get paid

At first, you will charge around $30-$50 an hour for your services. As you can see from the chart that precedes this chapter, there's plenty of room to grow as you build your reputation. Realistically, you won't be making a full-time living during your first year, but you certainly should in your second year. All you need is 15 productive hours a week to make $2,000-$3,300 a week. That's about $5,000 a month ($60,000 a year) for 25 productive hours a week. It's easy to see how many established copywriters make six figures annually, or close to it.

There are two ways to bill clients for your services. Most freelancers charge a fixed fee for each job because clients feel more secure being charged a definite figure. Other freelancers charge an hourly rate. In either case, you will look at the nature of the job and estimate how long it will take you to complete it. And then you make a proposal for doing X job for Y amount of dollars. You can make the proposal on the spot or promise to deliver one to the client (in person, by mail, or via e-mail) the next day. Strike while the iron is hot; don't wait too long to do this.

Get any agreement you make in writing. In other words, once your proposal is made, ask for a purchase order, contract, or a letter of agreement. If necessary, send the client a letter summarizing what was discussed. Label it a "letter of agreement." It is not legally binding because the other party did not sign it, but it may morally obligate the client to pay you.

Ask for half of your fee up front. Your attitude is *this is a normal part of doing business*. Say, "As soon as I have a check, I'll get right on this." The remainder of your fee should be paid on completion of the job. Make sure the terms of your work are understood up front. The value of your service decreases once it is performed. This is true for all services. People will pay a roofer anything if they have a leaky roof above their bed, but once the roofer has performed his service, the grumbling about his fee begins. Thus, you need to set your terms and get a commitment and some money when your service is most valued—*before* you perform it. If a client tells you the check is in the mail, say, "Fantastic. As soon as it arrives, I'll get to work. I'm looking forward to this project."

Make sure the client understands how revisions are handled. Usually, they are part of the job, but a complete change in the nature of the project should cost extra. Many small-business owners and entrepreneurial types will suddenly change the nature of a project as they are "inspired." The client should provide all research materials.

Be professional and be positive. Don't get chummy or too familiar with your client. Don't imply dishonesty of the other party. You ask for money up front and/or a purchase order because that's how you do business with everyone. If possible, try to find out in advance how your client usually operates and pays.

With any first job (or any job), make a positive first impression. Remember, you're more interested in establishing a relationship with the client and a basis for future sales than you are in getting a single job. Therefore, you will deliver work on time and deliver invoices on schedule. You will commit to these deadlines when you make the deal with the client. I am always amazed at businesses that pay tons of money for advertising to get customers into the store and then treat them poorly once they have finally arrived. It costs much less in time and money to retain clients and customers than to get new ones.

If a payment is late, make a phone call or a visit. That's much more effective than a late notice or letter. Ask the client about business. It may be you'll get another job. Of course, you won't start it until the previous one is paid for. Ask, "When will the check be ready?" Your last resort is to use a collection agency, Better Business Bureau, or small-claims court. You will need any purchase orders, signed agreements, and invoices for this. As a general rule, the larger the business, the more likely they are to pay you. When you are not paid, stop writing.

As your skills and clientele build, you may want to increase your rates. Before you do, put some thought into the matter; you want to create a strategy that won't backfire. Provide a sensible reason for the rate-hike. Always give ample warning of any increase in your fees. I recommend that you announce your new fee schedule about 60 days before they go into effect. Then, a week prior to that effective date, call each client and prospect and tell them they can still hire you at the lower rate this week.

The types of assignments you'll get

You'll be hired to write *marketing collateral*. That includes all company literature, including brochures, annual reports, catalogs, flyers, information sheets and booklets, newsletters, public relations materials, and so on.

Corporate brochures and annual reports. These are image-makers. They show off the company at its best, state its objectives and mission, and provide other company data. These are not usually direct sales pieces, but are informative. They are meant to impress people, especially the company bigwigs who commission it. Although these brochures may lead to sales, they are seldom focused on the company's products and services. Instead, they say *What a fine company are we!* These assignments are usually given to copywriters with a track record.

Sales brochures. I suggest you focus on sales brochures if you are a new freelancer. Sales brochures present a product or service in the most positive light possible. Sizes and lengths vary widely, but the most common brochure size is the *slim jim*, which folds twice like a letter and fits into a regular #10 business envelope. Some slim jims are designed as self-mailers with no envelope required. Businesses love these because they can be included in a direct-mail package, mailed out separately, or added to any public relations or promotional package. *Brochures are versatile.*

A brochure or any other piece of marketing collateral should grab the reader immediately. You will likely work with an art director in creating a headline to highlight the main image on the brochure. Jack, the Art Director, once gave me a photograph of a technical piece of equipment called a CAT and asked for a headline. I asked about the CAT's features and benefits, and Jack told me that this equipment was very quiet—that's what made it unique. I said, let's have a cat curl up next to it and write, "Can this cat purr."

Before writing a brochure or other marketing piece about a product or service, list its features and benefits. Features are the logical argument and benefits are the emotional argument. A life-insurance salesman will present the features of the policy, including the amount of money that will accrue and the payoff if you die. But the benefits will be more emotional: "Imagine, Mr. Jones, when your little girl graduates from college and says, 'Thanks, Dad, for making all of this possible.' How will you feel then?"

Brochures and ads are usually divided into short sections, each beginning with a descriptive heading. After you write a brochure, read just the headings for flow, continuity, and marketing appeal. Readers of brochures almost always glance at the headings before reading the content. For that reason, don't be afraid to write relatively long headings or subheadings.

Romance the product or service.

Every product has a story. My wife and I were in a jewelry store. The owner showed us some pieces and said, "The woman who crafted [not made] this jewelry travels the world in search of only the most beautiful and rare stones. And each one conveys the essence of its exotic origin." I smiled because the owner was literally *romancing the stone.* She understood the importance of painting a picture. Your writing should be visual and sensuous.

If you see an emotional hot button associated with the product, push it with your deft writing skills. Look for points of comparison to illustrate your point. I wrote copy for a financial company and contrasted Smith and Jones, each of whom invested $10,000 over a period of ten years. For example, Jones invested "wisely" (with my client); Smith invested in less-productive investments. Jones invested monthly, using *dollar cost averaging,* while Smith invested at whim. And the comparison continued.

Do a rough layout of the marketing piece without stepping on the art director's toes. In fact, the art director will likely present you with a model. One of my all-time favorite writing experiences resulted from a call from an ad agency. They needed me to do a Honda brochure. A mock-up of the entire brochure was given to me with boxes marked as follows: "70 words, emphasize performance," "85 words, luxury feel," and so on. These people knew exactly what they wanted, and it certainly made it easier for me to write the copy. When you receive assignments, get as much specific information as you can from your client. You will avoid many unnecessary revisions.

Ask yourself and your client questions. Why is this product or service or company important to the reader of the brochure? How will the reader come to emotionally identify with the item? How will the reader benefit? Make it exciting! Sell the sizzle, not the steak. Make sure you provide enough information to bring the reader to the goal.

The goal is what the client wants the reader to do when she reads the brochure. Make sure this goal is specific. Many clients will say, "The goal is to buy the product," when the real goal is *to get the reader to call a phone number*. Your brochure should tell the reader exactly what she should do next, whether it's one small task or several steps.

Direct mail and catalogs. Think of this as junk mail. This area pays well, although fees vary tremendously. Even though this is the one kind of writing where results can be measured, many direct-mail experts claim that 30%-50% of their success depends on the mailing list they use. Usually, clients will supply their own mailing lists, but many projects will benefit from a fresh list from the right mailing-list broker. These lists and brokers can be found in the Yellow Pages and trade or industry publications such as *Advertising Age*.

Magazines and newsletters use a great deal of direct mail to encourage renewals and attract new subscriptions. Besides subscriptions, direct mail is used to sell products or generate leads. In the latter case, the purpose of the direct-mail package is to get people to say they are interested in more information.

A direct-mail package will include a sales letter, a visual accompaniment such as a brochure, and a means to get a response such as a business-reply envelope or postcard. Other pieces can be added to the package as deemed necessary. Make sure you know how much all of the proposed pieces will weigh before you produce them. You don't want your client paying extra postage. Also, encourage your client to *test* direct-mail ads before spending a bundle on a campaign. Send the direct-mail package to 5%-10% of the client's list and monitor results before mailing to the entire list.

When you create direct-mail packages, you will want to consider including one or more of the following points: trial period to use the product, money-back guarantee, billing option, free offers associated with the main offer, a discount, and a sense of urgency. Here's an example of urgency you'll recognize: *Respond in 30 days and get a free Ginsu knife set!* The urgency statement is usually the P.S. at the end of the sales letter.

Write copy from the reader's viewpoint, usually in second person. Wrong: *Widgets Inc. is proud to announce its newest widget.* Right: *Are you tired to the same old widget?* Follow the AIDA format: Attention, Interest, Desire, Action. Get the reader's attention, build interest in the product/service, and then a desire for it. Get the reader emotionally involved. Then ask the reader to act.

I will not address the topic of *spam* (junk e-mail) at length. Naturally, you will want to write copy for e-mail advertising directed at established customers who are voluntarily on your client's e-mail list. I don't recommend spamming because, in doing so, your client places himself in unsavory company in the minds of most consumers.

Advertising. Everywhere you look, you'll find advertising. I saw a recent news item of college students selling advertising space on their foreheads. Some ads simply project an image or promote a brand, such as many TV ads or the Nike swoosh on athletic apparel, but most of the ads you will write will ask for some kind of specific response—call a phone number, send in an order, request information, go to a store.

Full-page print advertising is a great area you'll want to break into, and since it takes about the same amount of time to write a full-page ad as it does a quarter-page ad, you want to encourage your client to commission a full-page ad. In most cases, you will work with an art director or graphics person.

Make sure every ad has an image and/or a headline that will grab the reader instantly. As the poet said, "Words are things," and some words have proven themselves over the years in myriads of advertisements. "You" might be the most important of all, but "free," "easy," and "guaranteed" are eye-stoppers as well. I'm sure you can think of a few more that you have bitten on. When you write copy, have the "You" attitude; that is, write copy that will reach your market and bring results.

Make sure you understand the specific purpose for each ad. Most of the pointers I gave for brochures apply to advertising as well.

Once you have an assignment to do an ad, talk to your client in terms of *campaigns*. This is good for you and good for the client. If you are fighting a war, you don't throw a grenade here and drop a bomb there in hopes that you somehow will win. Instead, you create a plan—a unified campaign—to win the war. Tell your clients that they should not only think in terms of campaigns, but should correlate their advertising and marketing collateral so they have a similar, identifiable look.

Since TV advertising is usually written by ad agencies, you will want to get assignments for these by connecting with ad agencies. However, you may be able to write local TV ads for established clients. You have a better shot at radio advertising where there is less competition. Hook up with producers of radio and TV ads, station managers, and companies that advertise on the radio. Again, talk to your client about a campaign rather than a radio "spot" here and a TV "spot" there.

Standard Rate and Data Service (www.srds.com) is a major source of advertising information. You can find all kinds of advertising data there and even advertise there yourself once you are established.

2. Public relations writing

In the previous chapter, we discussed brochures, ads, and other marketing collateral. All of these can be a part of a public relations campaign and would certainly be included in any press kit.

Press kits and press releases. Press kits are great fun because they include several different items. Clippings of appearances in the news or other publications are important to a press kit. If your client has not been written about, then you should offer to make that happen. In such cases, sell your best efforts; do not guarantee results. However, getting your client into the media is not as difficult as it may seem.

First, what is noteworthy about your client? Have there been any promotions within the company? The business section of the newspaper may publish that. Will the company be hiring soon? That's a benefit to the community. Is the company involved with a trade event or show? That might be newsworthy. Is the company doing anything that might benefit the community? Examples include sponsoring a run for cancer, contributing to a clean environment, cleaning up its manufacturing process, keeping jobs in America, and so on. Business trends; new, large contracts; and unusual products and services might also be of interest to a newspaper.

Once you have identified something that might be newsworthy, match it to the appropriate publication and send a press release. Connect with an editor's needs. Timing may be important. Feature and Entertainment sections are developed up to two weeks in advance. Magazines need early notice of your trade show, etc.

Press releases should be sent to an individual at the newspaper or magazine. At the top of the press release, written on your client's letterhead, write NEWS RELEASE or FOR IMMEDIATE RELEASE. Double- or triple-space and center your headline; your headline needs to grab the editor's attention. A press release should be written exactly the way it will appear in the newspaper. That's what editors want. Put on your journalist's cap and write in that style. Open with a general paragraph that presents the central idea of the press release. Present the most important information in the early paragraphs and the less important information towards the end. When newspaper editors cut the size of articles, they start with the final paragraph and snip their way up. Always include glossy photographs, JPEG files or GIF files—whatever is preferred by the paper. Strive for action-oriented shots. The print media builds articles around visuals.

As a rule-of-thumb, press releases should be about 300-600 words with short paragraphs and double-spaced. Be sure to include contact information in the upper right corner so that the newspaper can contact you if they have questions. Sometimes press releases are handed to reporters who do more research and write an article or feature.

End the article with "30" or "####"; that's journalistic lingo for "the end." Many newspapers and magazines provide writer's guidelines for writing press releases. Because newspaper editors are always looking for content to fill their sections, and because your client would love to appear in print, you can rise to hero status by succeeding in public relations.

If something exciting is happening at your client's company that can be captured on videotape, then you might be able to get on the local TV news. The key is providing interesting video footage. That could be a new and exciting manufacturing process. I just saw on the local news how a local company makes individualized stuffed animals for children. The child is actually involved in the process, including the placement of a heart in teddy's chest. Today, I saw a TV news feature on a company that implemented a new employee plan. Footage was shown of the exercise area and the meals provided to employees.

Product releases and case studies. Many magazines carry "new products" sections. This is a specialized type of press release. Companies with new products benefit greatly by appearing in these "new products" sections. You will earn about $300-$600 for each new product description you write.

Case studies essentially show how a company solved a consumer or industry problem. These often focus on customer interviews that first convey the problem and then present the company's solution. For examples of case studies, visit search.microsoft.com/us/business/casestudies.

Specialty letters and speeches. Some clients may simply need a placement letter. For example, I walked into a wonderful little shop called Sweet William Cottage one day. I loved the herbs, dried flowers, small antiques, hearty foodstuffs, and wonderful old-style linens. In particular, I enjoyed the sparkling personality of Judy Heideman, the proprietor. As we chatted one day, Judy shared her dream of being featured in *Victoria* magazine.

So, I wrote a one-page letter to the editor of *Victoria* complimenting her on a recent article and then described Sweet William Cottage in the style that she might employ in her own publication. In the concluding paragraph, I suggested that she send a contributing editor to "drop by and see for herself." Nine months later, a feature article on Sweet William Cottage appeared in the magazine. Other magazines picked up on this, and soon the little shop was famous. (Story shared with permission.)

Some businesses may simply ask you to write a query letter that sells their article idea to a magazine's editor. Promise your "best efforts," not "results." This is a form of ghostwriting.

Still another form of ghostwriting is crafting speeches for business leaders and executives. We'll address speechwriting in Chapter 6.

Newsletters. Most company newsletters are public relations tools, whether it's the mini-newsletter you receive with your utility bill or the university newsletter (or magazine) you receive just before the annual drive. Many companies employ a staff to write their materials, but most companies are looking for articles to include in their newsletter. Often, small companies want someone to do the whole shebang. In such cases, your ability to handle graphics and formatting on a computer (act as an art director) is a plus. Finally, there are many companies looking for a writer and/or an editor only. As you can see, understanding your client's specific needs is key.

Why would a company need a newsletter? An internal newsletter can enhance employee relations. Newsletters can help create or enhance an image, especially for a small business. All business people know the value of staying in touch with customers. And, of course, newsletters can be used as a selling tool. You can provide helpful information to customers plus descriptions of new or existing products and services.

Once you have an assignment, correlate with other marketing efforts in which the company is involved. This is a way to broaden your work (and income) within a single company.

Incidentally, one networking opportunity is with the Public Relations Society of America. They have a membership of nearly 20,000.

For information on creating your own newsletter for profit, see Chapter 15 of this book.

3. Writing for causes, education, and government

If you are just starting out as a freelance writer and you'd like to apply your skills to a good cause, then consider contacting non-profit organizations. There's less competition in this area because non-profits generally pay less than regular businesses, and you can feel good about your contribution to humanity. In fact, you may even want to donate your services and take a tax deduction.

Keep in mind that you cannot take such a deduction unless other companies have paid you at the same rate for similar work. In other words, you have to be in business to be able to make the deduction. Of course, donating your services and doing great work on the first job will likely result in finding more work and getting paid for the second job, so this strategy might work for you, and you might be able to take the deduction. For more information on tax deductions, talk to a CPA.

Political organizations, charities, crisis centers, consumer groups, ecological causes, churches, foundations all need to have someone write their materials. Most of these organizations use marketing collateral and place ads like any other business. They also engage in fundraising activities through direct mail and telemarketing. Someone has to write those fundraising letters and telemarketing scripts.

If you believe in a cause, why not give that cause a discount? You can start your writing business immediately, get some experience, and begin building your arsenal of work samples to show prospective clients. Educational institutions and local governments also need your services. Since they often pay less than regular non-profits, you may find opportunities there. Many local churches, governments, private schools, and charitable organizations would like to find a writer to write their histories.

State and local government departments often advertise in the classified ads of newspapers. Look for the "Bids and Proposals" section, or similar section, in the classified ads of your newspaper. Or contact the city manager or Chamber of Commerce.

And don't forget the federal government, the biggest non-profit organization of all. Billions are spent each year by government departments for editorial services, pamphlets, training programs, newsletters, books, reports, manuals, proposals, articles, and video scripts. Most of this writing is done by freelancers and independent companies. Contracts are usually awarded as a result of proposals, and also by sealed bid, although there are some exceptions.

To learn of these opportunities, subscribe to The Commerce Business Daily (CBD). You can order it from the Government Printing Office in Washington, DC 20402, or visit www.gpoaccess.gov. An introductory six-month subscription will cost about $187. You will also need to complete a Bidder's Application Form. Some state and local governments will require a similar form to be completed.

One of the fastest-growing markets today is online learning. If you're interested in creating web-based training or educational program for corporations, private educational institutions, and other organizations that offer continuing education programs, then conduct a web search for current opportunities in this high-paying area. What makes online education attractive to writers is that online learning is almost entirely a writing environment. The words must do everything. The online environment is also more informal than traditional learning situations, allowing you to truly write to your audience.

Writing curriculum for traditional venues is still an excellent opportunity to make good money. One of these is the National Network for Curriculum Coordination in Vocational and Technical Education. If you are interested, contact them at www.ed.gov/pubs/TeachersGuide/nnccvte.html or call 217/786-6375. Purchase a copy of the *NNCCVTE Directory*.

Most non-profit organizations, educational institutions, and government entities produce videos, DVDs, and audiotapes. That's a great way to break into the lucrative scriptwriting business. Let's discuss that area next.

4. Scripts for business and education

This area of freelance writing may be one of the least-understood with the most potential.

Did you know that more money is spent producing business and educational videos, films, infomercials, and DVDs than on the entire U.S. motion-picture industry? Businesses create media for both internal use (such as training videos, Intranet, satellite, etc.) and external use (marketing and sales, product demonstrations, trade shows, etc.). Multi-level marketing companies (MLM; sometimes called "network marketing") use videos and audiocassettes as direct-response, informational, or image advertising.

How to find work

Approach the producers of business and educational media themselves. They make films for specific companies or to be used by specific industries. Where can you find listings of these people? First, check the Yellow Pages and Business-To-Business Yellow Pages. Look under "audio-visual," "video producers," "video production companies," "film producers," and other related subjects. You'll find a variety of listings from bona fide full-service production companies to guys who take videos of weddings.

The International Television Association (ITVA), the International Association of Audio-Visual Communicators (IAAVC), and the International Association of Business Communicators (IABC) all provide directories of members. You may have to join to get a directory.

A third source of names is video and film catalogs provided by film distributors such as CRM Films and Salenger Films. Many film distributors are also producers. You'll be amazed at the types of films that are made. For example, I wrote and co-produced a short film that spoofs the sales process. Entitled *Hercules and the 7 Secrets of Sales,* it is used at sales conventions as an icebreaker. There are many generic films that can be used by almost any company to improve sales, administration, marketing, and motivation. One of the early successes in this field is "Second Effort," a motivational film with Vince Lombardi.

How do you approach these producers of films, videos, DVDs, and other media? It helps to have a credits' résumé of videos you have scripted and work you have done in other media, including your copy-writing portfolio. Stress your skills when you talk to them. Consider writing a script for a bogus company as a sample of your work.

Ask producers if they hire freelance writers. Some hire full-time writers; most use freelancers. Your goal is to get a writing assignment. Another approach is to pitch an idea for a project to the producer or production manager. Naturally, you'll want an idea of the producer's needs before you pitch. Write a project proposal that presents your idea as practical and feasible. The proposal should define the problem and offer the solution. It should clearly communicate the value of your project to the client and to the people who will eventually view the film.

Approach ad agencies in the same manner.

If you decide to approach corporations directly, you will want to find a production manager or other executive in the video production department or marketing department or communications depart-ment. Understand their needs and convince them that you can meet those needs. These days, corporations are turning more and more to independent contractors (freelancers) for all or some of their media projects.

Other areas to look for work include non-profit organizations, the government, and military markets. Government at every level creates media projects, while non-profit organizations use media to reach their support base and solicit donations. Some may sponsor programming for PBS and other cable channels.

Medical centers, clinics, and hospitals create videos for staff, patients, and for the public. Drug companies and medical equipment manufac-turers make videos to be seen by doctors and other medical staff. As a general rule, you will need to do much of your own research in the medical area. For all other areas, the research is usually done for you.

If you enjoy medical writing, contact the American Medical Writers Association at www.amwa.org.

One area that is relatively easy to break into is the educational and informational area. That's because they don't pay as well as the others. Besides videos, there's a need for writers of interactive software.

Writing the business video/DVD script

The writing process begins with a story conference. During this conference, you will identify the following crucial parameters that will guide your writing.

Client needs, expectations, and the specific purpose and goals of the video. Make sure you understand the concept. Many short videos simply identify a problem and solve it. In any case, your script will present information while involving the ultimate viewer emotionally. What does the client want the ultimate viewer to do and/or feel at the end of the presentation?

Get a copy of previous scripts the company has filmed. You will learn something about their approach and philosophy.

Viewer needs. To whom will the client sell the video? What are their needs?

Ultimate viewer needs. Sometimes, the ultimate viewer or end user of the video is different from "viewer." For example, the client may sell the video to distributors (referred to as "viewer" above) who, in turn, sell to their customers (referred to as "ultimate viewer" above). You need to take into account the needs and expectation of both of these audiences. Focus on each viewer's needs and concerns. The strategy of your script will likely be to empathize with the viewpoint of the ultimate viewer while encouraging some change of behavior or way of thinking.

Venue. Will the video or DVD be shown in a large auditorium or on a computer? If shown in a large auditorium, you may need to script more *production values*. Production values include visual elements, interesting locations, and action (including demonstrations). If shown on a computer, then you may opt to include a lot of headshots of people talking.

Writing deadlines. At what date is the treatment (synopsis) due? The first draft? The final polish?

Budget. Know your limitations in terms of what your client can afford. For example, voice-over narration (where the narrator is not seen) is less expensive than a narrator who is visually present on the silver screen.

Length. How long will the finished product be? Most business films are about 10-12 minutes in length.

You will have help in defining the parameters of the film. Most companies will provide you with a *content expert* to help you understand the subject. Your challenge is to get the expert (and you, especially) to think about the subject in a new or different way. Recall what we discussed in Book II about creativity.

Other project parameters. Before writing an outline, create a design summary of project parameters. Identify the problem, purpose/goal, viewer(s), viewer key characteristics, viewer knowledge, and attitude. Complete this statement: After seeing this video, the viewer will _____ _____. Identify information categories, main points, and supporting details. Will the video be written in narrative style (telling a story), informational style, documentary style, or some other style? Will it be animated? Will there be a "round up" of testimonials—one person after the other bearing witness? What is your creative strategy? Sometimes, a metaphor of some kind can be powerful and create a sense of unity. Do not confuse the viewer; be absolutely clear. Since "show is better than tell," action, movement, and product demonstrations are helpful to any video.

Outline. Your outline will contain three main sections—beginning, middle, and end. The middle section, or body of the film, will be the longest section. Your outline will be followed by a synopsis (usually referred to as the "treatment") of a couple of pages or so. Once done, you are ready to write the first draft, then subsequent drafts, and then, finally, the polish. You will want your content expert and/or client to review your work at each stage. This gives the client a sense of security that the work is being done, and it gives you the security of knowing that the client has approved each step of the process.

Format. Use standard script format or video/audio format, depending on the needs and past experience of your client. In fact, try to get copies of past scripts to see what has been done in the past in terms of format, organization, content, production values, and style.

Here's a brief example of standard script format.

```
EXT. BURNING HOUSE — DAY

A cat runs from the flames, but a dog drags his
master out of the house and from danger.

                    NARRATOR (V.O.)
               Gives new meaning to the term
               scare-dee cat.
```

The V.O. stands for *Voice-Over*. We hear the narrator's voice, but don't see him or her.

What follows is an example of video/audio format. The visual element appears on the left and the audio on the right.

```
EXT. BURNING HOUSE — DAY

A cat runs from the                     NARRATOR (V.O.)
flames, but a dog                  Gives new meaning
drags his master out               to the term
of the house and                   scare-dee cat.
from danger.
```

116

Getting paid

Payment for visual presentations can vary. Generally, the writer ends up receiving about 5%-12% (usually close to 10%) of the budget. Most writers are paid by the finished minute (about $200-%500 per finished minute). Payment is usually rendered in increments: 25% up front, 25% on treatment, 25% on first draft, and 25% on completion.

Get a contract or purchase order. Ask about residuals or royalties. Some clients will pay a small royalty. Consider suggesting ancillary materials to accompany the video, such as a booklet or brochure. Always think of ways to expand your business and assist your client.

5. Technical writing

There is a huge demand for technical writing in our increasingly technical world. This includes reports, prospectuses, manuals of every kind, including sales manuals in technical areas, instruction manuals, and other technical documents.

The trick is to be able to write, research, and understand technical material, and then be able to simplify it so that a teenager can understand it. I get frustrated with computer software manuals that assume a certain level of knowledge that I don't have. Simplify difficult material using clear, accurate language. I personally feel that intelligent writers with little previous technical experience often do better than writers already steeped in a technical area. The former seem to be better able to communicate to the Average Joe. Of course, much technical material is not intended for the Average Joe, so understanding your audience (your reader), as always, is key.

There are many full-time and freelance opportunities. Freelancing is sometimes referred to as *job-shopping*. Possible clients include software and computer firms, especially fledgling companies, medical institutions such as hospitals, pharmaceutical firms, universities, electronics companies, chemical manufacturers, manufacturers of every kind including toy manufacturers, processing plants of every kind, engineering companies, advertising agencies with industrial or technical accounts, and technical and non-technical companies that need technical or semi-technical manuals written. In one of my writing workshops, an attendee shared in class that he made a living writing safety manuals for California companies. Companies hire him because he understands the many laws regarding employee and customer safety.

Look for opportunities to write training manuals, reports, and instructions. Corporations publish internal documents of every kind, including business plans, proposals, and marketing plans. Most companies of any size need employee manuals, policy manuals, and training manuals. The same goes for network marketing companies. Many of these areas require some expertise; however, even without expertise, you can help a company express what they want to say, you can help them organize their thoughts, and you give any piece a polish and/or an edit.

You might start at about $20-$40 an hour, but, with experience, you can make up to $100 an hour. Approach and handle potential clients in the same manner as any other business client. Consider joining the Society for Technical Communication (STC). For information, visit www.stc.org or call 703/522-4114. Freelancers and consultants (you are both) are welcome.

6. Your ghostwriting and editorial service

You can lift many spirits through ghostwriting. You may not see your name in print for your services, but you will see your name on checks. Most ghostwriting jobs pay very well. Many career ghostwriters specialize in certain subject areas; they find most of their work from referrals. Let's review the full spectrum of opportunities.

Books and publications. Most people think of ghostwriters as the real authors of celebrity books, but that is just one avenue. There are ghostwriting opportunities on every street. Although you don't usually get a byline for writing for other people, sometimes you receive an "as told to" or "with" byline. For example, *How I Broke the Mafia* by Herman Cappuccino with Dave Trottier. (If this were an actual book, I probably would want to keep my identity a secret and remain a ghost.)

You can make from $10,000 to $200,000 ghostwriting a book. If you happen to know a celebrity, politician, or famous expert, then make that luminary a proposal. Once you have an agreement of some kind, approach publishers to ascertain the viability of the project.

Many large publishers work with book producers or *packagers* to produce series books of virtually every kind. For example, the *For Dummies* series includes books on a variety of topics. I walked into a brand-new health food store the other day and saw *Marketing for Dummies* sitting on the counter. Now I know where that store's marketing secrets come from. Or do I? Many such books are written by several authors, and bylines are often not part of the deal. Such is the book packaging business. Although most packaged books are nonfiction, some are fiction. Book packagers are listed in *The Literary Marketplace* (www.literarymarketplace.com).

Some of your big-name authors do not write all of the books that bear their names. And some need the help of a good book doctor. This is someone who revises what is already written to make it more marketable.

Although ghosting books is an excellent opportunity, most ghostwriting takes place in other areas.

Professors, scientists, and technical people need help getting into professional journals and magazines. If you can write, have the patience to work with egos, and can subordinate your writing style to that of the person you're ghosting, then advertise or network where possible clients might find you. Advertise in publications that are read by the types of people for whom you've chosen to write. For example, if you want to ghostwrite for medical doctors, advertise in a journal they'd like to appear in.

Experts and other professionals need ghostwriters to put complex information into layman's terms. Offer to interview experts, professionals, and celebrities for an article, and then give them an "as told to" byline. Pharmaceutical companies often hire ghostwriters to write medical studies.

Some consumer health magazines use celebrity columnists, and those columns are often ghosted. Contact the editor of those magazines for leads.

Many professionals and business executives need someone to help them write their one-page autobiography. Others may ask you to write their 300-page autobiography. Some successful and wealthy people want their life stories or family histories written with no intent to make money. They just want to give books to friends, families, and business acquaintances.

In Hollywood, script doctors labor anonymously.

Business owners will want you to write articles for trade magazines or query letters. This might be part of a public relations campaign. TV and radio stations sometimes have their editorials written, and have disc jockey material written as well. Talk to the station manager.

Speeches. Politicians at every level need speechwriters who can coin the right phrase and express ideas in an effective manner. Executives must give speeches in many public arenas, not to mention within their own companies. They need you to write that speech for the next stockholder's meeting or convention. Some clergy have their sermons written.

Speech writing is actually a form of public relations, so contact the public affairs office of large and mid-sized corporations, where many opportunities await you.

When you write the speech, keep in mind the ideals and style of the person who will deliver the speech. Put words in that person's mouth that sound like they belong there. Give the speech phrases that people will remember. Open the speech with a statement, fact, humorous comment, question, story, or other attention-getting device. Speeches must be focused and well-organized, and end with a bang. All speeches inform, entertain, or persuade. What is the purpose of the person paying you? Maybe she wants to persuade in an entertaining way.

Grants. Non-profit organizations, businesses, foundations, and schools need help writing grants. Billions of dollars are awarded each year in grant money, but that money must be applied for in the form of a grant proposal. An Internet search will reveal many grant sources. Most companies or charities you contact will already know what grants they want to apply for. Nevertheless, you can include "grant finding" as part of your service. Many grantors have submission guidelines and proposal forms at their websites.

A lot of thinking and some research becomes part of the writing process. Offer your "best efforts" to write a proposal that will get the grant; do not guarantee results. As part of your contract for doing this work, suggest a small bonus if your grant proposal is successful.

The proposal itself needs to show a genuine need for the money, a description of the project, a responsible plan for the use of that money (including a budget and timeline), and the benefit that will be ultimately derived. Make sure you understand the grantor's application requirements and its preference for the makeup of the proposal. Your proposal should resonate with the grantor's purposes and philosophy.

Include a cover letter highlighting the proposal and offering more information. The letter should be signed by the company or non-profit executive. In Book IV, under "Support and Resources," I present information on grants for writers, including an outline for a proposal.

If you are interested in grant writing, I strongly urge you to visit the Grantsmanship Center's website at www.tgci.com. Other resources to consider include www.fdncenter.org and www.nsfre.org.

Résumés. There are always plenty of people looking for jobs, and most of these need help putting together an eye-catching résumé. This form of ghostwriting can be lucrative. I knew a résumé writer who made nearly $50,000 annually part-time. As an alternative to developing an independent service, you can apply to the many résumé writing services and employment consultants already in business. They're listed in the Yellow Pages.

Editing. Virtually every writing job we have discussed or will discuss in this book can also be an editing assignment. Often, business clients and publishers have editorial needs. Don't overlook these opportunities to add to your income, even though the pay is a little less for editors than writers. Proofreaders and copy editors are always in short supply, especially for small publications across the country. You'll see want ads for these services in *Publisher's Weekly.*

The contract. Don't write anything for anyone unless you are paid up front or in increments. You will want a contract or agreement if you are paid in increments. Keep in mind that ghostwriting often includes research and meetings with the "author" in addition to the writing itself. Once the work is published or produced, it will seem less valuable to the person who hired you than it was before it was published. Remember, the client has the final say on all writing decisions.

How to multiply your profits

We've touched on this topic several times already. Now I want to emphasize it. I've continually advised you to expand your work with your clients, even if it is no more than writing on-hold phone messages for them.

If you get hired to write a brochure or ghostwrite an article, do an incredible job. In fact, give your client more than she had hoped for. When the time is right, ask her about her advertising, and then, instead of talking about a TV spot and a full-page ad, sell her on the wisdom of a full campaign. And design the marketing collateral to match the look of the ads, and so on. It's so much easier nurturing a relationship than starting one in the first place, so nurture your clients, build loyalty, and suggest opportunities that expand your work and their market share.

An unexpected (or expected) byproduct of the above approach is referrals and word-of-mouth advertising. Your client will talk to other business people inside and outside the client company about you, for good or for ill. If he is pleased with your work, you will find new business coming your way.

This advice also applies to your relationship with editors, ghostwriting clients, video producers, or anyone who might hire you to write.

7. Articles for magazines

The key principle I want to emphasize is this: Don't write the article and then try to sell it. Instead, sell the article *before* you write it. That way, you can sell just about every word you write. To see how that is done, let's return to the writing process and adapt it for article writing.

The article writing process

1. An idea for an article or essay bubbles into consciousness. You think this could be interesting.

2. You conduct your marketing research. This is simply thinking through your potential market. Who would benefit from this article? What categories of people would find it interesting?

3. Think of publications that cater to your identified market. There are two general categories: trade publications, which meet the needs of a specific business or profession, and consumer publications, which are aimed at the general public. What specific magazines is your article right for? Make a list. Review the entries in *Writer's Market*, published by *Writer's Digest*. What is the editor of each publication looking for? Get a copy of the publication's "writer's guidelines" and review those. What are their current needs? What is the slant of the publication—traditional, counter-cultural, hip? For example, *Attaché* magazine prefers a "humorous view." *Parents* is more traditional in style than *Rolling Stone*.

4. If the article "feels" like a good fit for one publication or another, outline the article. Let the ideas flow. Freewrite. You'll use all of this later. You need to do enough work here to understand how your article is going to "play." In other words, you need to be able to talk intelligently about it in a query.

5. Write the query letter. (See the next chapter on "How to write a query letter.") Should you send the letter to more than one publication at a time? Check each publication's guidelines to see if they accept

simultaneous submissions. Also, check guidelines for an estimate of how long it will take to get a response. Once that time has elapsed, feel free to follow up with a phone call.

6. Evaluate the editor's response to your query letter. "No response" is a response; it's just like dating—once the other party stops calling, you know the relationship is over. Rejections usually arrive as form letters. Good news often comes over the phone. Occasionally, you might get a rejection, but with some suggestions or comments. See this as a positive. It means that the editor is open to something else, another query in the future, or another version of your proposed article.

7. Once you have a positive response, write the article in correct manuscript format (see the box below) in accordance with the submission requirements of the publication. Document any direct quotations and other sources. In all likelihood, it will be accepted. Pay varies from pennies per word to dollars per word, depending on the publication.

You may be able to increase your fee, depending on your negotiation skills. If the fee offered seems low, then say, "That seems a little low," and then listen. Make sure it's clear what rights are being purchased. For what rights to offer, see the box on page 126.

If you want to write a regular column for a magazine, you may need to write a few sample columns in advance. See Chapter 8 in this book about newspaper articles and columns.

Double your income, double your fun

Let's suppose you are able to sell your article for $1,000. How would you like to double or triple that amount? Here's how.

Create sidebars or boxes that elaborate on a particular point from your article. For example, if your article is on poisonous snakes, you could create a sidebar on "cobra myths." Open any magazine and you will see examples of sidebars or boxes. They are often shaded. Some publications pay extra for these or may simply pay more for an article that includes them. They may also pay extra for appropriate photographs.

Manuscript Submission Guidelines
for articles, stories, and other short works

- A title page is not necessary.
- Pages should be loose. No binding. No staples.
- Use 12-point Courier or Courier New as your font.
- In the upper left of the first page: Legal name, address, phone number, and e-mail address.
- In the upper right of the first page: Rights offered and word count. Do not number the first page.
- Center the title in CAPS one-third of the way down the page. Double-space and center "by." Double-space and center your name. Double-space twice and start the piece.
- Double-space the entire manuscript. Indent paragraph one-half inch. Margins should be 1–1¼ inches all the way around.
- On subsequent pages, create a header for the upper left of each page, stating your last name and a keyword from your title—for example, Trottier/Bible. Page numbers should appear on the upper right.

In fact, the right photographs add value to your article. Mention them in your query letter.

As you can see from the chart on "Rights you can offer," once your article appears in print, you can sell second rights as often as you wish. I have sold my essay "My Twisted Sister and How I Straightened Her Out" to eight different publications. In other words, I have sold second rights seven times. Naturally, I was not paid as much for second rights as for first, but I was paid.

Another tact is to revise the same article content for different markets. You don't want to undermine your sale to any publication, but sometimes you can adjust the material of your article for non-competing publications. If you sold "Ten Tips for Taming Tantrums" to a traditional magazine, revise the content, approach, viewpoint, or style of that article for a New Age publication. The title might be changed to "Calming the Inner Child of Your Child."

There may be foreign markets that your article is well-suited for. For example, travel articles and celebrity interviews do well overseas. For

Rights you can offer

—**All Rights.** This means that the publisher gets the exclusive rights to the article. You can never sell it to anyone else, nor can you include it in a book. This is a poor option for you.

—**First Rights**, also known as **First North American Rights** and **First North American Serial Rights** and **First Serial Rights**. This means that the publication has the right to be the first to publish your piece. Once your piece appears in print, all rights revert back to you and you can sell the piece again. This is almost always what you'll offer.

—**Second Rights**, also known as **Reprint Rights** and **Second Serial Rights**. This means that the article has already been published. You can now sell second rights to as many publications as you'd like and you may do so simultaneously. To summarize, you can sell first rights to your article, and once it is published, you can then sell second rights forever to as many publishers as you'd like.

—**One-Time Rights**, also known as **Simultaneous Rights**. These are seldom offered because there is no guarantee that the publication will be the first to publish your offering. "One-time rights" simply means that the publication has the right to publish the work once.

—**E-rights**, also known as **Electronic Rights**. These are the rights to publish your work on the Internet, at a website, via e-mail, on CD-ROM, as an interactive game, or other electronic means. E-rights can be broken down into First Electronic Rights, One-Time Electronic Rights, and so on.

—**Subsidiary Rights.** These are usually associated with book contracts, and may include e-rights, translation rights, audio rights, movie rights, and so on.

—**TV, Motion Picture, and Dramatic Rights.** These are rights to use the material on TV, in a movie, or on stage.

—**Copyright.** You own your copyright to anything you write from the moment you first write it. If you wish, you may *register* your copyright with the copyright office and pay the fee. Registering your copyright gives you more legal remedies, but it also "dates" your work. Once your work is registered, it must bear the © copyright symbol and notice. Place that copyright notice in the upper right of your first page. However, registering your copyright for a short work (such as an article) is unnecessary if you are submitting your work to a copyrighted publication. To determine if a publication is copyrighted, just look for the © symbol on the "contents" page. Sometimes it is on the editorial page. If you're unsure, simply call the publication and ask. Realize that you can't protect titles, names, ideas, facts, and concepts. You can only protect your original written work, such as a book. For more information, contact the copyright office or visit www.copyright.gov or call 202/707-3000. See an "intellectual property" attorney if you have any questions.

a directory of foreign writing markets, visit www.worldwidefreelance. com/markets.htm.

Write a sequel. In other words, write a different article on the same or similar topic.

If there is enough material, expand it into a book. That's exactly what Laura Hillenbrand did with her article on the celebrated racehorse Seabiscuit.

Write such a brilliant article that you get on the editor's list. That way, she contacts you. I remember an editor called me once, and I said jokingly, "Could you query first?" I can't tell you how good it felt to hear myself say that. She replied, "Real funny, Dave."

◆ ◆ ◆ ◆ ◆

Shockingly, there are some publications that do not pay in a timely fashion or even at all. One guide to the paying practices of publications is *The Writer's Market*. That book will tell you if publications pay "on acceptance" or "on publication." The difference between the two dates can be as long as a year or so. Some publications request invoices to create a paper trail for accounting purposes.

If a publication has not paid you in a timely manner, then start the collection process with an invoice, then follow up with a phone call a couple of weeks later. Your next invoice and follow-up call will be with the accounts payable department, if one exists. Your final round will be with the owner.

To solve payment problems in advance, make sure you get a signed contract, especially if the publication pays "on publication." Make sure the contract stipulates what "rights" are being purchased. There should also be a clause for a "kill fee" of 20%-50%. That protects you if the publication later changes its mind and decides not to publish your article. At least you'll be paid something.

How to write a query letter

Query tips

Query letters are always addressed to a person, not a company or agency. Write queries on a conservative 24-pound or 20-pound stock. You don't need a fancy logo or the title "writer" anywhere on the letterhead.

A query letter is a one-page pitch letter, no longer. It's a "soft" sales letter. Use crisp prose, but creativity is always a plus. The shorter the letter the better; most pitch letters are overwritten. Since your query makes an immediate first impression of your writing ability, use compelling, error-free prose.

As a general rule, write it in the same style as the eventual article, book, screenplay, or whatever you are pitching. Since it is a business letter, it should be written in standard block format—everything to the left margin, double-spacing between paragraphs, and no indentations. Use a 12-point readable font such as Times New Roman or Arial. Don't get fancy. Your query needs to accomplish four things.

1. Get the reader's attention.
Open with your strongest point, a hook. That might be your concept, a relevant and intriguing question, your unique approach to the topic, or 25-word summary of the project. If you were referred to the agent or editor by another industry insider, then that may be your strongest point. In some instances, #2 or #3 below will be your strongest point with which to open. Many writers open their queries with the first paragraph of their article. In my view, that practice has become cliché. Still, it's not a bad approach if you have something short and hot.

Your opening hook basically says, "This is what your readers will hear that they've never heard before." Of course, you won't use those exact words. That would be "telling" instead of "showing." Make your hook so interesting that the editor, agent, or producer believes that this article, book, or screenplay will be unique or "just right." Use active verbs and specific language.

"What if" questions can be effective. For example, here's an opener for a screenplay query: *What if the president of the United States were kidnapped?* The following is for a persuasive essay or article: *What if there were one simple solution to all of our environmental problems? There is, and it's called hemp.* By the way, that question and answer could be written as two separate paragraphs.

2. Sell your project.

Show the reader why she needs this writing project. If you are pitching an article, convince the editor that your idea fits the magazine perfectly. Write your pitch letter as if you are fascinated with the topic. The first two paragraphs are the sensuous and sensual part of your letter. Mention something about the content, the slant (if relevant), how you will write it (if relevant), and why you want to write it (if relevant). Think in terms of features and benefits.

If you are pitching fiction, summarize the core story—beginning, middle, and end—in a brief paragraph or two. Some writers choose to set up their story situation without revealing the ending. That can work if your "set-up" is particularly strong.

Don't mention your toil, tears, and turmoil over the project. Don't brag about how others love your article or story idea. And don't share your midnight longings to appear in that magazine or write for that producer. Instead, address the apparent needs of the reader of your letter.

3. Sell yourself.

Prove you can write the piece. Mention your qualifications, and be honest. If you have none, then omit this section. Don't mention the fact that you don't have credits or clips (photocopies of published articles). Never mention a negative in a pitch.

You prove you are qualified by stating or summarizing your professional writing credits (work sold) and/or by virtue of your expertise. For example, if your article is about how lawyers rip off the elderly, and if you are a lawyer, you are qualified on that basis. Your education is usually irrelevant, but an advanced writing degree might be worth mentioning. If you've won a contest, that might be worth mentioning.

Never say that you want to be a writer and you hope the editor will give you a break. Don't make wild claims that you can't substantiate. Don't tell the reader that your article will get her a promotion, that your book is destined to be a bestseller, or that your movie is going to make him millions.

4. Tell the reader precisely what to do.

"Call, e-mail, or use the enclosed SASE if you'd like to see my article on spec." You don't have to use that sentence, of course, but you need a specific and brief call to action. The phrase "article on spec" means that if the editor gives you a go-ahead, you are willing to write the article on the speculation that the editor will buy it once she sees it completed.

If you are pitching a book, then you want the reader to request the book proposal. If you are pitching a screenplay, then the request is for the completed screenplay. Yes, you must write it before you pitch it.

If you are pitching an article or short story, then include a couple of clips of past relevant work if you have them. Your clips will be more important to the editor than the query itself because they prove your ability to communicate with the written word. Some writers create their own websites and display "clips" there; don't refer editors to your site to see your "clips" unless you feel they would be open to that from what you read in their submission guidelines. (See Chapter 17 for more on setting up your website.)

Be sure that you have read the writer's guidelines carefully. If anything in those guidelines contradicts what I have told you, follow the writer's guidelines.

Don't mention fees, advances, or rights in your query. Don't try to sell more than one project in a query unless you 1) are approaching a magazine editor, 2) you have some past sales behind you, *and* 3) you have two or three solid ideas that can be presented concisely and effectively in one-paragraph descriptions. In every case, focus on the specific needs of the reader and on your specific purpose—getting the reader to request the project(s) you are pitching.

The term SASE is an acronym for "self-addressed stamped envelope." I recommend that you use a stamped, pre-addressed postcard instead. On the back of the postcard, give the editor some choices to check:

_____ Send me the article.

_____ We are not interested at this time.

_____ Please keep us in mind for other ideas.

And then type the name of the magazine or the editor at the bottom of the postcard. Otherwise, you might get a returned postcard and not know who sent it.

Another school of thought holds that the SASE or stamped card is unnecessary. Use them if you enjoy collecting rejection notices because that is what they are mainly used for. Additionally, SASEs are often lost. Besides, good news often comes via e-mail or the telephone. The day is coming, I am certain, when SASEs will be a relic of the past. If one is specifically requested in the writer's guidelines, then include it.

Another angle is to tell the reader that you will call him in a few days. I've seen this strategy work, but I have not mustered the necessary faith to actually try it.

Notice that the above advice emphasizes *lean writing*. With pitches of any kind, less is more. Your goal is to accomplish as much with as few words as you can. If brevity really is the soul of wit, then that dictum applies most perfectly to the realm of pitching projects. Because editors and other readers must sift through piles of queries and manuscripts, my personal goal is to write three-paragraph queries, although some of my letters are longer than that. My unstated message is: *I respect your time, so here's my pitch in as few words as possible.*

Before you send out your query letter, let it sit and get cold for a few days. Let the emotion surrounding it subside. When your head is clear, look at it with your Inner Critic and ask yourself if it is professional, fascinating, clear, enthusiastic (without going over the top), and concise.

Most importantly, will the letter convince the editor that the article must be written? Will it convince the reader that the project is a winner? Once you have done that, send the letter out.

Many publications accept queries via e-mail. Don't e-mail queries to any publication that does not explicitly state that it accepts e-mails.

Once you sell the "first rights" of your article and it appears in print, you can sell "second rights" or "reprint rights." In such cases, your query will highlight the article, and then state where it was originally published and the fact that you are offering "second rights." (This is the exception to my rule that you should not mention rights, advances, or fees in a query.) Enclose a clip of the published article with your query.

e-queries

More and more publications are accepting queries via e-mail. The beauty of e-queries is speed. The editor receives the query instantly and, thus, the response time is shorter. Another advantage is because the editor is Internet-connected, you can direct her to your website to view your previously published work (your "clips") displayed there. (See Chapter 17 for more information on creating your website.

Since an e-query is a query, the points discussed earlier apply. But there is one difference: The first thing an editor sees in an e-query is the subject line. That subject line must grab the editor's attention in very few words without looking like spam. Review the section "Get the reader's attention" earlier in this chapter. The premise *What if the president of the United States were kidnapped* becomes the following subject line: *U.S. president kidnapped.* The concept *There is one simple solution to all of our environmental problems and it's called hemp* becomes something like this: *One solution to environmental problems.* If the title of your proposed work is captivating, consider using that.

Sample queries

Sample Query 1

The following query is an actual query that I wrote to tempt my chosen publisher to ask for the book proposal, which appears later in this book. Incidentally, the term "evergreen" is an industry term referring to any book that is a perennial favorite. Although headings are not usually used in a query, I decided to use them here. Notice that the letter is addressed to an actual individual.

Dear Ms. F-------:

I am a published writer who's ready to tell all:

The Freelance Writer's Bible:
What you must know to sell your work

A sensible selling guide to every profitable writing area

Book concept: My proposed book is based on my national seminar, "17 Ways to Make a Living as a Writer," and will include a section entitled "Your One-Year Plan For a Successful Writing Career." This "evergreen" will address the most profitable (and most popular) commercial and traditional writing areas.

Market: The appeal is to writers (primarily developing writers) who want to make money. Most writing books address writing issues only. My book will be a marketing book. Its main competition, the Writer's Digest publication *Writing For Money* (1994), helps writers earn "extra money." Mine will focus on "bigger" money, full- and part-time.

Author's Credentials: *The Screenwriter's Bible* has sold more than 160,000 copies, despite the fact that it was published by a small publisher. Most recently, I self-published another book, *Dr. Format Answers Your Questions*. In addition, I have published hundreds of articles and stories while three of my feature screenplays have been produced. I was a marketing VP before devoting my time to teaching and writing.

Please contact me for a proposal for *The Freelance Writer's Bible.*

Sincerely yours,

Sample Query 2
This letter pitching a screenplay is provided by Kerry Cox, former editor of *Hollywood Scriptwriter.* As you know, an actual query would be addressed to a specific individual. First, he sells the story, then he summarizes his qualifications, and finally he asks the golden question. Notice how easy-to-read and engaging the letter is.

Dear Mr. T-------:

Thirteen years ago, J.T. Wheeler woke up at 5:30 a.m., showered, ate a light breakfast, and savagely murdered his family of four. He then hopped into his Lexus and vanished from the face of the Earth.

Or did he?

It's a question Susan Morgan, wife of prominent attorney Lawrence Morgan, has to answer fast. The chilling fact is, the more she learns, the more she realizes that Wheeler's killing spree not only wasn't his first . . . it may very well not be his last.

And she might be married to him.

BED OF LIES is a psychological thriller and dark mystery with a strong female protagonist, a deeply horrifying villain, and a series of disturbing surprises that build to a shocking ending. It is also the story of trust and betrayal, and the fine line that divides the two when secrets are buried between husband and wife.

I've written professionally for television, radio, and print, including network TV credits and two published books. I've also worked extensively as a marital crisis-intervention counselor.

May I send you BED OF LIES?

Sample Query #3

When I was a college freshman, I wrote a silly process-analysis essay that all my classmates loved. Many years later, I came across it and decided to sell it. I wrote my successful query in a tongue-in-cheek style and sent it to a humor magazine. The first sentence indicated my understanding of the editor's readership. Note the short length of the query.

Dear Mr. D----:

Did you know that college students spend more time squeezing their zits than they do squeezing each other?

It's a fact, and I have written a 450-word process analysis on how to properly conduct the aforementioned activity. I would like to send you this carefully researched piece entitled "Zit Squeezing—Key to a Clear Complexion."

Clearly yours,

Sample Query #4

A car mechanic broke into writing with the following query. Notice how the writer uses specific details to communicate his mastery of the topic and his passion for it. There is also a hint of humor to convey something of the tone of the article.

Dear Mr. F---------:

Corvette is an American legend. . . .

It's also the first American sports car. Prior to the Corvette, sports cars were manufactured primarily in Europe. So what events led to the advent of the Corvette on June 30, 1953? And how can it be "the true American sports car" when the bow-tie logo was inspired by the 1908 wallpaper design of a Paris Hotel?

As a certified car nut, I have researched this topic over the years. I now propose an article that chronicles the rise of the Corvette, and explains why it is the quintessential American sports car.

In addition, I have access to the rights of historic photos and fascinating early designs.

An SASE is enclosed so that you can express your level of interest.

Sincerely yours,

Sample Query #5
This successful letter resulted in a piece for *Writer's Digest*.

Dear Ms. D--------:

Screenplay formatting is the last great mystery in the world of film.

As a script consultant, professional screenwriter, and author of the highly acclaimed *Screenwriter's Bible*, I am asked more questions about formatting than about any other single screenwriting issue.

What most developing screenwriters don't know is the difference between a *spec script* and a *shooting script*. My proposed article, "The New Spec Style," will solve this mystery and clarify the basics of screenplay formatting in about 1,200 words.

I have written for numerous national publications. Enclosed are a few sample clips. May I send you my article on spec?

8. Newspaper articles and columns

Most articles for newspapers are staff-written, but many needs are met by freelancers. This is particularly true of the travel and lifestyle sections, where you can earn hundreds of dollars for the right piece. Sometimes, the editorial section presents opportunities. Some newspapers will pay more than $1,000 to add your brilliant insights to the Op-Ed page. (The term *Op-Ed* means "Opposite the editorial page.")

Although there are high-paying opportunities, the pay is generally lower for articles in newspapers than in magazines, sometimes even nothing. On the other hand, you can be published quickly and start building a credits' résumé. And you can publish in several papers simultaneously.

Some sports editors will pay you $50 as a *stringer* to cover a high-school football game. You can become a stringer for other editorial departments as well, offering to cover news in a certain town that is not normally covered, or addressing editorial areas that are not being covered.

Approach editors by mail, just as you do magazines. However, newspaper editors are usually more open to phone calls and even e-mailed queries. Some papers won't mind you skipping the querying process. Call the paper in advance for their guidelines and needs.

A nice feature of newspaper writing is that you can resell your articles all over the country. That's because the rights you sell are one-time rights or "exclusive to your circulation area." Seldom will a paper ask for "first rights." Thus, the travel article you sell to *The Boston Globe* can also be sold to the *Los Angeles Times*. In a sense, you syndicate your own work.

Don't forget that there are often magazines associated with newspapers, such as the *Los Angeles Times Magazine* and the Sunday magazine *Parade,* which currently pays a minimum of $2,500 for an article.

◆ ◆ ◆ ◆ ◆

Writing columns requires a great deal of dedication before results are seen. To break in, it helps to be an expert in some field, but a lot of limitations can be overcome with research. Of course, some columns only require an understanding of life or a unique perspective on events. Before you decide to write a column, make sure you are interested in your chosen subject. How does it measure up against the writing values you identified for yourself in Book I and Book II? Once you are satisfied that you have a passion for your topic, angle, or concept, make sure there is an audience for your viewpoint. I am mainly asking you to think through your market. What can you tell the newspaper or magazine editor that will make him see that your column is going to be read by a lot of people?

On the other hand, your column idea might appeal to a niche market, in which case you will need to find publications that cater to that niche. There are likely some magazines, particularly trade magazines, which serve that market niche. Some large newspapers might be open to your idea if they feel it fills a gap in their coverage or meets a valid need. Your column idea must be different from anything out there, but not too different or too narrow. Some small niche markets become larger over time. Such has been the case with topics like herbal/natural cures and emergency preparedness.

Your next step is to define your parameters. As with article-writing, choose your publications carefully and understand what they want from writers. Besides newspapers and magazines, some newsletters (such as *BottomLine/Personal*) contain columns. Even in-house or external business publications sometimes publish columns.

Is there a particular format or style your chosen publication prefers? Will it be informational or conversational? Will it be written as a personal essay, in question-and-answer format like "Dear Abby," or in bits-and-pieces format? My column for *scr(i)pt* magazine, "Dr. Format Answers Your Questions" is written in question-and-answer format. My favorite newspaper sports column, "Rock On" by Brad Rock, is written in a bits-and-pieces style, presenting tantalizing tidbits of information that are loosely related and almost always funny.

What is your personal writing style? Will there be a humorous tone to your column? Many newspaper columns are funny. Or will it be more serious or authoritative? What is your unique viewpoint, opinion, philosophy, or insight? Do you have a provocative or evocative title? Will it catch the eye? Identify your project parameters and write about five columns (for newspapers), fewer for magazines. Newspaper columns are about 500 words in length. Magazine columns will usually be longer.

Once you have some sample columns written, then you can approach your chosen publication. Some publications may want to be queried first before they actually see the columns. If so, send them a one-page query. Most newspapers and many other publications will want the sample columns plus a cover letter.

The cover letter will contain information on your proposed column—title, subject, and approach or slant. Include any factual information about the need for your column. For example, if you have some statistics about your topic or can show how you fill a gap, then great. However, don't make general, unsubstantiated claims such as "Your readers will love it." You're better off saying nothing about the needs of the market than to make such general, unsupported claims. Finally, summarize your qualifications. Close your cover letter with a call to action, and enclose an SASE or postcard. Include your sample columns in the package you send, and follow that with a summary of ideas for additional columns. The editor will want to make a judgment as to whether or not your column can sustain itself for a long period of time.

It's important to follow up on your proposal. If the editor is nearby, call and set up an appointment to meet with her to discuss payment, deadlines, and rights. You want to retain the rights to your columns so that you can use them in articles for other publications or even a book.

Newspapers will pay from zero to $50 per column. Some pay by the column-inch. Magazines will generally pay more than newspapers.

Your ultimate goal, if writing for a newspaper, is to get your column syndicated. Syndication houses prefer columns with some kind of track record. Once a few columns have been published, you can approach them, or you can syndicate the column yourself.

Begin by requesting a copy of the National Newspaper Association's media guide (www.nna.org). It provides information on every member publication. Also, visit your library and ask for the *Editor and Publisher's Yearbook*. Do the necessary research for each publication you want to contact. That might include securing sample copies of those publications. Consider phoning the editors of small papers. They are usually open and interested in including quality material in their newspapers.

Once you have gathered all the information you can, create your proposal as already discussed.

Start with these smaller markets and work your way up to the larger ones. Contact large newspapers across the country that are not in competition with each other. In other words, choose only one Chicago paper and one Miami paper, and so on.

If you don't want to do all of that research and contact work, approach syndication houses. There is a lot of competition in syndication. However, one column syndicated by King Features (you've seen their syndicated cartoons in the Sunday paper) can earn you more than $20,000 a year. A syndicate house has the connections to get your column into newspapers across the land. Usually, they split the proceeds 50-50. Syndicates are listed in *Editor & Publisher Syndicate Directory*. Be sure to review what each prospective syndicate syndicates. You don't want to submit a column that is too similar to something that house already syndicates.

An alternative way to get a column published is to get advertisers to buy space in a publication. In return, you advertise their product for them in the column itself.

9. Short fiction and poetry

Much of what I've written about magazine article writing (Chapter 7) applies to writing stories and poems. Naturally, there are fewer outlets for short fiction than for articles. Most of those markets are listed in *The Writer's Market*. All are listed in the *Novel & Short Story Writer's Market*, also published by Writer's Digest. Many markets pay extremely well. For example, *The Atlantic Monthly* pays $3,000 for a story. Most publications pay less.

The process is simple, but the competition is fierce. First read and study the various publications (including online publications). Read their submission guidelines and follow those instructions. Many publications have websites where further information may be found. Once you have done this, write the story. Submit it to the publication in accordance with the publication's guidelines. Often, you can include a cover letter that includes the title, word count, and a couple of sentences about the story. In a way, the cover letter is a query letter or pitch for the enclosed material.

As to the writing, a story has a beginning, middle, and end. The beginning sets up the situation or story problem. There is usually some kind of twist or turning point that defines that story problem. The long middle section should contain a rising conflict that culminates in some kind of crisis or decision. The conflict can take place within the character. The crisis leads to a climax or resolution. The central character is often a changed person at the end. This is a general description of how most stories work. In terms of plot, a story is simply a series of events or key moments that lead to some kind of resolution.

◆ ◆ ◆ ◆ ◆

Poetry begins with "p," and that stands for poverty.

It is tough making a living as a poet. Those who have succeeded in recent years have written free verse (Rod McKuen) or song lyrics. Poetry often runs deep and fewer people have the time to concentrate. I don't write much poetry anymore, but I recall with affection those days when I labored for hours over a few verses. It sharpened my mind and senses, and enlarged my soul. I even made a few bucks. Most poetry that fails is overly sentimental, and most poetry that succeeds touches the heart and often the mind.

Most poetry journals and publications pay little, but they accept all kinds of poetry and verse, including experimental. Some consumer magazines, such as *The New Yorker*, pay relatively well for a poem. You are wise to sell poems to a variety of poetry magazines before trying to publish a book of poems. You will need some kind of track record to attract a publisher.

Writer's Digest publishes *The Poet's Market*. If you are serious about writing poetry, then you'll find this guide very helpful.

Be leery of poetry anthologies that will publish your poem if you'll buy their book. Realize that you're paying them to get published. Be sensible about poetry contests as well. Enter those that are reputable and that have a track record.

◆ ◆ ◆ ◆ ◆

Poetry put to music is lyrics, and lyricists can become millionaires. Songwriters connect with the emotions of general audiences. You've listened to them all your life on your radio or CD system. The music business is tough to break into from any angle, but if you can write poetry, you can write songs. You will want to find a composer partner, someone who can write the music. Perhaps you are that partner. You query with a demo (demonstration tape), and that will cost some money, but not as much as you think. It is not unusual to create one for $500. Be on the watch for publishers who ask you to pay to have your tape reviewed. That's not standard practice.

As you might guess, Writer's Digest has published a guide to the marketplace entitled *The Songwriter's Market* by Tara Horton.

10. Greeting cards and humor

How would you like to be paid $5 for each word of poetry you write? You can. Just write and sell a great greeting-card message. The smaller card companies pay about $25 per idea or verse, and the larger ones pay about $150 per idea or verse, and sometimes as high as $250 or more. A few may even pay a royalty. Some companies pay a little more for humorous ideas simply because they are more difficult to write.

Greeting card messages are simple. Don't multiply words to make a point. Most companies will prefer a condensed verse, so distill your thoughts into a minimum of words. Those words should penetrate the heart or tickle the funny bone or both. In effect, your purpose is to make the card buyer think that he is brilliant, clever, and/or sensitive by buying your card. Keep in mind that women between 18 and 55 are the biggest card-buyers.

There are a variety of ways to submit ideas, so always read the card company's writer's guidelines before making a submission.

Most greeting card companies will ask you to submit your ideas on 3" x 5" index cards. Some prefer 4" x 6" cards or folded paper of various sizes. At the top right of your submission, type your name, address, phone, and e-mail address. Near the top, write the *caption*— the category of card such as "sympathy" or "wedding anniversary" or "get well."

Then, simply sketch out the visual idea or concept on the left and the accompanying verse on the right. If there are several images, list each on the left with the corresponding words on the right. You don't need to illustrate the card or provide original artwork; just convey the concept. Also, investigate the Greeting Card Association (www. greetingcard.org).

If you are an artist, some companies will accept your artwork with your greeting. Check the company's writer's guidelines.

Once you have about a dozen cards for any one company, send them out with a very brief cover letter addressed to the editor, indicating what's enclosed. Put your best ideas at the beginning and at the end. Many editors read the first two and last two before deciding whether to read the rest. Allow six months or more lead-time for seasonal messages. Since the marketplace is always changing, stay in touch with current needs of card companies.

Many card companies also produce novelty items such as T-shirts and posters. Take advantage of these opportunities, too, especially if you've already sold card ideas to the card publisher.

Don't overlook the e-card market. Contact such companies as BlueMountain.com for their writer's guidelines.

◆ ◆ ◆ ◆ ◆

Humor requires using the right words and right amount of words. This is why Dave Barry reportedly wrestles over every word he writes.

Humor relies on the unexpected and the exaggerated, overstatement and understatement, surprises and reversals, an unusual viewpoint, giving someone a pretense and then bringing him down a notch. And the purpose is often to reveal some human "truth."

If you have a sense of humor, you can write for your local disc jockey on the radio (contact the local station manager), or gags for comedians, cartoonists, and nightclub performers. For more information, see the *Humor and Cartoon Market* by Bob Staake.

To write comedy for national radio programs, contact the many radio networks. Here are two: American Comedy Network (203/877-8210) has a great website at www.americancomedynetwork.com. You can even submit your work there. The Premiere Radio Networks can be found at www.premrad.com.

There are a few publications dedicated specifically to humor, but there are also many trade and consumer magazines that buy filler pieces. These are listed in *The Writer's Market*. Religious and juvenile publications buy humor; many also purchase puzzles that are built around a theme. In most cases, you will need to submit the complete manuscript as part of your query.

Most game manufacturers are open to new ideas. Some syndicates (discussed in Chapter 8) are devoted to providing humor for top comics. Occasionally, a humorous column (also discussed in Chapter 8) makes it big.

Experienced comic-book writers make more than $1,000 per comic book. Besides the Big Three (Marvel, DC, and Image), there are many independent comic-book companies that you can approach. The market is decidedly male and young. Drop into a comic book store and ask the owner how things work. I did that as part of my research for this paragraph, and I couldn't get the guy to stop talking.

11. Movies, TV, and stage

Writing for the movies. Most screenwriters break into the movies writing a few *spec* scripts. Let me explain.

The first step to becoming a screenwriter, animation writer, or TV writer is to write screenplays and teleplays on *spec*. You must do the work first. Agents and producers are simply not interested in your proposal or synopsis because there are so many other writers out there who have completed screenplays to market. So learn your craft and write a great screenplay of 100-120 pages in correct format. Even if you want to write for TV, you will want to write an original feature-length screenplay as a sample of your work.

Once that script is written, you will approach agents or producers or both. The large producers are not approachable without an agent. So your gameplan is to craft cogent and creative query letters to send to small and intermediate producers and WGA signatory agents. A WGA signatory agent is one who uses contracts approved by the Writers Guild of America (www.wga.org). The WGA has offices in Los Angeles and New York, depending on which side of the Mississippi you reside. Contact them for a list of approved agents.

You will choose producers of films that are similar to the type of film you envision for your script. You will choose agents that are listed by the Writers Guild of America. Directories of producers and agents abound, so it is not difficult to find names. One company that produces such directories is Hollywood Creative Directories (5055 Wilshire Blvd., Los Angeles, CA 90036, 800/815-0503, www.hcdonline.com).

Do your research first and create a list of possible producers and agents to contact. (Review the chapter on "How to find an agent" in this book.) Agents prefer that you approach them first before approaching producers so that they can be the first to enter the market. So if you have written a blockbuster, consider approaching agents first and producers second. However, if your script project is designed as a low-budget film for a small, independent producer (meaning independent of the studio system), then an agent is unnecessary. In fact, most first scripts are sold to producers *without* the help of an agent. Some of my clients have sold large producers who later referred them to agents.

If your script is perfect for a specific star (called *talent* in the business), check to see if that talent has her own production company. If so, query the production company. The second best way to get a script to a star is to accidentally meet somewhere. The worst way is to approach the star's agent. Most likely, that agent simply will not be interested in your script unless there is a money offer tendered with it.

Of course, the best way to get your script to anyone in the film business is by referral. If your Aunt Minnie went to school with Robert Redford, then try to use that. I know it sounds lame, but consider exploiting any connection that you can find. Industry people often read referred scripts.

Once you have chosen five or ten agents and five or ten producers (which might include talent), craft the mother of all query letters. A query is a written pitch. See the section "How to write a query" in Chapter 7 of this book. Never query anyone until your script is completed and ready to show. Premature pitching is the hallmark of broken dreams.

Pitch letters can be mailed with a stamped self-addressed postcard or faxed. You may e-mail if your research shows that the recipient will accept e-mailed queries. Follow up by phone two weeks after the query is sent. You are very unlikely to be put through to the agent or producer, so speak to the assistant on the phone respectfully and talk with him about your query as if he were the agent or producer. Ask, "When should I expect to hear from Ms. Bigbucks?" or, if the assistant can't find a record of receiving your query, say, "May I fax you a copy right now, so you'll have it handy?"

Evaluate the responses you receive. No response means "no." Decide if you need to revise your query. Once you receive a favorable response to a query, you will send that person your script with a very brief cover letter saying that this is your script "as requested." The script will have a blank front cover and back cover, a title page, and the script itself.

Do not sent proposed cast lists, production art, or synopses unless specifically requested. The script should be three-hole punched and bound with two brass brads or fasteners. The middle hole will have nothing in it. Photocopies are acceptable and expected.

If the producer likes the script, you will be paid anywhere from one dollar to $5 million. More likely, he will want to option the script. That means he will pay you a small sum of money or nothing for the exclusive right to "show" the script for six months or a year. During that time, you can't contact anyone else about the script, and he can't produce it until he pays you the full price for it. The option agreement will define the full price. If the option period expires, then the producer must pay you full price, renew the option for a stated amount, or allow all rights to revert back to you. During the option period, the producer is using your script to try to attract financing, talent, and/or another producer.

If an agent responds to your query, she will offer to represent your work. She may not give you a contract immediately, but all WGA-signatory agents take 10% of any sale. If an agent does not succeed in any 90-day period, you are free to search for another agent. Some agents will charge you for photocopies of your script. Beyond that, there should not be any agent fees. The agent will send your script to the highest-level executives (producers) she knows. If an executive likes it, your agent will negotiate a deal. More likely, the executive will want to meet you. A meeting will be arranged.

At that meeting, the executive will ask you about your work and you'll have the opportunity to pitch a couple of projects. Then, the executive will pitch some projects to you and get your reaction. He may then say something like this: "Well, if you have more ideas about this one, I'd love to hear them." That's your cue to go home and develop a sound story around the executive's idea. Your agent will arrange another meeting and you'll deliver the 20-minute pitch. If the executive likes it, he will offer you a development deal, a deal to develop (write) the screenplay. Most of the deals in Hollywood are development deals. That's because producers already have their own ideas; they just need a writer to write the scripts. Your first development deal for a large producer will be around $60,000-$80,000.

As you can see, in Hollywood, life is just a pitch. You will need to express yourself orally with these people. Naturally, when you pitch, you can bring note cards. If you want to hear some sample pitches, rent *The Player*. Most of the pitches are pretty bad and delivered for comedic effect, but you'll get an idea of how things work.

In essence, what happens to most successful writers is that their script(s) becomes a sample of their writing ability that finds them work. For more information on writing, formatting, and selling your screenwriting, buy *The Screenwriter's Bible* by Yours Truly, or visit www.keepwriting.com.

Television and cable. TV movies and TV shows such as sitcoms and soap operas work in much the same way. Your script finds you work. Even with TV, it is smart to write a feature-length script as a sample. Then, if you are interested in writing for a particular show, write a spec script (on speculation that you will sell it later) for a similar show, but not the same show. Don't write a *Will & Grace* script if you want to write for *Will & Grace*. There are a lot of reasons for that, one being that your script is very unlikely to meet the producer's expectations of what she needs right now. Thus, you write for another show that's similar. Your agent sends these sample scripts to the producer of the show you are interested in, and then a meeting is arranged for you to pitch several episode ideas.

Although you don't have to live in Los Angeles to be a screenwriter, you will probably need to be near the production company of the TV show you are writing for. Incidentally, sitcom writers make tons of money, but they work long hours.

There are numerous cable channels these days, and all are looking for programming. So don't overlook these markets. Some are large (such as HBO and Showtime) and some are relatively small (such as PBS local stations like KCET). I remember an 18-year-old student telling me that he had pitched a project to the Discovery Channel. They liked it, but they wanted to see a sample script. He told me, "I'm not going to write a script unless they pay me." I remember thinking that he had missed a wonderful opportunity to break in.

Writing for the stage. In the world of the theater, you will need to write on spec (just as screenwriters do) or be part of a theater workshop. The pay is not nearly as good as with screenwriting and TV writing, but you are usually paid a royalty. Thus, if your play is successful, you can do well. Some playwrights sell directly to publishers for a flat fee. Helpful websites include the Drama Workshop at www.chdramaworkshop.homestead.com/Home.html and the Dramatists Guild of America at www.dramatistsguild.com. You will find a list of resources at www.artslynx.org/theatre/playwright.htm

Other opportunities. Some writers become film producers. That's rather daring and extremely expensive, but perhaps you could start at a smaller level.

Many local TV stations and radio stations have the time or staff to produce community programs. You could fill this need by picking a topic of interest to you and to the general public, such as travel, health, weight control, and so on. Or perhaps you could focus on a cause or social issue such as suicide, alcoholism, back-to-school tips, senior-citizen challenges, or local history. Talk to station managers and program managers about needs.

The next step is to name potential advertisers that might be willing to sponsor 1-5 minute programs in the category of your choice. If you chose something like alcoholism, maybe the Mothers Against Drunk Driver (MADD) would want to get involved.

Once you have sponsorship, produce the program "spot," or public-service announcement (PSA). A producer is essentially a general contractor; that is, a person who contracts the services of a writer, a cinematographer, a production manager, talent (actors), and so on. Once the program has been produced, you keep the remaining sponsor money not needed to produce the program. The radio or TV station would, in turn, solicit sponsors for the program and receive those advertising dollars. Everyone wins. Especially you. That's because you have made money without having to invest any, and you have gained a valuable producing experience.

12. Nonfiction books

The chapter on selling articles to magazines prepares you for selling your book to publishers. And like article-writing, you should sell your book *before* you write it. Most people who write books write novels. Most books that are sold are nonfiction books. Do the math and it's easy to see that you will experience much less competition selling your cookbook, self-help book, historical commentary, current-events book, or other nonfiction book than you will selling your novel.

Getting published

Be sure to establish your project parameters before approaching agents and publishers. In effect you are matchmaking. You are searching for the right partner for your book idea. Agents and producers are listed in the *Writer's Market,* in *The Literary Marketplace,* and in Jeff Herman's *Writer's Guide to Book Editors, Publishers, and Literary Agents.*

Approach these potential partners with a query letter first unless you know in advance they prefer to receive a proposal first. The book proposal is a marketing piece and must be written with the marketing needs of the publisher in mind. The same is true if you are writing the proposal for an agent. The agent will need all of the marketing ammo you can give her.

The proposal itself will be accompanied by a cover letter. Think of the cover letter as a query letter that highlights the key points of the book proposal. Your proposal will have a title page that will contain the title of your proposed book, the author (you), your address, phone number, and e-mail address. There's no set format for the title page, although most proposals will center the title and author about a third of the way down the page. The remaining information can be placed in the lower right corner of the page.

Your book title will consist of the main title and a secondary title. The primary title is the hook. Its job is to grab people walking down the bookstore aisle. The secondary title explains the first or focuses on a feature of the book. The main title of this book is *The Freelance Writer's Bible*. The secondary title is *Your Guide to a Profitable Writing Career Within One Year*. The main title is often emotional in nature, while the secondary title is often more logical and specific. Study the titles and book covers of successful books to see how they are marketed.

On the title page of a book proposal the main title would appear in CAPS; the secondary title would appear in upper- and lower-case letters, centered below the main title.

If the cover letter does not outline the contents of your proposal, then consider inserting a Table of Contents after the title page.

An abstract or overview of your book will appear next. It should be about one page or so in length. That overview or synopsis will begin with a sentence or two that describes the entire book. You must be able to encapsulate your book in just a few words, because that is what the agent will pitch to the editor and what the editor will pitch to the final decision-maker at the publishing company. Your overview will also convey your passion for the subject. Don't write, "I have a lot of passion for this book." That's "telling." Instead, write this overview in such a way that the reader senses your passion. That's "showing." And "show" is better than "tell."

Once done, you need to move to your selling points. Identify your audience—the ultimate reader. Explain how your book is better than other books on the same subject. Be realistic. In order to do that, you'll need to research your competitors. I suggest four places to look to find books and titles similar to yours: *Books in Print* and *Forthcoming Books* are reference books that you can find at any library. (The publisher's website is www.bowker.com.) *Publisher's Weekly* is an industry magazine that features new books, among other things. Finally, visit Amazon.com and see what is currently being sold on your topic.

In addition, the agent or publisher will want to know what you intend to do to promote your own book. Do you already have a following or conduct a seminar? Are you willing to do book-signings and interviews? Can you get on *Oprah*?

Follow this marketing section with some specific information about the book itself. On what date will the book be completed? How many words do you project it will be? (Estimate a range, such as 60,000-80,000 words.) Do you envision any complex graphics, photographs, or illustrations? Will you need to get "permissions" from people you are quoting?

Essentially, you are asking for an advance without asking for it. That's the purpose of your book proposal—find a publisher who will give you an advance. The bigger the advance, the more committed the publisher will be because the decision-maker will want to recoup that advance and prove to others she made the right decision.

Somewhere in this proposal, you should list your qualifications, both in terms of your writing credits and in terms of the subject matter. Do not include a résumé or write your bio in standard résumé format. You are creating a marketing piece, not an academic paper.

One important feature of any book proposal is the chapter-by-chapter outline. Summarize each chapter in a page or less. Follow that with one or two sample chapters. The first sample chapter does not need to be the first chapter in the book. It can be any chapter.

If your proposal is accepted, you will be paid an advance against royalties. That means the advance will be subtracted from your first royalty check. Traditionally, that royalty has been 10% of the cover price of the book and 5% of overseas sales. Special deals, such as book-club sales, are always less. Some contracts call for a 10% royalty of net instead of gross, defined in any number of ways. Some publishers may offer less than 10%. Read your contract carefully or have an attorney do so. If you have an agent, that person will negotiate all of this for you. We discuss getting an agent in a later chapter.

How long should the proposal be? Long enough to do the job. You want to be concise while, at the same time, provide sufficient details to sell the book. Write the proposal in your own, inimitable, style. Engage the reader. Remember, if the reader likes what you have written, she will use your words to pitch your book to higher-ups.

Once the proposal is accepted, the writing begins. Follow the steps of the writing process discussed in Book II. I recommend that you do your main research early. Gather plenty of examples, statistics, stories, and other support information. One of the pluses of a book proposal is that it forces you to outline your book in advance. That becomes a huge help in writing the book later.

Do what is necessary to meet the deadline in your book contract. If, by chance, you see that you are not going to meet the publisher's deadline, tell your contact person in advance. Never send anyone shoddy work just to meet a deadline.

For more ideas on books and book promotion, read the chapters in this book on self-publishing, novels, finding an agent, writing queries, and the sample book proposal. You are sure to glean information that you can apply to your particular book project.

If you write with another writer

Many books are written by more than one author. One reason to consider writing with another person is if that other person is already published. A few writers have broken the publishing barrier by creating a great book idea and asking a published writer to co-author it. You would only approach that other person if you believe the idea would appeal to him and because he has the connections to get the book published. As a precaution, try to get a sense of how well you work with this other person. Do you enjoy being with this person?

Most writing partners, however, are at the same rung of the ladder and are friends, co-workers, or acquaintances. In any situation where you choose to write with another person, make sure you have a signed, written agreement with that other writer *before* you write. Determine what each will contribute. Define this in specific terms and decide how performance will be measured. Settle the issue of whose name will appear first on the byline. If you don't have an agreement before the writing process begins, then you will likely experience a great deal of pain towards the end of the writing process. If fences make good neighbors, contracts make good writing partners and even preserve friendships.

Sample book proposal

The following is the actual book proposal that got this book published. When you read the book proposal, you should notice how (like any good copywriter) I use headings and subheadings. You will also notice that many elements of the book have changed in the writing and revising.

(sample)

BOOK PROPOSAL

THE FREELANCE WRITER'S BIBLE:
Your Guide to a Profitable Writing Career
Within One Year

by David Trottier

BOOK CONCEPT

The Freelance Writer's Bible is the only book that <u>mentors</u> the aspiring writer through four career levels, culminating in the creation of a **one-year master plan**:

1. Discover your creative vision and channel your passion
2. Write, and keep writing, with freedom and confidence
3. Sell to 17 key writing markets
4. Create your one-year master plan

The Freelance Writer's Bible is actually more of a workbook than a text. Driven by a unique feel-write, think-write holistic cycle, the writer learns to write from both her heart and her head, one step inspiring the next. Thus, visioning, writing, and selling become an upward spiral where blocks become steppingstones, uncertainty becomes passion, and dreams become reality.

Carefully designed exercises in freewriting, mind-mapping, dream-writing, reframing, values clarification, "what iffing," and other visioning and writing tools inspire the writer to find his creative direction and passion. In the process, he identifies 17 profitable writing areas—all clearly explained—and chooses which are best for him.

Most writers don't write because they're waiting for their Muse to fly down from Parnassus, or they're staring at a blank page in front of them and they feel pressured to create the Great American novel or the Great Honda Acura brochure in one fell swoop. The "Bible" keeps writers writing by breaking down this "wall" and converting it into a creative path. Writers learn to free themselves from pre-defined ideas about this journey and to summon the subconscious "inner voice that knows" (their Muse).

Selling is often a mystery to the developing writer because she lacks the industry savvy, specific knowledge, and confidence to succeed. Proven principles and useful tools, worksheets, and exercises reveal the marketing mountain she must climb and empower her to climb it.

The Freelance Writer's Bible is the ultimate success system for writers, and it is writer-friendly, creative, and practical. It's a mentor's helping hand and kick-in-the-pants when needed. It's the way of the wealthy writer—a whole-souled, whole-brained journey that leads the writer to his writing dream, frees him to write it, and guides him to sell it.

MARKETING & COMPETITION

Why am I writing this book?
I have worked with writers for 16 years. For that length of time I have been a writing consultant and teacher. In addition, I have made my living as a writer, having succeeded in 14 of the 17 areas discussed in my book. Two of my most popular seminars have been *17 Ways to Make a Living as a Writer* and *Free at Last! How to Get the Inner Writer Out and Working for You*. I have seen the frustrations that writers have, but also their joys when they see a sensible plan for success. I give writers both what they want and need. So there is a powerful desire to reach out to those who are struggling or want direction.

Years ago, I felt the same way about screenwriters in particular, so I wrote *The Screenwriter's Bible*. This book, as you know, was written for a niche market but has sold more than 160,000 copies. And that is with very little promotion except for my web site. To be honest, I feel it is possible to make *The Freelance Writer's Bible* a top-selling writing book.

Who will buy this book?

There are several categories of writers who will have an eye out for this book:

1. Novices and aspiring writers. These are writers who are looking for encouragement and a plan on how to get started. I often receive calls and e-mails from people who don't know what they want to write. There is something inherently comforting about a "plan for success." If you can put words together and have a strong desire for success, then I believe you can succeed at some level.

2. Developing and struggling writers. These are people who have already dived into the pool and found the water is cold. My book is a warm blanket for these folks who are looking for exactly the same thing the first group is looking for. Writers want advice "from the shoulder"—honest and straightforward. But they also have a side that wants to be coddled a little. They get both from me. I agree with Mary Poppins, who sings, "A spoonful of sugar helps the medicine go down . . . in a most delightful way."

3. Professional writers. There will be fewer of these than the first two groups. Even established writers, however, have down times. About 90% of the membership of the Writers Guild of America is out of work, meaning they haven't sold anything in more than one year. In addition, many "paid writers" are still somewhat naive about the business. Many others simply need a way to get organized and focused. That's what my book offers the professional.

4. Owners of *The Screenwriter's Bible*. I get e-mails every week from writers who have benefited from my book for screenwriters.

Every writer and aspiring writer wants and needs four things: 1) To be mentored, 2) To be published, 3) To make money, and 4) To feel the joy of creation. The order of importance varies, depending on the person. The owner of *The Freelance Writer's Bible* has a plan to get all four needs met.

Demographically, you have the young, aspiring writer (17-26), but there are just as many older people who have sent their last kid to college and want to satisfy that urge to write. For example, I have a large number of middle-aged attorneys and doctors as clients. It seems that many people either get bored with their careers or simply yearn to express themselves creatively. In past seminars, I would say that nearly 45% of my students have been 35-50 years old—yes, the baby-boomers. Another 45% are 18-30. And the rest are retired folks looking to realize their long-held dream to write.

Why will they buy this book?
Just the title *The Freelance Writer's Bible* is a grabber. It is the final authoritative word on the subject, and it will benefit from the franchise created by *The Screenwriter's Bible*. The tag, *Your Guide to a Profitable Writing Career Within One Year,* is positive and encouraging, and it implies a personalized approach. Suddenly, the writer's dream seems doable. It can happen!

Once the writer picks up the book, she will see that this is actually four books in one. It is a sensible plan. And there are plenty of involving worksheets and exercises. Oh! So it's a workbook, too!

The style of the book is inviting: "I am your mentor, your Uncle Dave, your very own Jiminy Cricket. I'm going to be honest with you. I am going to be realistic. But I am also going to be nurturing and empowering. Buy me."

Once the writer is into the book, she finds that, indeed, her career is taking shape. She discovers her creative direction, her issues, her talents, and also her blocks (which she reframes into steppingstones). She writes with abandon. And she learns how to get into print, and how she can have a full- or part-time career within a year of creating her plan.

She tells her friends to buy the book.

What makes it different from other writing books?
It is four books in one.

And each of the four "books" is integrated into the greater whole, giving the writer a clear "keep writing" plan to create his career, write, and sell. With *The Freelance Writer's Bible,* the whole truly does become greater than the sum of its parts. Let's look at each of those four "books" or "parts."

Part 1. Discover your creative vision and channel your passion. There is no book on writing currently available that helps writers find the writing career that is right for them. Think of this section as *What Color Is Your Parachute?* for writers.

Part 2. Write with freedom and confidence using the "keep writing" method. Well-received books in this area include *Writing Down the Bones* by Natalie Goldberg, *The Artist's Way,* and *Writing the Natural Way* by Gabriele Lusser Rico.

The above books help writers improve their creativity and write intuitively, but then what? How do the readers get their work into print? How can they use the other side of their brains to double their effectiveness? What type of writing are they best suited for? How does "finding the inner writer" fit into the writing process? How do they sell what they have written?

Part 3. Sell to 17 key writing markets. Virtually all books on writing focus on just the writing. There is less specific information (and fewer books) available about selling. Of those "selling" books, there are two main types.

A. The book that focuses on one type of writing. *How to Get Happily Published* and *1001 Ways to Market Your Books* are good examples. These are excellent books for novelists and non-fiction writers. My book provides an information-dense distillation of how to sell to those two markets and 15 other markets as well. In addition, my book helps the novelist/nonfiction writer develop a marketing plan to sell to any or all of those 17 areas. Now novelists can make money as writers in other writing areas while working on a novel.

B. The book that provides an overview of different writing areas. Perhaps the best is *Writing for Money* by Loriann Hoff Oberlin. Another is *How You can Make $25,000 a Year Writing* by Nancy Edmonds Hanson. Both present a good summary of several writing areas, but they do not include very much on how to specifically sell to these areas—the nuts and bolts. My book will provide the specific steps for selling to a given writing market.

Part 4. Create your strategic marketing plan. I know of no book that guides a writer in developing a strategic marketing plan for his career and a marketing plan for his written work <u>before</u> he writes it.

In summary, my book competes well in all areas. It's both broad and specific. And *The Freelance Writer's Bible* is the only book that does it all—it is four books in one. It's the mentor all writers wish they had.

PROMOTION

Seminars and book-signings

I have led seminars for The Learning Annex (a national speaker's bureau) in the past; in fact, they have contacted me to do more, so that's a definite option. I also plan to do a few university workshops and online courses. (I currently conduct online writing courses.) Book-signings are always fun. I would promote these events along with radio interviews, press releases, and perhaps publishing something of interest in the local paper.

keepwriting.com.

I have operated my own website since 1997 and have used the name keepwriting.com for two years. I have recently created a page entitled "For All Writers" where I will feature this book once it is published. I will provide updates, resources, and a "writers' group" page. I will create other promotional ideas to support the book. I will completely revamp the site, but the look and style will remain the same, as will my policy of no banners or advertising at my site except on the "hot links" page. As mentioned, I will continue to conduct online courses there.

Views From Your Muse

I intend to publish an online newsletter that focuses on success stories, motivational themes, and information for writers. This will be free for the freelancer.

Advertising

I will create a direct-mail campaign for my mailing list of 6,000 screenwriters plus an additional 4,000 on my e-mail list (voluntary registrations). I believe there will be crossover appeal to the 160,000 screenwriters who have purchased my book. Thus, I will probably run a couple of ads in screenwriting publications and in writing publications as well. These would be small classified or display ads. Keep in mind that I have a marketing background.

Articles
I will write articles intended for publication in *Writer's Digest* and other writing publications.

Interviews
Since I love the question-and-answer format, I am always available for interviews. I have interviewed for local television and radio before.

ABOUT THE AUTHOR

As mentioned earlier, I have succeeded (made money) in 14 of the 17 areas covered in Section 3 of this book. I live the dream.

My book, *The Screenwriter's Bible*, has sold more than 160,000 copies. I recently self-published another book, *Dr. Format Answers Your Questions*, a compilation of writing columns written for *scr(i)pt* magazine during the past decade.

I have sold several screenplays and developed projects for The Walt Disney Company, Jim Henson Pictures, and York Entertainment. Titles include *Igor's Revenge* (produced), *Zorro, the Gay Blade* (produced, but uncredited), *A Window in Time* (for ABC), *Kumquat*, and *The New Musketeers*. Most recently, I wrote *A Penny Promise* (released in 2001) and co-wrote *A Summer with Hemingway's Twin* (now in pre-production).

As a writing consultant, I have helped dozens of clients sell their work and win or place in contests. I have published more than one hundred articles in *Writer's Digest, American Writer, Writer's Journal, Creative Screenwriting, Road & Track, Disney Channel Magazine, COINage, Vision, Gift & Stationery, Single Parent, USA Today,* and other national publications.

With a B.A. in business administration (from Cal-State, Fullerton), I have a strong business and marketing background. I served for five years as a marketing manager and then marketing vice president for a distributor of precious metals and memorabilia (about 150 employees). As a business writer, my past clients include The Walt Disney Company, Honda Acura, American Premiere, Lucasfilm, Nutrex, Mitsubishi Materials, Ivy Communications, and Citizen America. For four years, I edited the quarterly newsletter *Precious Metals Today*.

I have an M.A. in communications from Goddard College (Vermont). Currently, my career is divided into thirds: writing, writing consulting, and teaching (including leading seminars). I have spoken at more than 30 American universities. Four years ago, I married Virginia artist and educator Marsha Sawyer, and we have two children.

OUTLINE OF CHAPTERS

PART 1. Discover your creative vision and channel your passion.

1-1 Writers Write.
One night, shortly before a great man died, he was standing with a friend and staring out the window. It was a stormy night, and the rain beat against his window pane. He turned to his friend and said, "When I was a boy, I'd stare out the window on nights like tonight and I'd dream about the man I wanted to be. And I can only hope that I've become that man."

Today, at this moment, you are gazing through a foggy window and dreaming about the writer you want to be. I am that friend standing next to you who is going to help you see clearly through the window to your career so that one day you can say, "I've become the writer I dreamed I would be." To that end, I am your mentor, and today we begin a journey together.

Bear in mind that writing is not for sissies and that markets are competitive. But you can succeed. And if you are willing, you will succeed. It won't be easy, but the world is waiting for the next great writer to appear. My great desire is to keep you writing. That is why I'm sharing my secrets with you.

In this chapter, I will relate how I got started. I will explain why discipline and commitment are important. I will even ask you to sign a formal commitment that will start you on your writer's journey, which is similar to Joseph Campbell's "hero's journey" in *The Hero with a Thousand Faces*. I will urge you to develop the four archetypes that live (or die) within you. The King creates the quest, and the Magician conjures the strategy or plan. The Warrior serves the King through purposeful action, and the Lover gives counsel along the way. You will want to draw upon your Warrior energy to make your writing dream come true.

[Note: In the original book proposal, each chapter was outlined in the same manner with about the same number of words as the summary above.]

SAMPLE CHAPTER: 4-2 Your strategic marketing plan

[Note: The book proposal concluded with the above sample chapter. I chose the above chapter so that the publisher would see that the "Bible" was not only informative but practical and applicable.]

13. Novels

Only one in ten novels breaks even or makes a profit. That's an average of the dozens of estimates and statistics I have seen. The message to you is this: Novel publishing is a risky business for publishing houses, and so they are nervous.

Before delving into this area, get acquainted with the business side of writing novels. Some areas of fiction are easier to break into than others. Romance novel writing is such an area, but the pay is not as good as that for other types of novels. Novelists are usually specialists, meaning that they write in the same genre each time. If you have an idea for a "series" book, that's usually a plus. In a "series" book, the same characters continue from book to book. John Clancy's Jack Ryan and Thomas Harris's Hannibal come to mind.

Getting published

Virtually everything in this tired old world is sold on concept, and novels are no exception. Because publishing houses are nervous, their marketing departments strongly influence acquisitions. In fact, the marketing department of your chosen publisher may have greater say than the editorial department in deciding whether or not to publish your book. Like Hollywood, publishing houses want to repeat last year's hit with something similar.

Naturally, you don't want to imitate last year's hit. By the time your novel is written and published, years will likely have passed. However, you will need to capture the essence of your novel in a single sentence that appeals to marketers. "This love story is more affecting than *The Bridges of Madison County* because . . . [in 25 words]." Review the covers of some of your favorite novels and look for those concisely written pitches.

Of course, you may not want to compete with mass-market novels. You may wish to write a sweet little story aimed for a niche readership. Nevertheless, you still need to clearly articulate the strengths of your project in marketing terms in order to sell it.

In times past, entire books were submitted for publishing consideration. These days, you can write the proposal first and then the book. Some publishers will require a query first. Your query's objective will be to get the editor to request the proposal. You'll find an example of such a query letter in the chapter "How to write a query letter." Simultaneous queries are okay. Choose publishers who have already had success with your type of book.

Once the editor or agent responds positively to your query, you will send your proposal with a brief cover letter that reminds the editor that she requested your proposal. It may also highlight the contents of the proposal itself, including the one-sentence "book hook." (See item #1 in the chapter "How to write a query letter.") Like queries, cover letters are *never more than one page*.

A proposal begins with a title page. About one-third of the way down the page, your title will appear as follows:

A Proposal for

The Incredible Shrinking Sugar Daddy

by David Trottier

In the lower right corner, write your name, address, telephone number, and e-mail address.

The entire proposal should be double-spaced and written in a conservative 12-point font. The title page may be followed by a Table of Contents. (In virtually all cases, a Table of Contents will not be necessary.)

Follow with a brief overview or synopsis of your book, about one page or two, followed by information about yourself, including a summary of your writing credits. This synopsis must be dynamite.

Some writers add a section that highlights the 5-7 main characters in the book, with a brief character sketch of each. I see that as optional. Do it only if those descriptions are tantalizing and you cannot find a way to adequately introduce characters in your outline of chapters, which comes next.

If you include chapter summaries, devote about 1-8 pages to each chapter in your outline of chapters. You'll notice that's quite a range, but some books contain long chapters and some contain short. *The DaVinci Code* contains 105 chapters plus a prologue and epilogue. Be sensible in how you summarize the chapters or sections of your book.

Make sure that these chapter summaries are fascinating and the plot is clear. If you find yourself essentially writing, "Then this happens, then this happens, then this happens," then nothing will happen when the agent or editor reads it. Include the same sparkle and fizz that will characterize your style in the completed book. Highlight the emotions and feelings of the characters.

Finally, include at least three sample chapters. I suggest you include the first three chapters of the book to maintain continuity of storyline.

Some publishing houses do not request chapter summaries, but prefer a synopsis and the first 30 pages, so carefully read the publisher's writer's guidelines. If you are sending just a synopsis plus the first 30 pages, the synopsis should be about 3-5 pages in length or more.

What I wrote about chapter summaries also applies to synopses. The story should be presented chronologically, completely, and enthusiastically. Emphasize the big event that changes the central character's life and gets the story moving. Don't withhold information: Be sure to include the ending. Add only a few bits of dialogue if you add any. *Writer's Digest magazine* (August, 2002) suggests you write the synopsis in present tense and third-person point of view.

Some writers will supplement the proposal with some writing samples. Only include samples that are published, relevant, and add value to your proposal.

In summary, your proposal will contain a title page, a synopsis, the first 30 pages (or first few chapters) of the book, and your credentials. Other sections may be added as discussed or in accordance with the publisher or agent's guidelines. The proposal (not the eventual manuscript) may be bound or stapled. Do not include artwork. Simultaneous submissions are okay, but don't shoot off dozens of copies at once.

You will send your proposal package to carefully researched agents or book publishers. Use the sources recommended in the section on nonfiction books. You do not need to voluntarily divulge to any one publisher or agent whom you've sent other proposals to.

The two golden keys to success

Once you have acquired interested parties, keep in mind the two golden keys to a novel's success:

Golden Key #1. The size of the advance equals the level of the publisher's commitment. The more the publisher pays, the more committed he is to making the book a success. The advance is against future royalties, so any royalties you earn will be paid to the publisher until that advance is recovered. If no royalties are earned, the advance is yours to keep. Therefore, it makes economic sense that they give the book all the necessary attention and publicity it needs to recoup that advance.

The first golden key leads to the next.

Golden Key #2. The pre-arranged distribution plan greatly influences your book's success. Ask you publisher what the "lay down" is going to be; that is, the number of books going to retail outlets and wholesalers before the official release date. The bigger the lay down to *retailers* (not wholesalers), the higher you fly. Thus, a book's success is often determined before the book is ever released.

Once the book is released, the most important things you can do to improve its performance is to give interviews and sign books. Bookstore owners look with favor on book signings not so much to sell copies of your book, but to bring people into their store. If you can arrange a tour with your publisher, then that's a big plus. Talk to your publisher's publicity department about ideas to promote your book. At the same time, think of ways you can get the publicity out to prospective readers. Don't expect the publisher to do it all.

Glean other possible promotional ideas by reviewing the chapters in this book on self-publishing and nonfiction books.

How to find an agent

Besides attracting publishers, you should consider luring an agent to your cause. For most first-time writers, it will be easier to find a willing publisher than a willing agent. This is especially true if you are writing romance, mystery, fantasy, and science-fiction. However, an agent will likely be able to get you a better deal than you can get on your own. On the other hand, although some agents are extremely helpful and can help you create a wonderful writing career, others are the devil's puppets, attempting to fit you and your material to their limited contacts and capabilities. You will want to make the decision to seek or not seek representation thoughtfully.

Both agents and publishers are listed in *Writer's Market*. I also recommend *Writer's Guide to Book Editors, Publishers, and Literary Agents* by Jeff Herman, which is published every couple of years. In fact, I recommend anything written by Jeff Herman. Another source of information is *The Literary Marketplace*. Finally, the Association of Authors' Representatives (AAR) in New York (www.aar-online.org) will send you a list of "approved" agents for a nominal fee. The above research sources will help you design a gameplan for approaching agents.

Be aware that some agents charge reading fees, retainers, and advances these days. In the past, that practice was looked down on, but it is becoming more and more commonplace. I would still be leery of it, so when you conduct your research for agents, keep that in mind. The Association of Authors' Representatives (AAR) has certain standards that agents belonging to that organization must subscribe to. For example, members may not charge a reading or evaluation fee. However, there is no judicial branch of the AAR to enforce those standards. Nevertheless, I recommend that you get a list of AAR-approved agencies. New York-based agencies are nearest the world of publishing, but that fact is not as significant as it used to be. There are many effective and successful agencies outside of New York.

In case you wonder, all of my books and screenplays to date have been sold without the help of agents, but that does not mean I won't seek one as I continue my writing journey. That's because more and more publishers are requiring writers to have an agent before considering their work. In the film business, virtually all of the studios and major producers will want your work submitted through an agent or attorney.

If you decide to seek representation, first get the names of several *individual* agents that you think would best represent your work. Approach agents in exactly the same way that you approach publishers—with a book proposal or a query. The query invites the agent to request the book proposal. The book proposal convinces the agent to represent your eventual book.

Some writers have met people who later became their agents or publishers at workshops and conferences. Sometimes you receive a tip or get a hunch at such gatherings.

Remember that the agent's primary motivation for doing anything is money, not helping writers with passion, although that can be a secondary motivation. The agent has many other clients, most of whom can bring in a higher commission than you. The agent decides to represent you because he sees bigger sales down the road and believes you can write the material his contacts want.

Therefore, communicate to the agent your desire for a writing career and your willingness to work hard. Your passion should carry that message through without your having to come out and say it. Don't be afraid to ask agents questions. Some, such as how long they've been in business and what books they've sold, can easily be answered by your research. Some you may need to ask yourself, such as does the agent charge for certain expenses.

If the agent is serious, she will offer a contract, although it's not unusual for an agent to "test the waters" by approaching a few contacts first before offering the contract. Before signing a contract with any agent or publisher, read it. What is the agent's commission? It should be 10%-15% for domestic sales and about 20% for foreign. There should be some escape clause if the contract is made for a long period of time.

In the film business, the standard commission is 10%, and there is a standard 90-day escape clause. If an agent fails to find you work in any 90-day period, you can escape. Of course, 90 days is unrealistic for both screenplays and books. Switching agents every several months is a bad habit, and the news of it will get around.

There are two things an agent will seldom do—act as your editor and act as your therapist.

14. Writing for children and teenagers

Do you like and respect children and teenagers?

That's the first qualification to write for them. The rewards and joys are many. You view the world anew and revel in little pleasures. You also re-experience the basic problems that confront children. You explore new ideas with them. You deal with simple themes and values. It's a heckuva lot of fun, but much more difficult than most writers think.

You will need to be unique and watch out for pits such as presenting stereotypical animals or trying to relive your own childhood. *Sleeping Beauty* has already been written, and *your* problems may not be the same as *theirs*. Be careful that your story characters are not purely evil or purely good—that's generally true for any work of fiction. Don't preach; don't let your message or personal cause overwhelm the story. Focus on direct action and crisp dialogue. Kids laugh at things people do, and they've seen too much TV to endure long speeches. Give your work a satisfying ending.

Editors like books that are serious with a touch of humor, and they *love* series books that feature characters that return book after book. *Harry Potter* is just one example.

Generally, you will approach the writing markets yourself. Agents of children's literature do more bookkeeping than they do selling. Let's look at the variety of markets for children.

Magazines. There are only a few dozen magazines aimed directly at children under 12, and about as many for teenagers. Many are sponsored by religions that are generally more interested in teaching values than in indoctrinating readers. The pay is not high.

Picture books for children 1-3, 3-5, and 5-7. There is a great deal of innovation these days. My wife brings home books for our children that sing, pop up, interact, and make noises. All are illustrated and contain anywhere from 100 to 1,000 words depending on the age group for which they are intended. The buyers, of course, are parents, guardians, grandparents, and other loved ones. In terms of content, remember that little children need to feel safe. Mr. Rogers taught all of his neighbors that.

When you write picture books, you are most often writing rhyme, but don't expect to illustrate the book as well. Most often, publishers draw from a stable of illustrators. Expect a royalty of no more than 5%. The illustrator gets the other half of the royalty. However, these days, most publishers pay a flat fee for a picture book, which may be a few thousand dollars. Your mass-marketers are Golden, Random House, and Grosset & Dunlap.

Picture books aimed at ages 5-7 are called **easy readers.** There are usually about 1,000 to 1,500 words in length, although some are up to 2,000 words long. Plots are usually predictable without much else going on.

As a general rule for all children's books, the characters should be about one or two years older than the intended readers.

Chapter books. Chapter books are aimed at ages 7-10. These are books of 1,000-10,000 words that have real chapters like grown-up books. *Horrible Harry* is an example. I asked a highly successful children's book writer to distill her wisdom in just a few sentences. She said, "I'd hate to say it, but there are only two storylines out there—*Cinderella* for girls and *Jack the Giant Killer* for boys." Those relationship and action fantasies extend well beyond the 7-10 age group.

Middle Readers (or **junior books** or **middle-grade novels**). These are the books that you are most likely to recall reading as a child. They are intended for 8-12 year-olds. The main characters will be about 12 years of age or young teenagers. The characters should have flaws, just as do your readers. Descriptions should be clear and simple. I remember reading mysteries and adventure stories at that age. Those genres are still popular along with horror (R. L. Stine), and some fantasy and sports. Staples from the past (and these are all "series" books) include *Babysitter's Club*, *Nancy Drew,* the *Hardy Boys,* and *Encyclopedia Brown.*

Middle-grade novels are about 15,000-30,000 words and about 10-12 chapters. Think of those numbers as guidelines and not rules.

Pitch your ideas with a book proposal, as you would pitch books for adults. With series fiction, present the setting and describe each of the characters; make sure there are no stereotypes. There should be a sub-plot or two.

Advances are about $1,000-$2,000 with a royalty of 10% or less. Keep in mind, when negotiating your contract, that there might be spin-off opportunities for certain books.

Young adult novels for teenagers. There is a thriving market in paper-backs, particularly in romance novels for girls. Royalty is about 3%-6%

for paperbacks, 10% for hard cover. Once children reach about age 14 or so, they begin reading novels intended for adults, or they stop reading altogether.

Once your children's book is published and has gone out of print, request the rights to it. That will force your publisher to re-evaluate the book.

Licensed books. If you have an idea that would be just perfect for Donald Duck or Cookie Monster, you will need to contact the publisher of books that feature those characters. These publishers have agreements that allow them to use copyrighted characters in books. They pay a licensing fee on anything they sell, and they must get approval for each book published.

Your job is to contact that publisher with your excellent idea. A track record of some kind in the area of writing for children will be helpful. This will not be an easy road, but it certainly can be a profitable one.

Children's plays. There are some theaters built just for children. In these little theaters, school theaters, and church theaters, 45-minute plays are performed. Staging and costuming are usually simple. In fact, avoid set changes or anything else that might increase production costs.

In plays written for middle school or high school, there should be more parts written for girls than for boys. Consider including a couple of parts that could be played by either boys or girls. Some plays contain speaking parts for as many as 20 people. That's to give everyone a chance to be in the play.

Plays for children ages 6-10 are mainly fantasy (such as talking animals) while plays for children 10 and above lean more towards adventure. Make sure there is plenty of physical action, even if it is simple. Plays for ages 6-10 often involve the audience.

There are many play publishers, including Samuel French, that buy plays to license to schools, community theaters, and professional theaters. The author is paid a royalty based on performances.

Children's nonfiction and writing for education. There is a growing market for educational videos and audiotape programs. The first major success was *Hooked on Phonics* and the market has grown from there. My own babies are hooked on the *Baby Einstein* series.

Another growing market is the home-schooling market. Write curricula or books to meet the needs of this market. Textbooks for public or private schools are usually sold with proposals. Nonfiction books are usually educational in nature; if you have an idea for one, talk to a children's books librarian—she'll know more about this market than anyone. Nonfiction books need to be imaginative to pull children into the material.

These days, children learn from computers as well as from live teachers. Interactive software scripts need to be written by someone. If you have an idea for an educational game, query the smaller game companies. Naturally, you'll want to do more research in these areas before jumping in.

Resources. If you interested in writing for children, you'll find the following resources helpful. Join the Society of Children's Book Writers and Illustrators (www.scbwi.org) at 8271 Beverly Blvd., Los Angeles, CA 90048, 323/782-1010. Writer's Digest publishes *The Children's Writer's and Illustrator's Market*. *Publisher's Weekly* puts out a "children's books" issue every spring and fall. You'll learn about what's new in children's books.

15. Self-publishing books, reports, and other media

What do you do when you can't find a publisher for your book? You decide whether or not self-publishing would be wise. Self-publishing is risky for books of fiction, anthologies, and poetry, especially if aimed at the general public.

There is also a risk with nonfiction books. However, there are many notable successes. *The One Minute Manager* was self-published. Ken Blanchard and Spencer Johnson sold 20,000 copies in three months. It has now sold more than 12 million copies and is currently published by Berkley Publishing Group.

Tom Peters self-published *In Search of Excellence.* It took a year to sell 20,000 copies. Ten million have been sold since.

Richard Paul Evans self-published *The Christmas Box*, and it has sold more than a million copies. Of course, he took a huge financial risk. On the other hand, he was a skilled marketer, having worked previously in politics. Now, he's a millionaire with a fat book contract with a major publisher.

Obviously, self-publishing is not the same as subsidy or vanity publishing, in which you pay a printer to publish your book so that you can see yourself in print and hand off copies to friends, family, and acquaintances. Self-publishing is a for-profit business. In the world of self-publishing, marketing precedes the miracle. To understand the business, regardless of what type of materials you want to self-publish, let's first discuss the ideal situation for self-publishing books, reports, newsletters, and similar materials.

Marketing to a specific market segment

1. Identify a market with unmet needs. The first step is not to write the book. The first step is to identify a *niche* market and the needs of that market. Any professional marketer will tell you that identifying first the market and then the product to meet that market's needs gives you a huge advantage in the marketplace. The more specific that market, the more likely you will succeed in penetrating that market.

For example, Robert James Bidinotto published *Criminal Justice? The Legal System Versus Individual Responsibility.* He had a lot of success approaching law-enforcement and crime victims' groups (*Writer's Digest,* February 1997).

Suppose you decide to write something for men. That's a big market. What's the need? I predict you will find several good books already published for any need you can name. The market is too broad for a self-published book. Ideally, you want to identify a market for which you can find a mailing list. Let's try to narrow the market down.

What kind of men would you like to reach? How about men who like sports? That's better, but it's still too broad. What sport? The moment you ask the question, you realize the answer is too broad. You think for a moment and suggest Little League fathers. That's a good choice, but how are you going to reach them? Do they appear on a mailing list? Then, it hits you—Little League umpires. There is probably a list of these somewhere. And boy, do they have needs. No one appreciates these guys.

Now brainstorm until you have listed several unmet needs that Little League umpires might have. One need is how to handle out-of-control fathers. Conflict management in general is another. Maybe there's a need to commiserate with other umpires. Are there any legal concerns? There sure could be. Is there an unmet need related to baseball? There might be. Your research will tell you.

2. Get a list of names to contact. Once you have identified your market, what that market's needs are, and whether those needs are being met, make sure you can get a list of names of Little League umpires across the country. Many companies and brokers rent mailing lists, including www.ParaPublishing.com. If umpires belong to an association, see if you can get a list from the association. You might have to join.

What form should the information you provide take? A book? Newsletter? Report? Perhaps it should just be an article for a publication read by umpires. Is there such a publication? Maybe you should deliver a speech or conduct a seminar or produce an audiotape. Let's say you decide on a short book. Good.

3. Create a detailed outline of the book. The purpose of this step is to make sure you have sufficient content for a book and to better understand the features and benefits of your proposed book.

4. Brainstorm alternate ways to present the content. Maybe, after writing the book, you can offer to keep umpires informed or connected with a newsletter. Perhaps the book can send them to a website. If there is no umpire association, you could create a formal or informal organization with a newsletter as part of membership. If there already is a newsletter for that organization, write an article for the newsletter. Do you see what you are doing?

You're not only creating different ways to package the same information, but you are also identifying promotional tools. The article might interest readers in the book. If you give a speech, it indirectly promotes the book. And the book indirectly promotes the speech. Readers of the book might want the newsletter or a sequel. What might make a good sequel? How about a book of true/funny umpire stories? If you're going to research the information, then you might as well optimize your use of that information. Would a CD-ROM be appropriate for your market?

The next three steps are critical—the design of the marketing plan, the test, and a go/no-go decision.

5. Design the marketing plan. How can you promote this book? Well, you have already identified some ways. Perhaps you get an expert or baseball celebrity to write a foreword to your book or provide a quote for your sales letter. If there is an association of Little League umpires, would it help to get the endorsement of the president? Yes, it would. What else could add value to the book? Illustrations maybe. Personalized copies perhaps. How about a free first issue of a newsletter, if you decide to write one? Keep the ideas flowing.

Identify the features and benefits of your book. Once done, you must design your direct-mail campaign or ad campaign. Refer to Chapter 1 of this book on "Copywriting" for helpful advice. Although sending direct mail to your mailing list is usually the best way to go, an ad in the right publication might work for the market you have chosen. Some self-publishers have done well with small display ads and classified ads in the right magazine or journal.

So far, you have *not* spent any money! Now you will.

6. Run a test. You need to run a test of your advertising materials to see if they will bring you the results you need. That means you'll have to pay for some printing to be done. Send your direct-mail materials to a small percentage of your mailing list. I recommend at least 250 names. You can buy stamps for your mailings, or you can buy a bulk-mail permit or a first-class mail permit. Talk to your post office about bulk-mail options.

Now because you have yet to write the book, your campaign will be a "pre-sale." You will communicate that the book is nearly ready for release. If the umpire will order in advance, he'll get a 10% discount. Otherwise, he'll strike out. Your P.S. on your sales letter will emphasize urgency and the benefit of acting now.

The book should sell for at least $20-$25. You'll need that much to recoup your marketing costs.

What is your percentage of return? In a direct-mail campaign to a general audience, you are looking for a ½%-to-1% return. However, when you aim at a specific market with a specific unmet need, you are shooting for a 5%-10% return. I had a student who simply created directories for organizations that didn't already have them and earned a consistent 30% return on his direct-mail campaigns.

When I self-published the first edition of *The Screenwriter's Bible* to my specific market, my return was 12.5%.

According to an article in *The Orange County Register* (March 29, 1995), a writer mailed 18,000 flyers about *What to do When a Loved One Dies* to funeral homes and grief counselors, and had a response rate of 3%—and still made a profit.

7. Make the go/no-go decision. Regardless of your percentage return, the main thing is to do the math and *determine if your book will make money or not*. There are many costs to take into consideration: creation and printing of direct-mail materials, postage, cost of printing the book, cost of materials and postage to ship the book to buyers, and so on. Take into consideration the amount of time you will need to devote to your enterprise. Now make the decision—do you go forward or go to the latest movie?

If it's a no-go decision, you have just saved yourself a ton of time and money writing a book and failing to make a profit on it. If you made a "go" decision, then the real fun begins.

8. Write the book, report, or newsletter. *Rapido*! When you are both the writer and publisher, you do not need to worry about correct manuscript format. Simply lay out the formatting of your book during the revision stage. Eventually you will convert your word-processing file to an Adobe® PDF (portable document format) file, and you will be ready to send the disk or file to a printer. The printer will teach you how to do the conversion.

While you are writing, try to get a merchant account at a bank so that you can accept MasterCard and Visa card orders. You may also want to create a business name. See the first chapter in this book on "Setting up your writing business for almost nothing."

In addition, get any *permissions* to quote material from outside sources. Write the publisher or individual who owns the rights to the material you want to include. This may require a couple of phone calls or other research. Most publishers have a specific department that handles permissions. In your letter, state the fact that you are asking permission to use X-material in your forthcoming book. Include the entire quotation that you want to use and where it appears. Then ask for permission. Leave a place at the bottom of the letter for them to sign. In some cases, the other party may ask for a usage fee. The process can take from days to months, depending on whom are you dealing with, so don't wait too long to make requests.

Once your work is done, you need to design a cover or hire someone to do it, create any "fore" material (preface, acknowledgements, table of contents, etc.), and get an ISBN (if a book).

The ISBN (International Standard Book Number) is the 10-digit (soon to be 13-digit) number that precedes the price on the back of every book. If your book is ever going to appear in a bookstore, then get an ISBN for it. Contact R. R. Bowker (www.bowker.com or www.isbn.org or 908/665-6770) as a book publisher and apply for an ISBN prefix. The charge is a little more than $200 for a block of ten ISBNs. Once you have your

ISBN, have your book-cover designer create your bar-coding. If you are creating your book cover, look for software to create the bar code.

The ISBN may not be necessary if you foresee your book only going to your mailing list and never appearing on library shelves or in bookstores or on Amazon.com.

9. Print copies of your book. Don't print thousands and thousands of copies for your first printing or you may never get your car back into your garage. Print no more than 1,000-2,000. Find a list of printers that handle "short runs." You can order as few as 500 at most places. *The Literary Marketplace* lists short-run shops. You can also get this list and other self-publishing information from Dan Poynter's *The Self-Publishing Manual*. See his website at www.ParaPublishing.com.

Another printing option is to take your PDF file of your book and get it to a printer with PQN (Print Quantity Needed) printing machines or a POD (Print on Demand) service. (They are essentially the same thing.) That way, you can produce as few as a dozen at a time, or even one at a time.

As you can see, that allows you to keep your costs down. You can also send advance copies to reviewers, or simply print copies as they are purchased by customers. Some writers, instead of sending review copies to reviewers, simply invite reviewers to their website to read the book there. (If you display your book or portions thereof at your website, make sure there is a password system to prevent piracy of your work.) Naturally, you'll want to compare costs of the PQN and POD methods versus the old-fashioned method of printing 500-2,000 at a time. Ask several companies for quotes.

Be sure to send some copies of your book to publications for review and to experts for endorsements (testimonials). Realize that some publications won't review self-published books because they fear possible plagiarism or other legal liability reasons. Ask each selected expert for an endorsement in writing, and include a section in your letter (or on a separate piece of paper) for writing the 1-3 sentence "comments" and another section for his/her "printed name and title/attribution (i.e., how you want yourself listed)."

10. Make any adjustments to your marketing plan. Once you receive your initial orders from your test (Step #6), send the book out to those who ordered it, and then wait two or three weeks. Give them a chance to read it. Next, send those buyers a questionnaire about the usefulness of the book along with a self-addressed stamped envelope. In essence, you are asking for testimonials. You'll review these testimonials along with any endorsements and positive reviews you have received. Ask for written permission to use the testimonials (unless that permission is requested in your original questionnaire). Determine which to include in your direct-mail package or whatever promotional materials you have designed. That might mean adding a flyer or revising something you already created.

In the next printing or edition of your book, add the excerpts from reviews, endorsements, and testimonials to the cover or "fore" material of the book.

11. Send your direct mailer to your entire mailing list. Now that you have a little more ammo, fire away. And get ready to fill orders. That step is called *fulfillment*. Get books out as quickly as you can. Don't make people wait 4-6 weeks. In your materials, advertise a 2-3 week delay. That's so you can make sure checks have cleared.

12. Brainstorm alternate media for your content and alternate distribution channels. After a successful marketing campaign, direct your Warrior energy to ways to multiply your profits. In Step #4, you brainstormed several ways to get the information out. Review that information. Should you create that newsletter or audiotape now? Would it be worthwhile to try to schedule a seminar? Ask yourself these kinds of questions.

Do you have an idea for an article? Don't query a magazine; sell the article directly to the marketplace as a booklet or report, especially if it presents how-to information. Think in terms of 32 pages, which would include your cover, fore material (copyright, preface, etc.), and order form in the back for other materials you sell. The back cover should "sell" the booklet's contents.

On my desk at the moment is a copy of Jeffrey Lant's *Cash Copy: How to Offer Your Products and Services so Your Prospects Buy Them . . .*

NOW! At the back of this book is an order form and descriptions of more than 100 books, newsletters, reports, and other offers. He has perfected the art of self-publishing.

Next, think in terms of new distribution channels for your successful book—bookstores, libraries, e-delivery, and the Amazon.com Advantage program for self-publishers. Do any of these make sense for your project? What other distribution channels can you think of? Amazon.com provides a "Search Inside the Book" feature, where readers can read portions of your book before they buy. Likewise, Google has launched Google Print. These might be worth looking into.

Independent bookstores are easier to approach than chains like Barnes & Noble and Borders. You approach any bookstore as both the publisher and distributor of your book. Offer them a 20% discount on orders of 1-5 books (or 1-9 books), and then the standard 40% discount for orders above that. If they ask for a 40% discount for just two books, give it to them. Shrink-wrap books in groups of two. That way, bookstores must remove the wrap to display the books, allowing indecisive people to check the contents.

If you visit a bookstore for any reason, offer to autograph your books. Offer to conduct a 15-30 minute mini-workshop, or to deliver a short lecture on your topic and conduct a book-signing. If the store allows you to do that, be sure to sign every book, even those not sold. The bookseller will display these.

You can also approach distributors and wholesalers who cater to bookstores. All of these have specific requirements, so ask them what these requirements are before you pitch them. For a list of distributors and wholesalers, see Dan Poynter's *The Self-Publishing Manual.*

13. Identify new, related markets. Now that you have chosen other ways to package your information and have found other distribution channels for your successful book, think of other markets to approach with the same information. You already know that Little League umpires love your book. Who else would enjoy the same book or similar information presented differently? I would think that Babe Ruth League umpires, high school umpires, and other youth league umpires might be interested. How about coaches? Don't they have to deal with Little League parents, too? Others who might be interested are municipalities and parents.

Do you recall your idea for a second book, a collection of umpire stories? Little League parents might love these, and maybe the little tykes will, too. I realize that "parents" and "kids" constitute a "general" market, but you would create your "umpires stories" book for the more specific markets named, and then try to get it into bookstores for parents.

As you can see, throughout this process, you have found ways to maximize returns at every step. For many self-publishers, this business has a domino effect. One success leads to the next success, and so on. Not everyone makes millions as self-publishers, but the prospect of making six figures is very real.

Here are the statistics from a self-published audiocassette tape package. The tapes cost about $1,800 to produce (production costs, duping, studio time, cassette shells, labels, Norelco boxes, J-cards, and accompanying booklet). My marketing costs amounted to $3,500. The return was 11% on a mailing list of 6,000 names (from more than one list). That's total sales of 660 tapes at a price of $24.95 each plus shipping. That's not a bestseller, but my gross revenues amounted to about $19,100. You'd have to sell about 10,000 books using the traditional method to make that amount. Once orders were received, product was shipped. Fulfillment cost about $1,500. There were other administrative costs of about $550. The bottom line? My net profit amounted to $12,300.

And that's just one product sold through one distribution channel to one market using one medium. There are other distribution/marketing channels I tried to sell the same tapes. There are many media I could use to sell the same information to the same market or different markets. And there are other markets that might be interested in the same or similar information.

My total investment in this project was large. Of course, not all of the money was invested at once. I ran my direct-mail test on 300 names and then on 3,000 names. I used the profits from that mail campaign to approach the remaining names on my mailing lists.

In any business, there is a risk, and that is why you want to be able to predict with some certainty what your results are going to be before you lay your money down.

I mentioned earlier that I self-published the first edition of *The Screenwriter's Bible*. I sold 7,850 copies before Silman-James Press took the book over. About a third of those sales were to bookstores. My gross revenue was $157,000. After expenses, my net profit before taxes was just under a hundred grand.

14. Enjoy the fruits of your labors. Reward yourself in some way.

Writing franchises and subscription newsletters

One way to build an empire is to teach other people to do what you do under your name, and pay them to do that work. If you decide to duplicate yourself in this manner, be honest with writing assistants about fees and work parameters when you hire them. That will include asking them to sign a non-competition agreement. This protects you somewhat from those who decide to break off and become competitors.

Hiring assistants is a scenario I would consider only if my workload became overwhelming. At that point, you probably will have built a reputation in a particular area. Your efforts in self-publishing will have given you a recognizable name. Hiring assistants gives them a chance to make money from writing and allows you to expand your operations. In effect, you are offering writing franchise opportunities.

◆ ◆ ◆ ◆ ◆

I mentioned earlier in this chapter the idea of selling a newsletter to readers of your self-published book. That newsletter may be a freebie to build support, or it may be a subscription newsletter. Subscription newsletters succeed best when directed at a particular market—just as we discussed with nonfiction books. Thus, you will start by identifying a specific need of a specific group of people.

Newsletters are different from magazines. With a newsletter, you charge more for less information. With a magazine, you charge less for more information. The difference is in the specialized nature of newsletter information. Where magazines may report some *thing*, newsletters report to some *one* (the subscriber). That's the difference in editorial slant.

Business areas are usually the best to focus on, but *Contest Newsletter* has thrived for years, as has the *Car Rental/Leasing Insider*. Note the specific focus of those titles. There's even a *Newsletter on Newsletters* (www.newsletterbiz.com), which I recommend if you decide to create your own for-profit newsletter.

What makes or breaks subscription newsletters are renewals. You must be able to convince people to renew before their subscriptions lapse. If your content has truly met the readers' needs, then your chances for strong renewals are good, but you will still need to promote your publications and spend some money reminding people to renew. This is often the costliest part of running a newsletter business.

As you might guess, self-published subscription newsletters are riskier than self-published books. My recommendation is to achieve success in other areas of self-publishing first before designing a newsletter as a profit center. On the other hand, if you have the right idea for the right market segment, and you have created a great plan, the world is your oyster.

Marketing to the general public

Thus far, we have focused on the ideal situation of meeting a specific unmet need of a specific group of people. That's the best risk for your money. However, many writers succeed by focusing on some specific need that they feel is not adequately addressed in the mass market. Years ago, Robert Holt did that and made a ton of money on a book about hemorrhoids. Notice that he chose a very specific topic for his general audience.

If you want to self-publish your self-help book or novel or children's book to the general market, then there will be a great deal more risk involved, but there are many success stories, and even moderate successes can be very fulfilling.

I've already mentioned Richard Paul Evans and *The Christmas Box*. Julie Aigner-Clark was a middle-school art teacher who decided to quit teaching to become a full-time mom. When she couldn't find something educational for her baby, she created her own video and *Baby Einstein* was born. The first video cost her $18,000 to produce. Years later, she sold her business to the Disney Company for a reported $25 million.

The process of creating and marketing newsletters, videos, audiocassettes, and DVDs is basically the same as with self-published books. And the process for marketing books of fiction is similar to what we discussed earlier about selling to specific markets. Naturally, you won't be buying a mailing list, but you will need to form your own little book-publishing company.

Your first big step is to publish your book. You are the publishing company. Create an attractive cover and get about 500-1,000 copies printed, or use the PQN (Print Quantity Needed) or POD (Print on Demand) methods described earlier. In any case, don't print more than 1,000. Try to keep your initial investment as low as possible.

Once the book is published, try to get endorsements and positive reviews. Send out advance copies of your manuscripts for the reviews. Realize that some newspapers won't review your self-published book. They worry about plagiarism issues. They know that published books have gone through a legal scrutiny that self-published books have not.

Next, approach independent bookstores, chains, wholesalers, distributors, book clubs, and remainders houses. There are many independent bookstores across the country that are willing to work with small publishing companies like yours.

When I self-published *The Screenwriter's Bible,* I first went to independent outlets, and then to local Borders bookstores. Because of my success at Borders, I was able to approach the corporate office. At about that time, a publisher became interested and took over from there. That could be your goal as well: get a track record behind you, and then approach other publishers about picking up your book.

Marion Street Press, Inc. (www.marionstreetpress.com), produces a newsletter entitled "Independent Bookstore." You may find some of the articles helpful to your fledgling publishing company. Another helpful resource is the Publishers Marketing Association (www.pma-online.org).

With new technologies being created and improved virtually every day, getting your work out is becoming easier and easier, and that includes using the Internet, which we discuss next.

16. E-publishing and the Internet

The Internet is the cyberland of opportunity. Anyone can publish something online. For that reason, you'll find some poor writing on the Internet. On the other hand, you'll find a great deal of superb writing as well. It all depends on where you look. As a general rule, you will earn less for work distributed online than for comparable work sold through traditional means. However, that's quickly changing, and I've seen instances where the reverse is true.

The Internet is faster than traditional publishing. As a general rule, you will see your article or book "published" in record time compared to traditional printed publications and book publishers. Your book may appear within a year of submission and your e-zine article may appear within weeks. If you want a quick writing credit, this is one place to look.

There are three main e-markets: e-zines, websites, and e-books. Three areas differ in many ways from their traditional counterparts.

e-zines

Think of e-zines as newsletters and magazines written for the web-surfing public. Everything you learned about writing articles and columns is applicable to writing for e-zines (or just *zines*). See examples at www.fabjob.com, www.crescentblues.com, and www.womensenews. org. And, of course, book publishing is book publishing.

Some e-zines are laden with graphics, while others contain words only. In fact, an e-zine written in text only (TXT file or ASCII) doesn't even use bold, italics, or color. The words have to do it all. As a writer, I like that challenge.

E-zines are a wonderful way to spread the word. I receive e-zines from bookstores, magazines, specialty stores, and e-businesses. For most, the central idea is to provide information that attracts the reader to the website and, in many cases, attract advertisers to place banners. Many of these e-zines are free. That is one reason the pay is low here, and most e-zines already receive plenty of free material from other writers and people promoting their own products and services. Perhaps you should consider publishing your own e-zine for promotional purposes. We'll discuss that in the next chapter.

Web writing

The real money is in websites and product sites (which are dedicated to selling a single product or range of products). Writing for the web falls under the category of copywriting, so everything you learned in Chapter 1 of this book applies. Most businesses have learned, as I have learned, that it pays to have a website. I think of my website as a support to my regular business, not as a profit center. Though my website makes a profit, its main function is to provide free information to passers-by and information-seekers. A website is an interactive advertising billboard. People can click for more information or to place an order. I can hardly think of a business that wouldn't benefit from having a website, and someone has to write the material that appears at each business's websites. That writer (often called a *content provider*) does not have to be a technological genius either. He just needs to understand how webpages work. (For tips and information on online writing, read Chapter 17.) To get online writing assignments, approach businesses either online or by the traditional methods discussed in Chapter 1 on copywriting.

Many, if not most, traditional publications have web editions. That's true for newspapers and magazines. Some of this material comes under the category of copywriting, while much of it is similar (and even the same) as what appears in the printed editions. And that includes the e-zines e-mailed to subscribers.

e-books

As electronic technology continues to improve, I think we'll see more people purchasing and reading e-books. The University of Phoenix, which boasts an enrollment of nearly 300,000 students, has moved to e-textbooks. Specialty software has been developed to make reading on your computer easier. Examples include Microsoft® Reader®, tk3 Reader, eRocket, and Palm Reader (freeware). And, of course, Adobe® Acrobat Reader® reads PDF files.

The e-publishing industry is still in its infancy, and, although it's unlikely that e-books will ever replace paper books, you will see more and more opportunities in e-book publishing. As of 2005, e-books constituted about 3% of the book publishing industry. That's actually quite high when you realize how large the book publishing business is.

If you have a manuscript, you can choose to self-publish your book and convert it to an e-book (probably as a PDF file) that you can sell at your website, or you can go to an e-publisher, such as Xlibris (www.xlibris. com) or Booklocker (www.booklocker.com). For help in preparing your book and understanding your e-rights, visit www.e-rights.com. You'll find additional helpful information at such websites as www. knowbetter.com, www.openebook.org, and www.epicauthors.org. Also, *Writer's Online Marketplace* (a real, tangible book) by Debbie Ridpath Ohi is quite informative and lists hundreds of e-markets.

You will want to know if the publisher you contact wants e-rights only, print rights, or all rights. Usually, an explanation of how an e-publisher does business, how it promotes its books, and even a sample contract can be found at its website. Although royalty rates can be as high as 50%, there may be some costs you will need to cover, for example, converting your e-book into the right format (such as HTML, TXT, OR

PDF). Usually, royalties are paid for each time your work is "viewed." There is seldom an advance, but you will have instant global access.

Be aware that there is piracy on the Internet. It's reasonably easy to scan files and re-post them somewhere else. Most e-publishers have found ways to protect your work. However, if you display your work at your own website, you need to find a way protect it yourself. Some writers make a chapter or two available to anyone who visits the website, but the entire work can only be accessed with a password. Regardless of where you e-book is displayed, conduct a periodic web search of the content of your work to see if your book appears at some other site.

If you self-publish your e-book, you will save on printing costs. On the other hand, you will need to decide how to promote your self-published e-book on the web. You will probably need to create a website and find ways of drawing people to your site without spamming (sending unsolicited e-mails to people who have not contacted you). Choose a reliable web host. This is crucial if you are going to e-publish your work there. For information about web hosting and creating your own website, read the next chapter.

17. Teaching, consulting, and self-promotion

Who you are

You are a writer. You are a teacher and consultant. You teach through your writing. You are a consultant when you say you are. You act as an entertainment and information consultant to publishers, publications, and businesses clients. You are a marketer. You promote yourself primarily with your work. Your article promotes your book. Your speech promotes your copywriting services. You are a professional writer. Congratulations!

Another tool for your own self-promotion is press releases about your appearances and successes. In fact, why not create your own press kit? Just follow the tips discussed in Chapter 2 of this book. Make sure you have a good-quality photograph of yourself in case you need it.

Sometimes, a membership in a specific organization can help you network with potential clients, editors, or publishers. Attendance at writers' conferences can be helpful in that regard. Get interviewed on television and radio. Get involved in community events. If appropriate, advertise or create marketing collateral or a newsletter or an e-letter.

Most importantly, stay in touch by phone, e-mail, or regular mail (also known as *snail mail*) with people who are or can be beneficial to your writing career. By this I mean occasional notes, not regular correspondence.

Build your website and publish your e-zine

At some point in time, you may want to consider a website. Many writers now promote themselves with a webpage highlighting their credits, experience, and published work. You can refer people to your site in your queries, whether by phone, mail, or e-mail.

Owning your own domain name gives you control over the future of your website and business, and is a valuable marketing tool as well. For that reason, choose a domain name that is easy to remember. Domain names that end in .com have more marketing value than any other suffix.

As mentioned in the previous chapter, choose a reliable web host. A host is the "place" in cyberland where your website appears. Web hosts (such as www.xo.com and www.hostindex.com [Interland]) are rated at www.webhostingratings.com. Personally, I have had success with verio.com. I am leery about free web hosts (such as geocities. com). Some have disappeared without a trace, leaving customers with an entire website to rebuild or install over again. Look for web hosts with a track record and some longevity in this relatively new field.

Before publishing your work online, carefully review the user agreement or contract with the hosting service and make sure that you retain the copyright to materials published at the website. Some web hosts (mostly "free" hosting companies) claim the copyright to any material published through their hosting service.

Although you can learn Java and HTML to create your website, there are some freeware and shareware programs available that can make the process easier. Conduct a web search to see what is current. Some writers use Microsoft® FrontPage® to build their sites or pay consultants or *developers* to do it for them.

You will need to get a merchant account with a financial institution so that you can process credit-card payments and/or try one of the Internet-based pay systems. Obviously, any relevant experience in cyberspace will help you self-publish or promote your work, but make sure you understand the process before you plunge in. If you build a site, register it with the major search engines.

Online writing differs from "hard copy" writing. You need to catch the reader's attention quickly and make the reading experience as easy as possible. Write concisely with shorter sentences. I think of writing for the web as *designing*. That's because I usually have many tools at my disposal: graphics, bullets to make lists that can be easily seen and assimilated, color to highlight certain words and phrases, bold and italic, font choices, special headings, and hyperlinks (an underscored keyword that, when clicked, links the reader to a page containing additional information).

Your site should be well-organized. Catch the reader's attention with graphics, and write your *text content* to a lower reading skill level than you would normally. Don't go overboard with graphics. I recommend a simple design for the home page with a minimum of graphics so people can see immediately who you are and what you do. Of course, you should decide what best represents you in terms of design. (For more on this topic, see www.gerrymcgovern.com/la/writing_for_web.pdf.)

Create a way for site visitors to sign up for your e-mail list at your site. Once you have their e-mail addresses saved in an e-mail list software application, you can contact them with future news about your writing services, and there are no mailing costs. You may need the help of a consultant or developer to set this up for you. I know I did.

A benefit of creating a good amount of "text content" at your site is that you are more likely to get noticed by search engines. If you are promoting your book online (whether an e-book or a physical book), put your table of contents, the first chapter, and other promotional information about the book at your website. Search engines will index your content and direct interested readers to your website.

Promote yourself with an e-zine, and e-mail it to your clients and contacts, if appropriate. Never attach an e-zine to a document; many people will not open attached files for fear of contracting a virus. Your e-zine should probably appear in *text* format so that everyone on your list can receive it and so that you can save money for graphics. Of course, if you want something fancy, it will need to be formatted in HTML. Your e-zine should be sent monthly or quarterly. Consider asking for feedback, and archive past e-zines at your website.

Consider creating a *blog* (weblog), which is similar to a bulletin board. Discussion groups form in this way and may generate traffic to your site. There are many blogging software packages available if you conduct an Internet search. I recommend that you include www. typepad.com in your search.

Think about conducting online classes at your website or through existing educational websites.

Teach, speak, and promote

I love to teach. In fact, I teach occasional university courses just for the fun of it. However, I make more money leading seminars and workshops. This "Bible" is based on two of my one-day seminars. Teaching is the best way I know to get feedback on the information you present. I have learned a great deal about the unmet needs of writers by talking to writers in seminars and workshops. So teaching, if nothing else, is a great way to refine your material before placing it into book form. Read Chapter 16 of this book for more information

Teaching and speaking on the corporate circuit can be very lucrative. You can make thousands of dollars a day for the right presentation. In fact, some writers make money teaching corporate employees how to write reports, proposals, and even e-mail. You are a writing consultant or some other kind of consultant or expert—that's how you will sell yourself to executives and department managers. Emphasize your first-hand, real-world experience.

Although you can also sell your services to public schools, associations, and clubs, your best opportunity is college continuing-education programs. Virtually every community college and university publishes a regular catalogue of short, non-credit courses and seminars.

Program directors look for people with a degree, but they mainly want people who have real-world experience at something that will draw a crowd. Before approaching anyone, see what courses are currently being offered. Decide exactly where your workshop or seminar would appear in that catalog. Then, call the program director about your course idea. If the response is positive, ask for any application information and prepare a proposal.

Fees for a six-hour seminar can range from $100 to $1,000 or more. Some program directors will offer a contract where you earn anywhere from 30%-50% of the total take. If tuition is $60 and your program draws in 30 people, then your take would be $900, assuming a 50% contract. Since you do not pay for any advertising or administrative costs, this is a great deal. Once you make a deal for a specific date, work with your program director in getting the word out to the media. In other words, write a brilliant press release and include your photo. With experience, you will find your fees moving upward.

◆ ◆ ◆ ◆ ◆

Brainstorm other ways you can promote your services as a writer and consultant. Review the section entitled "How to attract clients" in Chapter 1 of this book.

Most importantly, enjoy this challenging and satisfying journey. Realize that with each step, you gather power and desire. You move closer to your dreams while you live them. And you set the stage for wonderful things to come.

It's time now to plan for those wonderful things.

CREATE YOUR STRATEGIC MARKETING PLAN

BOOK IV

Making dreams come true

Remember those dreams from Book I? Well, now we're going to create a master plan to make those dreams come true. By now, you are well grounded in reality (Book III) and you have a lofty writing mission-statement (Book II). Your feet are solidly on the ground, and your head is in the clouds. That's the balance we want.

Your power cycle

Let's begin by converting those dreams and your writing mission statement into specific goals, milestones, projects, and action plans. Put some thought to the following questions:

- In the next 12 months, are you aiming for a part-time career or a full-time career?

- Do you want this plan for one year or a longer period of time?

- If you are already an established writer, what do you want to accomplish in the next year?

I will ask for commitments in terms of education (developing your craft), writing time, and selling time. Realize that you will spend at least as much time with your selling, skill development, and administrative activities as you will with writing. And, of course, you will need to be flexible. What follows is the planning cycle, why it is flexible, and why it is powerful. In fact, let's call it your *power cycle*.

195

1. **Envision**. You start by setting project **goals** and **milestones** that emerge from your values.

2. **Plan**. The next natural step is to plan a path to those goals. That plan culminates in a plan of action, or (in your case) a **strategic marketing plan**. This is what you will do in the next chapter.

3. **Act**. The next natural step is to **implement** the plan. Write, sell, and learn.

4. **Evaluate**. Your actions will bring results, which can be evaluated, so you can create new goals and milestones.

And the cycle begins again.

YOUR POWER CYCLE

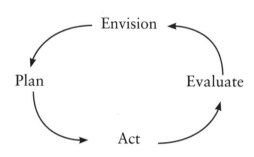

Making time your ally

In your writing journey, you will face tests and overcome obstacles, but you will also gather allies and resources. Many of these resources will be discussed in the chapter "Support and resources" at the end of this book. But let's discuss one key resource now—time.

It's easy to think of the lack of time as a problem or an obstacle. I invite you to reframe that view, and see time as an *ally*, a resource that requires your management skills.

You completed a time log in Book II. Please take a moment to review it. If you have not done that exercise yet, then now is the time. Before you can manage your time, you must be able to identify where it currently goes.

Time management does not need to be complicated. It's essentially prioritizing tasks in accordance with your values and goals. Some people like to make long lists and check them off. That's a great idea unless you are listing a lot of insignificant tasks and checking them off to get an emotional buzz. You are much better off accomplishing one quality task than several tasks that do not make a difference. *Focus on quality when you plan your time.* What activities carry the highest value? Think of this at the beginning of each day and week. That does not mean that some small and seemingly insignificant activities cannot be important. Dropping a note off to that editor whose support you want may pay off down the road.

In Books I and II, you committed yourself to write a certain number of hours each day or week. It's time to re-visit that commitment. Most professional writers spend only about half of their committed time actually writing. The other half of their time is divided between selling activities and skill-development activities.

Skill-development activities include reading the kind of work you want to emulate, studying writing books (such as the "Bible" now in your hands), attending seminars and classes, going to conferences, and completing writing exercises.

You may also need to spend some time on administrative activities (buying toner for your printer, keeping track of expenses). I suggest you think of those as part of your selling or marketing activities.

Here's a breakdown of time allocations that is accurate, or close to accurate, for most professional writers:

> Writing—50%
>
> Selling—30%
>
> Learning—20%

Judging from the goals you have set, how do you think those percentages will break down for you in the next 12 months? Will they be the same as what I have suggested for most professional writers, or will they be slightly different? Indicate any differences below.

Writing: _____%

Selling: _____%

Learning: _____%

Now, during the next 12 months, how many *hours per week* will you devote to your writing business? This means total hours. If you write on Tuesday and Thursday nights from 9-11 p.m., then that's four hours. If it is four hours a day, six days a week, no matter what, then that's 24 hours. How many total hours per week? _____

Let's see how this breaks down, using the percentages you estimated above.

Writing:
Total hours per week _____ x _____% = _____ writing hours per week.

Selling:
Total hours per week _____ x _____% = _____ selling hours per week.

Learning:
Total hours per week _____ x ____% = _____ learning hours per week.

Naturally, in some weeks you may spend 100% of your allotted time writing, and in other weeks 100% of your time selling. So think of the above breakdown as an average.

You will allow yourself two weeks of vacation time, so the above is for 50 weeks.

I don't recommend that you spend much more than four hours each day on writing. After that, your powers will begin to fail you. There are times when you will want to engage in an all-night writing marathon; just don't make it a regular practice. And always take a break after any two-hour stretch.

What happens if you do not meet your work commitment for a given week? Do not stop writing. What's past is past. Do not let it influence the future. This is a fluid, flexible process. Just make your commitment for the next week. And keep writing.

Your strategic marketing plan

Goals should be specific, measurable, and result-oriented, with deadlines for their completion. The following statement is a poor example of a goal: *I'd like to write a book.* That is nothing more than a vague wish. The following declaration is a goal: *I resolve to complete my 60,000-word novel, titled* Love Freight, *by January 31, 20XX.* A goal should be written down; otherwise, it is just a passing fancy.

Don't kid yourself with the common notion, "I know what I want; I don't need a written goal." That's often (not always) an excuse for lack of commitment. There may be a block or fear at the heart of that notion. I hear many of my students say, "But I gotta be free to follow my heart." That's a wonderful concept *if* it means that you are truly following your heart or intuitive nature. *Following* implies action. There's only one thing finer than hearing the "inner voice that knows," and that is taking focused action that brings the results that your inner voice seeks.

On other hand, if "being free" means following your *whim,* then you have become a whimsical writer. Forgive me for saying this, but true freedom comes from being responsible. You're an adult. So get serious, and make the contribution you want to make and earn the money and other rewards that come with that attitude.

Don't set unrealistic goals. Then again, don't be afraid to reach for your dreams. A goal should make you stretch, but not place you on the rack. Usually, it is unwise to broadcast your goals. The exception is to share them with someone who will take you seriously and who will be a faithful support while you are on your adventurous writing journey.

Be careful not to get so caught up in the goal that you become despondent if you don't achieve it. If you are shooting for $100,000 a year and you make $75,000, you still have a great deal to celebrate. After all, the $75,000 is more than you made the previous year. It is a testimony to the progress you have made. So be happy, evaluate your results, and set new goals. The entire goal-setting process is your servant, not your master. You are the King who set the quest. Your Warrior (that part of you that carries out the quest), Magician (that part of you that creates the plan), and Lover (that part of you that gives counsel, support, and love) serve you, the King.

You may choose an overall goal such as "Make $30,000 this year as a writer" or "Set a foundation for making $100,000 in Year 2" or "Acquire ten new clients in one year." Or the goal could focus on a specific project: "Write and sell an article to *Parents* or *Parenting* by X date" or "Find a literary agent by year's end."

With that explanation, let's dive into this magical, exciting process. Please feel free to make photocopies of the charts and worksheets that follow.

Set goals for the next 12 months

Before you set goals, review the worksheets in Book I and Book II. You want your major goals to emerge from your values—those ideals about your self, life, and writing about which you are passionate. You also listed some possible writing projects in the "If I were a rich man" exercise. Take a moment to review those as well.

Whether you see yourself as a part-time writer or full-time writer is irrelevant. This process applies to you.

List possible goals for the next 12 months. You are just throwing out ideas at this point. Include specific projects you want to write, or a specific amount of money you want to make, or specific publications (or categories of publications) in which you want to be published, or a specific number of clients you want to acquire. At this point these goals can be expressed in any way you wish. And they can even extend years into the future if you wish. You don't necessarily need to write a one-year plan; it can be a five-year plan. In the space below or on a separate sheet of paper, write down anything that occurs to you.

_____

_____

_____

_____

_____

_____

_____

_____

_____

_____

_____

_____

_____

_____

_____

_____

_____

_____

_____

_____

Now, let's refine the list. Choose those entries that make the most sense to you. Pick anywhere from 1-5 goals that you would like to accomplish in the next 12 months. Be sensible. Express these in specific language. Make sure they are measurable in some way or can be quantified (write an 80,000-word novel, sell three children's books, earn $50,000, publish five articles in "major" publications, set a foundation on which to build a full-time writing career beginning next year).

Feel free to add a learning or development goal; for example, read two books on writing for children and interview a successful children's book writer.

The deadline for each of these goals is one year unless you specify otherwise. (You will break these goals down into smaller chunks later.)

1. _____
2. _____
3. _____
4. _____
5. _____

You have taken the first steps in creating your master plan. Are you excited? Wonderful. Keep moving forward.

Are you feeling somewhat apprehensive, ambivalent, resistant, or even scared? If so, listen to your feelings. What are they telling you? Is there an underlying fear that needs be addressed, a mental block that needs to be broken? If so, consider returning to Book II, or marshal your Warrior energy, charge through the fear, and complete the exercises that follow. The more you build your desire by doing the necessary work, the more you diminish your fear. Carry on.

This is probably a good time to introduce *Trottier's Theory of Evolution.* It is essentially the idea that writing careers often evolve in unexpected ways. You may start your career with a firm idea of what you want and how you are going to get there. However, the journey may be completely different from what you expected. Often, it takes you to a different and better place than you had previously imagined. The same often happens in life. So my advice is to *be flexible* during your journey. When setbacks and rejections happen along the way, embrace them and make them your friends. They will teach you what you need to know. Thus, you will grow and progress, and your career will evolve.

Many artists, writers, religionists, and business people believe that if you have a specific goal that you plant in your heart and nurture with your thoughts and desires, then the milestones and plan of action will naturally emerge. I believe that, too. The purpose of a strategic marketing plan is to think through with your head what your heart is already telling you. Your "thinking through" inspires your creative, intuitive side to develop more ideas that will help you achieve your goals. As with all tools, use this one in a way that best suits you. If you truly operate better with an open-ended, go-with-the-flow *unplan,* then I salute you. But before you dismiss the idea of creating a plan, whether brief or detailed, I invite you most humbly to continue this journey with me.

As you might guess, you began creating your strategic marketing plan when you set your goals. That process now continues. In a later chapter, I will provide two examples of strategic marketing plans for your reference. Always keep in mind that this process is a tool that you should use in a way that best fits you. Adapt it to your needs and better nature.

Marking your progress with milestones

All goals break down into milestones. Those milestones can sometimes be expressed as project goals. In any case, they are the key steps that you must take to achieve the goal.

Milestones can be broken down into specific activities or task lists. Doing that makes the biggest project seem doable. For example, let's take that 60,000-word novel you want to write within one year's time. Assuming that you take two weeks off for vacation, that means you have 50 weeks to get it ready. The first milestone might be the outline, the second the rough draft, and so on. How long will it take you to sketch out the book? You estimate two weeks. Good.

Now, the rough draft. Let's assume that you only have ten hours a week to devote specifically to writing. How many words can you lay down in ten hours? Stephen King can write 3,000 words in a four-hour day. Let's say you can do less than half of that. Let's say you can write 3,000 words in a week. That means the rough draft can be done in 20 weeks. That leaves 28 weeks to revise and polish the book. It's doable, isn't it? Breaking down your big dreams into manageable chunks makes them *real*. You can do this!

◆ ◆ ◆ ◆ ◆

In the first section of the chart below, write down one of the major goals you set in the previous chapter. How will you know when the goal is achieved? The answer to that question should be evident from the goal statement itself, so use specific language.

Major Goal: I, _____, resolve to

_____

_____

by (target date) _____.

Next, think through the steppingstones to the major goal. I have given you room to list five such milestones, but you might only have two, or you might have six or more. Usually, milestones, or steppingstones, are listed in chronological order, but that's not always true. These intermediate goals are markers for your progress towards the major goal.

If your major goal is to make $60,000 in the next 12 months, don't subdivide that goal into incremental amounts of $10,000 every two months. Instead, think in terms of how many new clients you will have to bring in or how many articles you will need to sell, or apply the *Pareto Principle*. This principle states that 80% of your results will come from 20% of your effort. It follows that about 80% of your income will come from 20% of your clients or writing projects. Identify that "20% income source" and focus a milestone on finding more of that type of client or writing assignment.

It is always difficult to gauge time in the writing business. Realize that your first estimates may be way off, but as you continue this process, you will get a feel for how long things actually take.

Milestone #1 _____

_____

Milestone #2 _____

_____

Milestone #3 _____

_____

Milestone #4 _____

_____

Milestone #5 _____

_____

Note: If you set more than one major goal, then you will need to identify the milestones for each of those major goals.

Assets, resources, and contacts

Once a goal or milestone is written on paper, it should be written on your heart. Nurture your desire to achieve it, because that achievement will come at a price. But before you envision possible prices, obstacles, and challenges, take inventory of your strengths.

You have many resources and assets to carry you through to victory. These might include the following:

- your confidence in your writing ability

- the amount of time you have available

- specific skills and knowledge

- past sales and successes

- placement in a contest

- sizzling query letters and other marketing tools

Are you enthusiastic or have other personable skills? Those are assets. Can you separate your ego from your work? Do you have financial resources? Do you have access to reference books and other sources of information? List the resources that you believe will help you to reach the milestones you have named.

Assets and Resources: _____

_____

_____

_____

_____

_____

_____

_____

_____

_____

_____

_____

One specific resource that you might have is *contacts*. What contacts do you have that you think might be helpful to you in your writing career or with the specific milestones you have named? Take some time to brainstorm this. Your business will grow as your list of contacts grows. Even someone who has rejected a piece but who was positive about your work is an important contact.

Do you know people who have contacts or who might have contacts? Just pretend that you are an Amway distributor and list anyone and everyone. My students are often surprised at the results of this little exercise. (If you still cannot identify any contacts, then don't be overly concerned. You will acquire them as you continue the journey.) Do you know people or writers' groups who can lend moral support? List those as well.

Possible Contacts: _____

_____

_____

_____

Meeting challenges

What is a quest without challenges and tests? Take a moment to assess your milestones collectively or individually, whichever seems to make the most sense to you. You will see a variety of obstacles blocking your path to these achievements. These may range from family resistance to a perceived lack of writing experience to having been pigeonholed as a specialty writer.

Your addiction to television sports or daytime television might be a challenge. And you know whom movie matinees are for—lazy writers.

All or most of these may need to be sacrificed.

Other challenges might stem from the types of publications you are trying to break into; some may be particularly tough. You may lack some specific knowledge that is needed to reach a particular milestone. And, of course, there is sometimes a price in terms of money.

How much money do you need to earn to support yourself during your transition to a writing career? What start-up costs will you incur to establish your writing business or to move it to the next level? Will you need a new health-insurance plan if your quit your current job?

Having completed the exercises in Book II, you have already identified the blocks and fears that have defeated you in the past and have found ways to deal with them. However, list them again if they are going to cause you any trouble.

Some of the assets, resources, and contacts you named earlier will help you successfully overcome your obstacles. In the space below, name each challenge and how you plan to meet it.

Challenge #1 _____

_____

Challenge #2 _____

_____

Challenge #3 _____

_____

Challenge #4 _____

_____

Challenge #5 _____

_____

Other challenges _____

_____

_____

_____

_____

_____

_____

You may be surprised at how easily you will overcome some of your obstacles. Just going through this exercise may resolve some issues. An especially worthy challenge might suggest another milestone.

Before you go on to create project plans and action plans, put on your *marketeer* cap for a moment.

Putting proven marketing principles into action

The writing business is a business. To succeed, you must successfully market your product. Your product is your written work or your proposal to write it. Most writing markets are quite competitive. You need a refined approach, a laser-like focus. You need a strategic marketing plan in which you determine your target market, create marketing strategies that will help you achieve your sales objectives, and position yourself in the market.

Two key marketing concepts are segmentation and differentiation. *Segmentation* is identifying the market segments that seem best for your written work or proposed written work.

Differentiation is how you differentiate yourself from other writers competing for that same market segment, including writers who have already published in that market segment. Differentiation has to do with your product—your written work, proposal, or query—and with your marketing approach. What gives you that competitive edge?

In any persuasive presentation in any business arena, there are three planning steps:

1. Purpose

2. Audience

3. Strategy

Please recall our discussion of "The Writing Process" in Book II. First, identify your purpose, then understand your audience (your market, your reader) and, finally, create strategies to reach that audience. These key steps seem simple enough, but few writers apply them.

Purpose has to do with what *you* want to accomplish, what you want to sell. It derives from your point of view.

The *audience* is whom you want to influence. Once you understand your audience (market or reader), then you know what they need to hear.

In my earlier years, I was a marketing executive. I have since become a writer, writing consultant, and seminar leader. But I still do a little marketing consulting and even teach an occasional college-level marketing course. I can't tell you how many business people to whom I've given some version of the following speech:

> You cannot say what you want to say, you have to say what they want to hear. They don't care how much you sacrificed to build your business; they just want to know if the product will work for them.

So *strategy* comes from the point-of-view of your audience.

Here's an example of the Purpose-Audience-Strategy Principle. You want a raise. That's your purpose. Your audience is your boss. And your strategy is to state all the reasons you deserve the raise (using a lot of sentences that begin with "I"). Right? Wrong. Let's take a marketing view of this same situation.

Your *purpose* is not to get a raise. Your purpose is to get a 7% increase a year over the next three years. Do you see how much more powerful a specific objective or purpose is?

Who is your *audience*? It's the boss. That's not enough. Who really is your boss? What are his or her objectives at the moment? What are this person's concerns for the company? Will there be budget concerns when you ask for your increase? Does your boss personally like or dislike you? Why? And so on. You are conducting your marketing research.

The *strategy* step should come from the boss's point of view. Not "Gimme a raise because *I* deserve it and because *I* did this and *I* learned that," but "Boss, here is how *you* and the company will benefit from giving me a raise. . . ." Certainly, your qualifications for the raise are important, but the strategy step is mostly concerned with applying what you learned from your marketing research to reach your boss. *Strategy is involved with communicating the benefits to your audience so that you can accomplish your purpose.*

(Another example of the Purpose-Audience-Strategy Principle can be found at www.keepwriting.com/marketer.htm. On that page, you will find a short story I wrote using that principle. I also integrate the principle into the narrative.)

Your purpose is to sell your manuscript or get a writing assignment. Actually, that's a little vague. You need to identify a *specific individual* you want to sell your manuscript to. Once done, then you need to understand that person and his company. What is their buying history? What are they looking for now? Do they prefer query letters, proposals, phone calls, or e-mail inquiries? Who is *their* market? In the final analysis, they don't care if you're starving. They just want to know if your ideas can be used to reach their market. Or, they want to know if you are the writer they can trust with a writing assignment.

So you really have two audiences, don't you?

1. The eventual reader of your written work.

2. The person who can get your written work to that reader. I often call this second person your *real* audience.

Your strategy, therefore, derives from the needs of both of these prospects. How will each benefit from what you have to offer?

Another key marketing concept is *positioning*. This refers to how you will "place" your product in the mind of the prospect—the decision-maker who says "Yea" or "Nay" to your project. How does that person need to "see" your query, proposal, article, pitch, or completed work?

Clarifying your purpose, audience, and strategy

1. Select a specific unsold work you have written or a specific work you want to write. (If you are a business writer, technical writer, or other writer who is more interested in getting writing assignments than writing a specific work, then skip to 2b below. Naturally, this entire worksheet could be completed once you know what the writing assignment is.)

Title of project _____

What is your purpose for this work? What do you want it to accomplish? Why have you written it? This is really the goal of the work.

_____

_____

_____

Your response may include a *thematic* goal (the message of the work, how it will affect people) and a *selling* goal. Both are important because you need to achieve your selling goal in order to reach your thematic goal.

2a. Who is the intended, eventual reader of your work? Provide demographics (age, income, occupation, etc.) and psychographics (lifestyle, attitudes, needs, etc.); for example, teenaged boys (demographics) who see themselves as macho and cool (psychographics).

_____

_____

_____

2b. Who is your *real* audience? Your real audience is the person who will hire you to write, or who must love your written work or proposal enough to pay money for it. Or, it is the person who will love the marketing prospects of your work enough to represent it (an agent or manager). Provide relevant demographic and psychographic (lifestyle) information, if available, and include possible resistances this person may have to your inquiry. Here's a brief example: My editor is a 30-year-old female (demographics) who belongs to a literary society and wants to be thought of as an intellectual (psychographics). She is resistant to unprofessional manuscripts and errors in grammar and punctuation.

_____

_____

_____

_____

3. What strategies must you employ to reach the audience identified in 2b above? How will you *position* your work in the mind of this person? In other words, how will your reader know that your project is just what he or she needs? You may not have a clear idea of what strategies to take right now, but do the best you can. I'll provide more guidance later on.

_____

_____

_____

_____

4. What is your emotional reaction to this exercise? _____

_____

If you feel some small amount of excitement, then that means you are seeing more clearly how you might achieve your purpose. Keep moving forward!

If you feel some anxiety, then that is healthy, too. It means that you are seeing there is more to learn.

Likely, you are feeling some combination of those two emotions. The key, as discussed before, is to channel any emotion in a positive direction. Is there a little fear there, too? You know by now what to do with that—dismiss it, or go through it with your Warrior energy.

The features and benefits of your written work

In any sales situation, the "informed" sales person presents features and benefits. *Features* constitute the logical argument; *benefits* are emotional. This book features information on how to create a strategic marketing plan and presents two sample plans. The benefit to you is that now you have a proven tool for making your writing dreams a reality.

An insurance agent will show you the features of the policy and run the numbers, showing you the "face amount" of the policy and how values will accrue. Then the agent will turn to you and say in a most solemn way, "How will you feel 20 years from now, Next Great Writer, when your little girl looks up to you with tears in her eyes and says, 'Daddy, Mommy, thank you for thinking ahead and making it possible for me to graduate from college. I'll always be grateful.' How will you feel then?" That's the emotional appeal, right? (Please recall our discussion of "features and benefits" with regard to brochures in the "Copywriting" chapter of Book III.)

Some time ago, I was trying to sell my car, and an engineer dropped by. In a quick analysis of my audience, I guessed that he would be interested in specific features and facts about my car. After all, engineers are logical, emotionless people. But his reactions to this approach were all negative. During the test drive, however, I turned on the radio. And he said, "Whoa, what's that?"

I thought to myself, "It's your emotional hot button and I am about to use it as a strategy in presenting an emotional argument (or benefit) for buying the car." Here's how I applied my positioning strategy. I said, "What kind of music do you like?" He liked classical, so I dropped in a tape and said, "Imagine yourself driving through the Irvine hills. Just you, the road, and Mozart." Well, he bought a stereo with a car attached.

Here's a writing story. I was pitching to a magazine editor. I had in mind an article on writing. I was giving her a run-down of the important features of the article, including length, sidebars, and so on. She sounded interested. What cinched the deal, however, was this benefit: Her readers had never seen something on the *real story* within the story. I knew this was a real need and benefit to her, so I offered to write a separate sidebar on that topic alone. She offered me an extra C-note for the sidebar. I accepted.

In your strategic analysis, jot down the features and benefits of your writing project to the specific person to whom you will try to sell it.

Refer back to the application exercise above where you identified your purpose, audience, and strategy. In the worksheet below, list your project's features. Then, list the benefits of each feature as they might appeal to your two audiences—the eventual *reader* and the immediate *buyer* (the real audience).

Features	Benefits to reader	Benefits to buyer
_____	_____	_____
_____	_____	_____
_____	_____	_____
_____	_____	_____
_____	_____	_____
_____	_____	_____
_____	_____	_____

One of the most important features (and benefits) of your work is the *core concept*. The concept is a single sentence that communicates to the reader that your work is something that he or she must read. Marketers need a handle that they can grasp. Potential buyers will ask you, "Describe your story/book/article/script in 25 words or less." They will want to know this because this is what they will use to sell your project to higher-ups and eventual readers. (To see how this applies to specific writing areas, see Book III.)

If concept is king, then enthusiasm is queen. And the king is nothing without his queen. Your enthusiasm and conviction about your project are probably your most important assets after the project itself. The voice of conviction is what sells the concept. Enthusiasm is contagious. Your conviction and enthusiasm will be communicated through your most excellent creative-writing skills, via telephone conversations, and occasionally in person.

Always remember that in the world of marketing, perception is reality, and how you present your writing influences how it is perceived by others.

Let's create your project plan right now.

Project plan

The worksheet that follows will help you create a project plan and focus your marketing strategies.

Your project is the specific work you wish to write and sell. The exceptions are cases where you are seeking a writing assignment (as in business writing), and the specific project has not yet been identified.

After you identify your target market, complete the remaining worksheet. Naturally, you will adapt the plan to your specific purposes. You may not need to complete every section, and some sections you may wish to expand.

Title _____

Type of work (book, greeting card, brochure, etc.) _____

_____

Purpose or goal for the project _____

_____

Concept _____

_____

_____

Description of *eventual reader*, including any demographics and psychographics. (Psychographics is lifestyle information. What are your prospective readership's lifestyle choices. How do these readers see themselves? Hip, religious, on-the-edge, intelligent, open-minded, red-blooded American patriot, animal-lover, hunter? What reference groups do they identify with? Democratic party, Philadelphia Eagles, Joe's Bar?) _____

_____

_____

_____

Name and briefly describe the company (publishing house, business, magazine, agency) you wish to approach. (Note: If there is more than one possible company or person whom you might sell to, then see below.)

_____

_____

_____

_____

_____

Sometimes there are many different prospects for your work, not just one. For example, there may be several different agents and publishers that would be perfect for your proposed book. List each potential publication, client, or buyer below.

_____

_____

_____

_____

_____

_____

_____

_____

_____

_____

_____

_____

_____

_____

Note: Complete the remainder of the project plan for each entity named above. This might require making photocopies of this worksheet.

Name of specific person I must sell first (the *real* audience) _____

_____

Description of that person (if not available, rely on your description of the person's company) _____

_____

_____

_____

Current needs of that person or company _____

_____

_____

_____

Buying history of that person or company _____

_____

_____

How that person likes to be contacted _____

_____

How does your writing project or your writing services or other abilities differ from those with whom you are competing? What makes your project, services, or abilities original? What fresh twist do you add?

_____

_____

_____

_____

_____

List the features and benefits of your project and your writing services as they relate to the above-named project. The term "reader" refers to all of the people who will eventually read your work. The "buyer" is the *real audience*, the decision-maker you must sell your work to before it is distributed to the reader.

Features	Benefits to reader	Benefits to buyer
_____	_____	_____
_____	_____	_____
_____	_____	_____
_____	_____	_____
_____	_____	_____
_____	_____	_____
_____	_____	_____

What other strategies should be considered? _____

_____

_____

_____

Your action plan

Your strategic marketing plan is not complete without a list of the key activities that are going to bring you results. What will you accomplish by the end of this week? Here, you identify specific activities and tasks. And always remember to *keep writing*—that's the point.

What if the goal is not achieved, or a milestone is not met by a certain date? All is not lost. Expectations should be flexible. You will simply make a flight adjustment.

When you take the time to plan, you make your dreams real. Suddenly they are achievable, and you feel empowered as you do the little things that add up to the big things you want to achieve.

Here's what you have accomplished thus far: You have identified your personal values and writing values, and have created a writing mission statement. From there, you have identified goals, then milestones and project plans.

The next step is to implement your plans. This is where the rubber hits the road. The time for preparation has passed, and the time for action has arrived. For some writers, all that's needed is the answer to this single question: *What is the most important thing I can do this week to achieve my goal or milestone?* And that may be all *you* need before your mount your charger. However, if you want to sharpen your focus, then I hope you find the next worksheet to be helpful.

◆ ◆ ◆ ◆ ◆

Complete the Weekly Action Plan worksheet on the same day of every week. On that day, you should review all of your goals and evaluate what you have accomplished so far. Ask yourself: Do I need to make any course corrections? Make this action-planning session a weekly habit or ritual. If you prefer, use the same worksheet for a monthly action plan. Don't forget to reward yourself for a successful week or the achievement of a milestone or goal.

Weekly Action Plan

Main goal _____

Key milestones for this week:

1. _____

2. _____

3. _____

Time commitment _____

What specific actions and tasks will you undertake this week to achieve your milestones? *Note: To prioritize the action list below, place an "A" beside each of those actions and tasks that will likely bring the best results, and do those first.*

Writing _____

Marketing research _____

Meetings, pitches, groups, networking _____

Query letters and proposals _____

Cold calls and phone calls _____

Submissions of completed work _____

Follow-ups by mail, e-mail, or fax _____

Follow-ups by phone _____

Self-promotion activities _____

Competitions _____

Other _____

Other _____

Other _____

Notes: _____

Obviously, many activities regarding the same project or the same milestone can overlap. I don't think that you have to go so far as to create a PERT (Program Evaluation and Review Technique) Chart, but certainly with complex projects, you can estimate the amount of time it may take to complete certain activities and gauge which activities need to be completed before others can be begun.

Keep records

Keep track of every contact you make. Use the Queries & Submissions Log on the next page to keep track of queries and submissions you mail out. In the second column, the "Q" stands for "Query" and the "S" stands for "submission." Just use the applicable letter in that column. In the final column, you can jot down any comments you want to make to yourself, such as a reminder of when to follow up. When you get a response, jot down the date and results.

The Meetings, E-mail & Telephone Log is for any meetings you attend and any calls you make or that are made to you. In the third column, the "M" stands for "meetings," the "E" stands for "e-mail," and the "T" is for "telephone." Just write the applicable letter in that column.

Consider maintaining a file (or a 4" x 6" card) on each contact and jot down impressions and other comments in that file (or on that card). For example, if a client or potential client likes to talk about his daughter, jot that down. Next time you call him, ask about his daughter. If an editor tells you to keep her in mind in the coming year, jot it down.

You can't possibly remember everything that is said. You are a writer, so write things down. Include the date of the contact, so you'll know how long it has been and when you should contact that person again. Nurture your relationships. As Joan Rivers cleverly put it, "It's not *who* you know, it's *whom*." Your most important business assets are your skills and your contacts. And keep in mind the Purpose-Audience-Strategy Principle whenever you correspond or converse with anyone.

Besides the obvious marketing reasons for maintaining logs and records, you'll enjoy presenting these to the slack-jawed IRS agent at the audit.

Queries & Submissions Log

Date	Q/S	Title	Person/Company	Comments, response, follow-ups

Meetings, E-mail & Telephone Log

Date	Time	M/E/T	Person/Company	Comments, ideas discussed

A writing career within one year

If you are just starting out and seek a writing career, I recommend that you pick one of the 17 areas described in Book III. Choose one or two that appeal to you in terms of your values. Become reasonably proficient at them, and then add another writing area, probably one that is similar to the one or two in which you are proficient. Focus on those at first.

You can build your business quickly or slowly, create a part-time career or a full-time career. It's all up to you. In that process, continue to learn about writing and the writing business. Develop your craft and hone your marketing skills.

Roberto was a student of mine who did not believe it possible to have a full-time writing career within one year. However, once he focused on his desire and applied the principles explained in this "Bible," he saw his dream come true just seven months later.

For another writer, it was 18 months before she felt financially secure enough to become a full-time professional writer. Still another student made her "break" at the ten-month mark.

What will it be for you? While we can't say with absolute certainty, I urge you to set your goal and strive to achieve it.

Many people love their current jobs and only want to make some extra income as writers. I think that's wonderful! So is becoming the full-time writer you've yearned to be. *Whatever your desire, create a plan, and you may be surprised at what you ultimately accomplish.*

◆ ◆ ◆ ◆ ◆

What follows is an actual plan created for a beginner who had not yet sold a single article or story. His desire was to start out part-time, and then be able to quit his full-time job after one year to become a full-time, traditional writer. He wanted to eventually write a proposal for his Great American Novel, get a contract, and write the book he had always longed to write.

225

The plan has been adapted for this book. Names and other details have been changed. Some areas may contain more information than would normally be found so that you can follow the reasoning. In other areas, there may be less.

Sample Strategic Marketing Plan #1

Major Goal: I, Bob Dunn, resolve to establish a successful part-time writing business so that on this date next year, I can quit my teaching job and work full-time as a writer. A part-time writing business shall be defined as the ability to make a minimum of $30,000 a year in areas that match my talents and writing mission statement. Naturally, I'll be able to make more than that as a full-time writer. Although money is not an issue this year, it will be next year.

Milestone #1 – Define my time commitment within the next two days. I am thinking of somewhere between 12-20 hours a week.

Milestone #2 – Get published or sold within a month to establish some small level of credibility. At the moment, I have no writing credits and have not had anything published.

Milestone #3 – Continue my education by reading in the areas that I wish to write for.

Milestone #4 – Establish something of a regular income (and some writing credits) in the areas of video scripts for science education and article writing. If I can write five video scripts, I will earn a minimum of $12,500. I've already checked with my contacts listed below. I love travel, science, and sports. I want to publish two or three travel articles (with photographs) in several different newspapers, and then sell another article to a travel magazine. In addition, I want to write a weekly column or regular feature for a city newspaper. At some point, I'd like to self-syndicate my column, but I will not count on that for this first year. I have a science article idea, and I have targeted *ATV Magazine* for another article. I have selected mid-level publications that I think I have a good shot at. At my current writing schedule, the above efforts should take me only ten weeks at the most to write. I realize there will be a lot of time spent selling and learning the ropes, but I also see that I will very likely have time to write much more than I have mentioned in this plan. That would translate into more income. This milestone will be broken down into at least a dozen project plans, and probably many more.

These efforts should bring in at least $20,000, and will lay an excellent foundation for the second year due to my accumulated credits and experience. In addition, I'd be able to save about half the money I make as a writer because I would still have my teaching salary. Because I will make $20,000 in my first year as part-time writer, I can expect to do much better in my second year as a full-time writer. Thus, I will "easily" achieve my goal of making $30,000 a year as a writer in my second year.

Milestone #5 – Within one year, write and sell two short stories or personal essays to gauge my ability to succeed at my ultimate goal—sell a science-fiction novel.

List of assets and resources:
I am a science and science-fiction nut, so my knowledge of these areas is very strong. I have taught high school science for several years. I have read heavily, both fiction and nonfiction.

I know three producers of educational films. One has already asked me about my ideas. All three are approachable and open. They could also refer me to people and distributors who hire.

As a teacher, I am a communicator. I have a strong desire. I have a lot of story ideas in my head.

Current contacts: Slim, Bill, and Sally—educational video contacts.

Potential challenges and how met:
Challenge #1 – I am a single father with a teenaged boy. He is resistant to the idea of my becoming a writer because he's afraid of lost time together. I am going to involve him with my writing, ask his opinion of my work, share ideas with him, ask him to go with me to mail queries. I will also contact some publications aimed at teenagers, and maybe write a story

just for him. We can continue to take little trips and ride our ATVs as long as I use those trips as source material for some of my articles.

Challenge #2 – The financial sacrifice will be minimal. I still have my job, and the only costs are postage, paper, and incidentals. There will be a sacrifice of time. I'm going to choose only two football, baseball, or basketball games a month to watch on TV, and savor those with my son—make them real events. The others I will sacrifice. I know I can find time to write because I find time to read. In fact, I may need to cut back on the reading. I will make a commitment of 12-20 hours a week to my writing business [Milestone #1].

Challenge #3 – Fear of failure and making a fool of myself in front of my son. In science, there is a lot of failure before discovery, and I'm applying that mindset to this adventure. I am unsure of how much ability I have, so the prospect of testing myself in this area is scary. However, I've been scared before doing a lot of things in my life. I just need to press forward and realize that my abilities will develop.

Challenge #4 – I have no writing credits. To establish myself, I need to publish a couple of things quickly. I'm sure I can get something into the local paper—it's a start. I have an idea for a weekly column or regular feature on nature and hiking trails.

Note: What follows are two project plans. These two are representative of the many that were created.

Project Plan #A

Title: Happy Trails (Milestone #2)

Type of work: Articles

Purpose or goal for the project: Get published or sold within a month to get some writing credits.

Concept: Articles or a column about walking trails, hiking trails, equestrian trails, bike trails, mountain-bike trails, and ATV trails.

Description of eventual reader, including any demographics and psychographics: The target market is age 14-40, active, outdoorsy, and a lover of nature. This person likes to hike, bike, or ride trails for exercise or recreation. This person reads the recreation section of the newspaper, and probably the sports section. Income level is almost irrelevant. There may be more males interested in ATVs and mountain bikes than females. Otherwise, both sexes enjoy getting out into nature.

Name and brief description of company you wish to approach: The *Herald* is a local newspaper that does not feature anything about trails in its sports section.

List other potential publications, clients, or buyers: A second publication is *The Tribune*, a city newspaper that also doesn't feature anything about trails. In addition to a daily sports section, it has a weekly recreation section.

My plan is to place one or two articles in the *Herald* for free. I can't imagine them passing up the opportunity to highlight two beautiful but largely unknown trails in the area. Once accomplished, I want to propose a "Happy Trails" column to the *Tribune*. It would be a weekly or even monthly column, and it would be free for the first two months. After that, I would hope to earn at least $10 per column. The result would be two published articles and possibly a credit as a columnist. If the *Tribune* doesn't go for the column, I could probably place another article in their paper. That's three credits in one month.

Name of specific person I must sell first (the real audience): I have the name of the person to contact for each of the two newspapers, but I know nothing about them.

Description of that person or company: Not known.

Current needs of that person or company: The *Herald* needs these articles because trail users form a large portion of their readership. I got that information by calling the newspaper.

Buying history of that person or company: Nothing is being sold. This is a free offering.

How that person likes to be contacted: I talked to the editor's secretary, and she said he (the editor) responds to e-mails.

How does your writing project or writing services or other abilities differ from those with whom you are competing? What makes your project, services, or abilities original? What fresh twist do you add? It's unique because no one is addressing this area. Only occasionally do I see something along these lines in the newspaper. It's a gap in their coverage.

List the features and benefits of your project and your writing services as they relate to the above-named project. The term "reader" refers to all of the people who will eventually read your work. The "buyer" is the real audience: the editor or decision-maker you must sell your work to before it is distributed to the reader.

Features	Benefits to reader	Benefits to buyer
Article is 300 words, but can be longer.	Easy to read.	Small space commitment.
Photographs provided.	Can actually see the featured trail.	Photos add value because they catch the eye.
Article focuses on specific trail with tips for users.	Usable information.	This is a service to readers.
Article and photos are free.	N/A	No expenditure.

What other strategies should be considered? Perhaps, it would be best to go to the newspaper's office with the photographs. If the editor is not available, I can leave the photographs plus the article in an envelope for him. That would be better than an e-mail. Since papers are now built around visuals, the photos will catch the editor's eye and draw him in.

Project Plan #B

Title: "Runaway Genome"

Type of work: Short story

Purpose or goal for the project: 1) Get published in a literary magazine or science-fiction magazine. 2) Test my fiction-writing abilities.

Concept: A cloning experiment goes wrong, resulting in a wondrous-yet-dangerous new creation.

Description of eventual reader, including any demographics and psychographics: A science-fiction enthusiast, 75% chance of being male and young. Ages 14-30 would be the main demographic. Above-average intelligence. Likes to imagine other "worlds."

Name and brief description of company (publishing house, business, magazine, agency) you wish to approach: See below

List other potential publications, clients, or buyers below.

1. *Azimov's Science Fiction.* I am a subscriber. It's 98% freelance-written.

2. *Rosebud* (literary magazine), 85% freelance-written and publishes 1-3 months after acceptance. They're a good prospect for a quick, literary credit.

3. *Absolute Magnitude: Science Fiction Adventures.* It's 95% freelance-written. Publishes one year after acceptance. Pays up to $2,000 on acceptance.

4. *The Iconoclast* (literary magazine), 90% freelance-written, pays on acceptance, responds quickly.

5. *Analog Science Fiction & Fact.* I read this one on occasion. It's 100% freelance-written and they pay on acceptance.

6. *Starlog Magazine*, 90% freelance-written, responds quickly, and publishes three months after acceptance.

I like starting with #2 and #6, only because of their fast response and the chance of getting published rather quickly.

Note: For the remainder of Project Plan #B, Azimov's Science Fiction will be used as an example. Information on science-fiction markets is gleaned from The 2004 Writer's Market.

Name of specific person I must sell first (the real audience): Gardner Dezois

Description of that person: Not known.

Current needs of that person or company: Science-fiction. No explicit sex or senseless violence, and no "sword and sorcery." He likes character-driven stories, and serious but accessible stories.

Buying history of that person or company: Science-fiction mainly. Eighty percent freelance-written. He's open to new writers because some of his best stories have come from new writers.

How that person likes to be contacted: Accepts queries by mail, so I should flesh out the story and write a synopsis to make sure I understand the pluses of my story, and then begin the query process. I can write a draft of the story during the wait for a response.

How does your writing project or writing services or other abilities differ from those with whom you are competing? What makes your project, services, or abilities original? What fresh twist do you add? It's unique because most cloning stories are horror stories in which cloning is shown to be a bad thing. In this case, the clone becomes a new, wonderful creation. That brings many interesting issues into the story's subtext.

List the features and benefits of your project and your writing services as they relate to the above-named project. The term "reader" refers to all of the people who will eventually read your work. The "buyer" is the real audience, the editor or decision-maker you must sell your work to before it is distributed to the reader.

Features	Benefits to reader	Benefits to buyer (editor)
Original storyline that meets stated needs and avoids no-no's.	Captures interest.	No wasted time; positive reading experience.
Will query and submit according to instructions; I am a subscriber.	Likely to meet expectations.	He's found a writer who reads writer's guidelines and the magazine—relief! He's "connected" to readers.
Story will not be overly long.	N/A	Easier to find room for it.

What other strategies should be considered? I should state in my query that I am a subscriber and a science teacher.

Weekly Action Plan

Main goal: A successful part-time career during the next six months, so I can go full time next year.

Key milestones for this week:

1. Establish a regular income with scripts and articles.

2. Sell two short stories.

Time commitment: 14 hours.

What specific actions and tasks will you undertake this week to achieve your milestones?

Note: To prioritize the action list below, place an "A" beside each of the above actions that will likely bring the best results. Do those first.

Writing: Nine hours finishing a travel article for *Heartland* magazine. Two hours on my short story. Spend the remaining three hours with the following activities:

Marketing research: Investigate the teenage market for science-fiction stories so I can write one for my son. Write *Zoetrope* for sample copy ($6), but first check their writer's guidelines online.

Meetings, pitches, networking: None.

Query letters and proposals: Write a query to *Coast to Coast* magazine concerning my travel article idea. Wait a week before revising and sending it.

Cold calls and phone calls: None

Submissions of completed work: None

Follow-ups by mail, e-mail, or fax: None

Follow-ups by phone: Call Rod at *Rosebud* about submitted article.

Self-promotion activities: None.

Competitions: None.

Notes: _____

_____

◆ ◆ ◆ ◆ ◆

I hope you find the above examples informative and motivating. Naturally, it is not necessary to use these worksheets as they are laid out, or even use them at all. The main thing is to use both sides of your brain to create a workable plan. Don't think that just because the plan is in writing you must follow it religiously. The plan may need to be adjusted as time goes by.

How to make $100,000 a year

Think of yourself as a consultant, because as a professional writer, that is what you are. In many of the areas of writing that we have explored, you act as a general contractor or producer; that is, you put together the projects and bring in specialists or subcontractors to do some of the work.

In Book III, you learned how to multiply your profits. You also reviewed 17 writing areas. Writers have made six-figure annual incomes in each of the 17 areas. That is not the average income for any of those areas, so the question becomes, *What makes the difference?*

Part of the answer is in your vision and desire.

Part is in the development of your writing skills and in doing what you were born to do (Book I and Book II, and some aspects of Book III).

Part of the answer is in your knowledge of the business (Book III).

And part of the answer is in creating a focused, purposeful plan to achieve specific goals (Book IV). That gives you a laser-sharp focus.

The word LASER is an acronym for Light Amplification through Stimulated Emission of Radiation. A laser requires much less energy to accomplish its purpose than an ordinary flashlight because the process described in the acronym synchronizes all of the light waves so they have exactly the same cycle. Thus, no energy is scattered; everything is focused on the goal. The lasers you see in planetariums only require a few watts of electricity to produce those dazzling shows.

In a way, one of my goals is to help you become laser-like and supremely effective.

◆ ◆ ◆ ◆ ◆

Although you can make an excellent income in any of the 17 areas, some are more promising than others. Copywriting, direct-mail writing, book writing, DVD/video scriptwriting, certain kinds of ghostwriting, and all of the entrepreneurial areas are prime targets for the writer who wants to make the big bucks. Some novelists, screenwriters, and TV writers make seven figures.

Thousands of writers have earned and do earn six figures annually. Why not you?

◆ ◆ ◆ ◆ ◆

The following plan is adapted from an actual strategic marketing plan created by an experienced writer (whose name was changed as well as many of the details). You will find more explanation in some areas than would normally appear so that you can follow the writer's reasoning. In other areas (such as the list of contacts), there may be less.

Sample Strategic Marketing Plan #2

Major Goal: I, Marina Martin, resolve to make $100,000 by January 1. Once this goal is achieved, I will reward myself and my family by scheduling a *Bike Vermont* family vacation for the following fall or late summer.

Milestone #1 – Facilitate a 20% increase in business with current clients during the coming calendar year. Last year, I earned $73,500. A 20% increase will result in a total amount of $88,200 for the coming year.

Milestone #2 – Find at least ten new clients between May 1 and August 31 who will hire me to do a brochure or its financial equivalent. Ten brochures should bring me $6,000 at my current rate. I am waiting to start this campaign in May to allow time to get a strong start on Milestone #1.

Milestone #3 – After Labor Day, follow up on new clients and prospects that did not "bite" the first time. Make sure all of my clients' needs are being met. The results of these efforts will bring in at least another three clients ($1,800) and at least $4,000 additional business from the new clients captured during the spring and summer. That will bring my total income to $100,000. I realize that a few of my invoices will not be paid on time, and there might even be a bad debt or two, but that will be compensated for by the additional income I believe I will make beyond the above estimates.

Milestone #4 – Flesh out an article idea on the subject of pottery-making (my hobby) and identify a few magazines for it. Do this as time becomes available. I am doing this for fun and for a change of pace, and also to begin looking at other writing markets.

List of assets and resources:
Nearly a hundred people have hired me to do work for them. Most of those have hired me more than once. Seven clients have provided sterling testimonials. So I have a rather solid clientele.

My writing skills are getting sharper. It is taking me much less time to do the same work I once did. I have a variety of items in my "portfolio." I am doing work I enjoy and have no plans to change—I represent stability to clients.

My family is behind me all the way. I have all of the tools (computer, etc.) that I need.

Current contacts and possible contacts:
Let's summarize this section. I have 94 contacts, 7 of which have given me testimonials. Applying the Pareto Principle [80% of your earnings come from 20% of your clients], I've listed the clients who have paid me the most. As expected, there are 20 clients who comprise 78% of my business. I need to nurture these. I see this as still another milestone, a key point to keep in mind.

I identified the characteristics of these 20 clients. Most work for larger companies, but some own their own small businesses. Since these clients have been the most profitable for me, I want to identify more potential clients that resemble them. I will do that once I have achieved Milestone 1. However, during the first four months, I will keep this [Milestone #2] in mind, and certainly I will get ideas and see opportunities in the course of business. I may also get referrals from current clients.

Potential challenges and how met:

Challenge #1 – Affects the first three milestones: I'm still having some trouble asking for the business. Sometimes, I feel myself drawing back, restraining my cheery personality. I think the basis of this is the fear of being seen as the stereotypical salesperson. I have succeeded by seeing myself as a professional or consultant. I have a valuable service that helps my clients make more money. I just need to maintain that mindset. I'm getting more and more comfortable with the "people stuff" each month.

Challenge #2 – Affects Milestone #1: I need a carefully planned strategy to avoid a possible backlash from clients not appreciating being approached for more business. This is not really an obstacle. As my friend Dave puts it, I hit them with a velvet glove and they don't feel a thing. My approach is always "client oriented" and "solution driven." I talk about their needs. "How can I serve you better?" So far, I have only seen one negative reaction to my numerous direct questions.

Challenge #3 – Affects Milestones #1 and #2: There will be some additional costs to create the right materials to bring in the additional business. I will write and produce a newsletter to go out to current clients, but I will also be able to use it when I prospect for new clients this spring and summer, so I will be creating it for two different groups of people. Perhaps, I should include those seven testimonials. Since I can produce it myself, the only cost will be the printing. After reviewing my website, I would like to make adjustments that make it more relevant to new clients. My computer guy will charge about $150 for those. The big question is the campaign to get new clients. I've tentatively decided to mail out the newsletter with a brief sales letter. I will follow up by telephone or in person. The time to create all of the above will be about 20 hours at the most and cost about $500. Add another $200 for postage. That's well within my budget.

Challenge #4 – Affects Milestone #2: There could be a time problem in Months 4-8. It will take extra hours bringing in the ten new clients. I need to take into consideration vacations. I'm going to send out about 400 newsletters to targeted businesses. I've estimated about 20-30 hours identifying individuals to contact. I'll need another 20 hours to create all of the materials. Follow-ups will actually take much less time since I will use the phone or drive by as I am seeing another client or running an errand. I will use "motion efficiency": that is, plan a route to minimize my time on the road. So, all told, my efforts should not take more than three weeks combined time. I may have to put in a few nights.

Challenge #5 – Affects Milestone #3: I foresee the usual resistance from new clients. What do I have to offer? I have a variety of items in my portfolio now, a website, testimonials, and proven skills. And I will have a newsletter with useful information. In addition, I have some experience now handling objections and the resistance to change.

◆ ◆ ◆ ◆ ◆

Note: What follows is the plan for just one project, the creation of a brochure. Another project plan might have as its purpose the following: Find ten new clients in four months. The project plan worksheet below could be used to define that campaign. The concept for such a plan might be: Focus on meeting the writing and marketing needs of prospective clients.

Project Plan

Title: n/a

Type of work: Brochure

Purpose or goal for the project: Write copy that directs the eventual reader to call a toll-free number to order a commemorative medallion.

Concept: The magic of Disney is now captured in pure gold. Be one of the few to own this keepsake, treasured for a lifetime. The Disney name must be prominent because it catches the eye and conveys values that resonate with our target market. (Note: This is an actual project, though not originally a part of this particular strategic marketing plan.)

Description of eventual reader, including any demographics and psychographics. The target market is between 30 and 65, a parent or grandparent, and a lover of Disney. This person has positive associations with Disney. He or she may subscribe to *Disney Channel Magazine* or be on some specific Disney mailing list for having bought Disney products in the past. This person is probably more traditional than contrarian, and has a love or affection for his or her children or grand-children. He or she may read magazines like *Family Fun* that cater to parents of children ages 7 to 11. We are looking at middle-class parents and grandparents who will buy it for themselves or as a gift. The very poor and the very rich will be less likely to buy.

Name and brief description of company (publishing house, business, magazine, agency) you wish to approach: The *real* audience is already sold. This project has already been commissioned to me.

List each potential publications, clients, or buyers: N/A

Name of specific person I must sell first (the real audience): In this case, it is the person who has already hired me to do the brochure.

Description of that person: Linda is fastidious; likes things done on time according to specs. It is best to present exactly what she wants and then pitch alternative creative ideas. She is defensive; she does not like glitches. Let her feel in charge of the project, the creator of ideas.

Current needs of that person or company: Although cost is important, it is not nearly as important as results. She knows that she needs to spend money to make money. Her main personal need is to impress her manager and higher-ups. She needs this project to be successful.

Buying history of that person or company: N/A

How that person likes to be contacted: Always by phone. Do not use e-mail.

How does your writing project or writing services or other abilities differ from those you are competing with? What makes your project, services, or abilities original? What fresh twist do you add? N/A. I already have the assignment.

List the features and benefits of your project and your writing services as they relate to the above-named project. The term "reader" refers to all of the people who will eventually read your work. The "buyer" is the real audience, the decision-maker you must sell your work to before it is distributed to the reader.

Features	Benefits to reader	Benefits to buyer
The Disney name.	Recalls memories of happy times and family times.	Pride.
Gold piece.	Value, permanence, worth keeping.	N/A
Limited-edition proof of Disney characters.	Rare collectible to show others or give to a loved one.	N/A
Many options to order.	Easy to buy and pay for.	Encourages sales. Meets main objective of brochure to get people to buy now.

What other strategies should be considered? Make sure the brochure copy is ready before the deadline to allow for changes. Ask for visuals from clients in advance. In terms of the eventual buyer, the brochure must use language that evokes emotions the target audience associates with Disney—memories of fun, freedom from cares, family values and togetherness. The Disney world is a world apart, a world worth remembering. It must also convey a sense of timelessness and high value. We are presenting a very rare opportunity that should not be taken lightly. Use "second" person as always (use "you" rather than "we").

Weekly Action Plan

Main goal. Make $100,000 by January 1.

Key milestones for this week:

1. Facilitate a 20% increase in business with current clients.

Time commitment: 44 hours, a full week.

What specific actions and tasks will you undertake this week to achieve your milestones? (*Note: To prioritize the action list below, place an "A" beside each of those actions and tasks that will likely bring the best results, and do those first.*)

Writing: I need three hours to write the copy for the full-page ad for Sam (A). Also, Jack's brochure copy—five hours. Much less important is the corporate brochure; I still have a couple of weeks to write it, and there's the question over the visual elements, so I better call Suze about that.

Marketing research: None.

Meetings, pitches, groups, networking: From last week's efforts, I have four appointments scheduled with clients to discuss their needs for the next several months (A).

Query letters and proposals: I need to write a proposal for the referral I met last week—that's just an hour at the most, but an "A" priority (A).

Cold calls and phone calls: Call another 20 clients to follow up on the newsletter I sent them and ascertain needs. (I only call 20 a week so I have time to evaluate and adjust my approach, if necessary.)

Submissions of completed work: Sam's ad, already mentioned (A). Get Jack's brochure copy to him by Friday—e-mail it for review.

Follow-ups by mail, e-mail, or fax: None

Follow-ups by phone: Jim at X Company about that direct-mail/ad campaign—I would love to get that assignment (A).

Self-promotion activities: Look ahead for networking opportunities this spring.

Competitions: None.

Notes: _____

_____

Support and resources

The most important support you can get is from yourself. Be positive with yourself. Don't kick yourself if you fail to achieve a certain goal. Be kind, but not indulgent. The support you get from loved ones and other writers is a bonus.

Websites, publications, and books

Subscribe to *Writer's Digest* magazine. It is comprehensive and motivating.

Another publication I have mentioned is *Publisher's Weekly,* which keeps you up-to-date on book publishing. Go to a library and review a few issues before subscribing to this specialized magazine. You will also find *Books in Print* and *Forthcoming Books* there (or visit www.bowker.com).

Other books I have mentioned include *The Writer's Market*, published annually by Writer's Digest. It's a huge help to writers of articles, stories, poetry, nonfiction books, and novels. The same magazine has created a similar source book just for children's authors—*Children's Writer's and Illustrator's Market.* There are similar specialty books for photographers, songwriters, poets, and humor writers. A similar book is available in Canada, entitled *The Canadian Writer's Market* by Sandra B. Tooze.

For book writers, I like Jeff Herman's *Writer's Guide to Book Editors, Publishers, and Literary Agents.*

I should not forget an industry favorite, *The Literary Marketplace.*

It's not hard to find the right book for whatever special need you have. These books abound at libraries, bookstores, and on the Internet, and they are featured in writers' magazines.

If you are seeking sources for your book or article, start with www. google.com, www.profnet.com, and www.newslink.org.

◆ ◆ ◆ ◆ ◆

My website **www.keepwriting.com** is committed to helping writers succeed. You'll find "free updates" to *The Freelance Writer's Bible* and information on how to get more worksheets. (Incidentally, send any comments, success stories, or suggestions for future printings of this "Bible" to dave@keepwriting.com.) Keepwriting.com also provides a list of carefully selected books and links to other websites that I believe will help you the most. Look for other tips, resources, and services at keepwriting.com—as well as a list of writers' groups.

Grants, awards, and contests

There are numerous grants and awards available to writers. Grants are paid before you write. Awards are paid after. Contests are worth looking into as well. They can help you get a general sense of where you stand in comparison with other writers, and if you win, it's a plus you can add to your query letter. Some contests provide feedback on your work that can be helpful.

Information on awards and contests can be found in *The Writer's Market*. For grants, there are several sources. Perhaps the best is *Grants and Awards Available to American Writers* by the PEN American Center (www.pen.org) at 568 Broadway, 4th Floor, New York, NY 10012. Another is the *Annual Register of Grant Support* (www.infotoday.com) and *Foundation Grants to Individuals* (http://gtionline.fdncenter.org). For a list of every government-assistance program that exists, including grants, see the *Catalogue of Federal Domestic Assistance* (www.cfda.gov).

Grants are awarded by corporations, private organizations, and the government. As you search through the many grants available, make sure you qualify to apply. Many have very specific requirements. For example, one grant is only available to certain tribes of Native Americans. It's okay to call the grantor in advance to verify requirements. Don't call to ask what your chances are or to pitch your grant proposal to see if it's close to what they want. Of course, in a conversation about requirements, you may get a better sense of what they are looking for.

Most grantors seek projects that meet a need and that ties in with the grantor's goals or philosophy. Put yourself in their shoes. Why are they giving this money away? Who do they want to give it to? Why?

Your written proposal should be about 5-10 pages long. It will contain a title page, followed by an executive summary, overview, or abstract. This is not the same as an introduction; it is a summary of your entire proposal. Generally, a statement of purpose should follow the summary. Define your project and its objectives. Include your qualifications. If you've had a past success in a similar project, then definitely state that.

The next section is key. You need to sell the grantor on why the money is needed. You might include a budget, if appropriate. List the steps or procedures you intend to take once the money is granted. Be sure to outline the benefits of the project. What will be the happy result?

Keep in mind that the above is a general outline. The grantor may suggest a different approach. Essentially, you are showing the grantor that you are in agreement with its requirements and goals and that you have a clear vision and the ability to make it happen.

Colonies and conferences

There are probably at least 30 writing colonies across this country. If you dream of an idyllic natural setting where you can contemplate the mysteries of eternity and write in peace, then consider one of these. Each retreat is unique and has its own requirements and policies. As with grants, you must qualify with some kind of admissions proposal. Residencies can range from a week to several months. And although you will usually be required to contribute to your room and board, the amount will usually be low. Many are free. For a list, visit www.poewar.com/articles/colonies.htm or www.shawguides.com (which also lists conferences).

Writing conferences can be very energizing. You learn more about your craft, but I think you mainly benefit from the "good vibrations" and energy you feel at these events. The excitement is contagious. You often get ideas. There's something positive about rubbing shoulders with other writers. Of course, don't spend so much time with conferences and groups that you forget to write, but such adventures can give you an emotional and creative boost.

An additional benefit is that you can network with editors and other professionals. Be prepared to pitch your work and yourself. Keep track of any contacts you make. These may pay off later. I met an editor at such a conference, jotted down the gist of that conversation, and then forget about her. Three years later, I wrote something that I realized was suited just for her. Thank heavens I still had my notes from that earlier meeting. I got through her door when other writers could not.

I know one writer who found a mentor at a conference. Usually the best way to find a mentor is to connect with a successful local writer. In fact, you might even meet such a person in a writers' group.

Writers' groups and organizations

Writers' groups are everywhere if you know where to look. Here are five general areas to begin your search.

1. Network with fellow writers at conferences, workshops, and seminars. Ask them if they know of any writing groups.

2. Read the classified ads of writing publications. Many groups and individuals advertise, seeking to form or continue a group. Some groups may have special requirements.

3. Consider joining a large, professional organization such as The National Writers Association (www.nationalwriters.com), the Canadian Authors Association (www.canauthors.org), National Writers Union (www.nwu.org), or the Editorial Freelancers Association (www.the-efa.org).

4. Ask bookstores and librarians if they know of any writers' groups. Sometimes writers' groups form at book-signings and other bookstore activities. Ask non-writing friends who might know writers.

5. Surf the web. There are many online writing groups such as www.fmwriters.com and www.writing.com. Many writing lists (sometimes

called listservs) are available. Think of these as bulletin boards that you subscribe to with an e-mail. Begin your search at www.egroups. com and www.onelist.com. Sometimes editors pop in to these list-servs! Also, search for writing blogs (short for weblogs) and other online-discussion bulletin boards.

If your search for a writers group proves fruitless, there's only one thing left to do—start your own group. Here's how to attract writers.

Meet them at conferences and workshops. Network with them. Trade phone numbers. Hand out flyers. Ask the workshop or seminar leader to put your name and phone number on the board because you'd like to start a writers' group. That way, interested writers can call you. Post a notice or sign-up sheet on bulletin boards in classrooms and at conferences. Ask me to post a notice at www.keepwriting.com.

While you are forming the group, you will want to create some rules or guidelines that can be mutually agreed upon. Here are some things to keep in mind:

Include writers who are basically at the same level. One group might consist of beginners—people who are just getting started. Another group might set a requirement of having published something. Many screenwriting groups require at least one completed screenplay.

Keep the group small. Five people may be enough. Seven is an ideal size. If you start with 12-15 people, you'll likely end up with the magnificent seven who are dedicated. On the other hand, some groups function well with large numbers.

Make it a participative group. You may need a facilitator to head the group, but make sure everyone has an equal say in making rules. You might even rotate responsibilities (such as making reminder calls and assigning/bringing refreshments) so that no one is unduly burdened. Take care that your meeting does not become a social hour. There will be plenty of time to socialize before and after the meeting.

Have a place to meet. This will probably be someone's house. It might be easier to use the same location continuously, but some groups like to rotate. Many libraries, savings and loan associations, and other businesses have "community rooms" that are without cost for non-commercial use. You qualify if admittance to your group is free. Have a regular meeting time—the first Tuesday of every month, or every Wednesday at 7:30. Get people into a routine.

Decide on the purpose of the group. You might go as far as to create a mission statement.

Establish protocol. Some groups focus on one or two writers per session. Some groups require members to send the work to others in advance of meetings. It's often profitable to read selections aloud (or silently) at the meeting itself and evaluate them on the spot, or address writing ideas and specific writing problems. Members can keep each other informed on writing opportunities or coming events.

Make sure critiquing sessions do not deteriorate into slugfests. Writers should avoid a defensive posture. Listen carefully, avoid speaking, take the advice seriously, but remember that you are the writer of your work. Criticism should be given constructively. Members should avoid speaking in absolutes, but instead offer their opinions, reactions, observations, and suggestions. Each member should agree to a code of silence. Everything discussed or read is confidential.

After a period of months or years, a motivating routine develops into a fatiguing rut. Since all members of the group are creative, this problem can be solved by being creative. Here are some ideas to get you started.

- Organize a swap night• "I'll read yours if you'll read mine."

- Sponsor a contest, or challenge another group to a competition.

- Compile a collection of query letters or rejection letters.

- Have a special award or recognition when a writer passes a milestone.

- When groups get too large, create specialized areas such as "Nonfiction writers" or the "Travel writers' chapter." You can have a short, large meeting for everyone, and then break into the specialized groups. As a matter of fact, maybe your group should be specialized from the start.

In the best writers' groups and organizations, a feeling of camaraderie develops, enabling each writer to root for the other's success. It's an upward spiral of positive energy that revitalizes every writer. This is the fuel each writer needs to keep writing.

A personal challenge

I want you to know that I have enjoyed being your mentor and walking this path with you. Little did you know when you began that you would be standing on a mountain. There is much that you see about yourself and your future as a writer that is new.

And, of course, you see other mountains.

My hope is that your writer's odyssey will be increasingly satisfying, fulfilling, and profitable. You have not chosen an easy road. For that reason alone, I salute you. Continue to draw from your inner resources and believe in yourself.

When you get up in the morning, face the person in the mirror and say, "I am the next great writer." Then perhaps one morning, you may awaken to find that you *are* the next great writer.

Don't be surprised. Just keep writing.

Dave Trottier
keepwriting.com

Index of writing opportunities

Advertising . . . 73, 93-106, 112, 122, 149, 159
Animation . . . 145
Annual reports . . . 102
Anthologies . . . 142, 172
Articles
    children's . . . 169
    consumer . . . 120, 123-127, 242
    e-zines . . . 94, 98, 168, 185-187, 189-191
    foreign markets . . . 125, 127, 168
    ghosted . . . 119-120
    magazine . . . 123-136
    newspaper . . . 136-137
    trade . . . 123-127, 242
Audio cassette scripts . . . 111, 172, 181, 184
Autobiographies . . . 120
Automotive writing . . . 69

Bios . . . 120
Booklets . . . 102, 117, 179, 181
Books
    children's . . . 168-172, 242
    electronic . . . 187-188, 191
    fiction . . . 162-168, 172
    non-fiction . . . 150-162, 234, 242
    packaged . . . 119
    self-published . . . 172-185, 234
Brochures . . . 27-28, 70, 93-106, 122, 238-240, 241
Business plans . . . 118
Business writing . . . 91, 92-123, 186-187

Cable shows . . . 113, 148
Case studies . . . 108
Catalogs . . . 201, 104, 192
Cause writing . . . 110-111
Charities . . . 110-111, 121
Children's literature . . . 168-172, 242
Churches . . . 91, 110, 171
Columns
    business . . . 94
    magazine . . . 137, 138-139
    newspaper . . . 137-140
Comic books . . . 144
Commercial writing . . . 15-16
Consulting . . . 188-192, 234
Copy editing . . . 122
Copywriting . . . 92, 93-106, 107-117, 234
Copywriting fee schedule . . . 92
Curriculum . . . 111

DVD scripts . . . 111, 112-117, 184, 234
Direct mail . . . 93, 94, 98, 102, 104-105, 110, 175-176, 179, 181, 234

E-books . . . 187-188, 191
Editing . . . 111, 212-122
Editorials . . . 137
Educational games . . . 172
Educational DVDs/videos . . . 112-117, 172, 184, 226
Educational writing . . . 110-111, 112-117, 172, 184, 187, 227, see "Teaching"

Entrepreneurial writing . . . 15, 16, 101, 235

Essays . . . 67, 71-73, 129, 135, 138, see "Articles"

E-texts . . . 187

E-writing . . . 94, 98, 132, 185-192

E-zines . . . 94, 98, 168, 185-187, 189-191

Fantasy . . . 166

Fee schedule . . . 92

Fiction
ghosted . . . 118-119
novels . . . 162-168, 168-172, 172,187-188, 203, 235, 242
stories . . . 125, 140-141, 169, 172,231, 242

Flyers . . . 93, 95, 98, 102, 179

Foreign markets . . . 125, 127, 168

Freelance fee schedule . . . 92

Fundraising . . . 110

Gags . . . 144

Games . . . 51, 144, 172, see "Interactivesoftware"

Ghostwriting . . . 109, 118-122, 234

Government writing . . . 110-111, 113, 243

Grant proposals . . . 120-121 243

Greeting cards . . . 142-143

Histories . . . 110, 120, 149

Humor . . . 135, 142-144

Infomercials . . . 112

Instructions . . . 118

Interactive software . . . 114, 172

Internet . . . 93, 185-188, see "e-writing"

Job shopping . . . 117

Journalism . . . 19, 136-140

Licensed books . . . 171

Lyrics . . . 141, 142

Magazines . . . 123-136, 140-142

Manuals . . . 111, 117-118

Marketing collateral . . . 93, 102, 105,106, 110, 122, 189

Medical writing . . . 113-114

Military writing . . . 113

Movies . . . 145-148, 235

Mysteries . . . 134, 166

Newsletters
business . . . 93, 102, 104, 109, 111
self-published . . . 173, 180, 182-183,184, 185
subscription . . . 138, 182-183

Newspapers . . . 136-140

Non-profit organizations . . . 93, 110-111,113, 120, 121

Novels . . . 162-168, 168-172, 172, 187-188, 203, 135, 242

PSAs . . . 149

Pamphlets . . . 111

Placement letters . . . 108-109

Play writing
adult . . . 149
children . . . 171

Poetry . . . 62, 141-142, 142-143, 172, 242

Poetry anthologies . . . 142

Political writing . . . 110, 173

Press kits . . . 106-107

Press releases . . . 106-108, 188, 192

Print ads . . . see "Advertising"

Producing . . . 149, 234

Product releases . . . 108

Proposals
business . . . 110, 111, 118, 191, 211
book . . . 150, 154-162, 165
educational . . . 172

Public relations writing . . . 106-109

Puzzles . . . 144

Radio ads . . . 106

Radio writing 120, 144, 149

Reporting . . . 19, 136-140

Reports . . . 93, 102, 111, 117-118, 173, 180, 191

Romance . . . 162, 166, 170-171

Resumes . . . 121

Sales brochures . . . 102-104

Sales letters . . . 98, 104, 105, 175, 176

Science fiction . . . 166

Science writing . . . 226
Screenwriting . . . 145-148, 235
Script doctors . . . 120
Self-publishing . . . 16, 172-185, 187,
    188, 190, 234-235
Sermons . . . 120
Short fiction . . . 125, 140-141, 169,
    172, 231, 242
Sitcoms . . . 148
Slim jims . . . 102
Soap operas . . . 148
Song writing . . . 141, 142
Specialty letters . . . 108-109
Speeches . . . 108, 109, 120
Stories . . . 125, 140-141, 169, 172,
    231, 242
Stringer . . . 137

Teaching . . . 188-192, see
    "Educationalwriting"
Technical writing . . . 117-118, 119, 211
Telemarketing scripts . . . 110
Television ads . . . 105, 106
Television writing . . . 145-148, 235
Textbooks . . . 172, 187
Traditional writing . . . 16
Travel writing . . . 125, 136-137

Video games . . . see "Games"
Video scripts . . . 111, 112-117, 184,
    234

Web writing . . . 186-187
Writing franchises . . . 182

zines . . . see "e-zines"

General Index

AIDA . . . 105
Abstract . . . 151, 244
Accounting . . . 87-89, 110, 127
Action Plan . . . 219-222

Active voice . . . 79-80
Ad agencies . . . 93, 103, 106, 113
Advance, The . . . 152, 165, 188
Advertising . . . 73, 89, 93-106, 112,
   122, 149, 159, 175, 186, 192
Affirmations . . . 5, 21, 55
Agents . . . 145-146, 147, 150, 165,166-
   168, 169, 242
Aigner-Clark, Julie . . . 184
Alchemy . . . 4, 35-52, 56, 57, 62, 66-
   67
All rights . . . 126, 147, 187
Alpha state . . . 52
Alpha writer . . . 52
Amazon.com . . . 151, 178, 180
Ambivalence . . . 46-47, 202
American Comedy Network . . . 144
American Medical Writers . . . 114
Anger . . . 42-43, 53
Animation . . . 145
Annual reports . . . 102
Anthologies . . . 142, 172
Anxiety . . . 44, 213
Archetypes and the Collective
   Unconscious . . . 33
Art Directors . . . 95, 96, 102, 103, 105,
   109
Articles
   children's . . . 169

consumer . . . 120, 123-127, 242
e-zines . . . 94, 98, 168, 185-187,
   189-191
foreign markets . . . 125, 127, 168
ghosted . . . 119-120
magazine . . . 123-136
newspaper . . . 136-137
trade . . . 123-127, 242
writing process . . . 123-124
Association of Authors' Representatives
   . . . 167
Atlantic Monthly . . . 140
Attache Magazine . . . 123
Attitudes . . . 17-19, 45-46, 90-91, 95
Attorneys . . . 88, 126, 152, 167
Attracting clients . . . 93-99
Audience . . . 80, 111, 117, 138,
   151,171, 176, 183, 214, 219, 229,
   see "Purpose-Audience-Strategy"
Audience, real . . . 72, 211, 212,
   214,218-219, 229, 230
Audio cassette scripts . . . 111, 172,
   181, 184
Audio-Visual Communications . . . 112
Autobiographical . . . 42
Autobiographies . . . 120
Automotive writing . . . 69
Awards . . . 243-244

Baby Einstein . . . 172, 184
Bach, Richard . . . 6
Barriers . . . see "Blocks"
Best efforts . . . 106, 109, 121
Bios . . . 120

Blocks . . . 4, 29-35, 35-52, 62,70, 154, 157, 208
Blogs . . . 191, 246
Book hook . . . 163
Book proposal
    children's . . . 170
    non-fiction . . . 150-162
    novel . . . 163-165
Book signings . . . 151, 166, 180, 245
Booklets . . . 102, 117, 179, 181
Booklocker . . . 187
Books
    children's . . . 168-172, 242
    electronic . . . 187-188, 191
    fiction . . . 162-168, 172
    non-fiction . . . 150-162, 234, 242
    packaged . . . 119
    self-published . . . 172-185, 234
Books in Print . . . 151, 242
Boris the Bug . . . 58-59
BottomLine Personal . . . 138
Boxes . . . 124
Bradbury, Ray . . . 64
Brainstorm . . . 14, 29, 64, 65, 174-175, 179, 192, 206
Brochures . . . 27-28, 70, 93-106, 122, 238-240, 241
Business cards . . . 90, 94-95
Business license . . . 87
Business plans . . . 118
Business writing . . . 91, 92-123, 186-187

CRM Films . . . 112
Cable shows . . . 113, 148
Calling card . . . 94-95, 96, 98
Campaigns . . . 94-98, 104, 106, 120,122, 175, 176, 179, 181,237, 238
Campbell, Joseph . . . 4, 162
Canadian Author's Association . . . 245
Canadian Writer's Market . . . 90, 242
Case studies . . . 108
Catalogs . . . 201, 104, 192
Cause writing . . . 110-111
Chapter books . . . 170
Character/Draft Worksheet . . . 44-45
Charities . . . 110-111, 121
Children's literature . . . 168-172, 242
Children's non-fiction . . . 172
Christmas Box, The . . . 173

Churches . . . 91, 110, 171
Clips . . . 90, 91, 129, 130, 132, 136
Clustering . . . 65-66
Collective unconscious . . . 33
Colonies . . . 244
Columns
    business . . . 94
    magazine . . . 137, 138-139
    newspaper . . . 137-140
Comic books . . . 144
Commerce Business Daily . . . 111
Commercial writing . . . 15-16
Commission . . . 168
Commitment . . . 6, 35, 51, 162, 197, 198, 199, 220, 226
Concept . . . 75, 114, 128, 132, 133,138, 143, 163, 215
Concept importance . . . 163
Conferences . . . 69, 167, 189, 197, 244-245, 246
Confidence . . . 40, 95, 205
Conscious . . . 48, 53-56, 62
Consulting . . . 188-192, 234
Contacts . . . 166, 168, 191, 206,208, 222, 245
Contacts file . . . 222
Content 62
Content provider . . . 186
Contests . . . 129, 142, 205, 243, 247
Contracts . . . 91, 100, 107, 111, 117, 121, 122, 126, 127, 145, 147, 152, 153, 168, 170, 173, 187, 189, 192, 225
Copy editing . . . 122
Copyright . . . 16, 126, 189
Copywriting . . . 92, 93-106, 107-117, 234
Copywriting fee schedule . . . 92
Cosmopolitan . . . 72
Courage . . . 29, 32
Cover letter . . . 121, 129, 141, 143,146, 150, 151, 163
Cox, Kerry . . . 134
Creative artist . . . 54, 56
Creative bubbles . . . 65-66
Creativity . . . 52-63, 128
Curriculum . . . 111

DVD scripts . . . 111, 112-117, 184, 234

Darlings . . . 46
DaVinci, Leonardo . . . 55
Demographics . . . 212, 216, 228, 230, 238
Dickens, Charles . . . 81
Differentiation 209
Direct mail . . . 93, 94, 98, 102, 104-105, 110, 175-176, 179, 181, 234
Discipline . . . 4, 6, 21, 44, 162
Distribution . . . 166, 179, 180, 181
Doubt . . . 27, 30, 40-41
Dramatic rights . . . 126

E-books . . . 187-188, 191
E-cards . . . 143
Editing . . . 79-82, 111, 121-122
Editor & Publisher's Syndicate Directory . . . 140
Editor & Publisher's Yearbook . . . 139
Editorial department . . . 163
Editorial slant . . . 183
Editorials . . . 137
Editors . . . 46, 107, 108, 122, 130, 131, 137, 140, 143, 150, 169, 189, 245, 246
Educational DVDs/videos . . . 112-117, 172, 184, 226
Educational games . . . 172
Educational writing . . . 110-111, 112-117, 172, 184, 187, 227, see "Teaching"
Electronic rights . . . 126, 187
Empiricist . . . 55
Endorsements . . . 178, 179, 184
Enthusiasm . . . 21, 95, 215
Entrepreneur . . . 87
Entrepreneurial writing . . . 15, 16, 101, 235
E-publisher . . . 187
E-queries . . . 132, 137, 146
E-rights . . . 126, 187
Essays . . . 67, 71-73, 129, 135, 138, see "Articles"
E-texts . . . 187
Evans, Richard Paul . . . 173
Eventual reader . . . 211, 212, 214, 216
E-writing . . . 94, 98, 132, 185-192
Exaggerating . . . 39-40
E-zines . . . 94, 98, 168, 185-187, 189-191

FEAR (as an acronym) . . . 39
Fantasy . . . 166
Faulkner, William . . . 46
Faust . . . 69
Fear . . . 4, 27-35, 35-48, 61, 70, 199, 202, 208, 213, 228, 237
Features and benefits . . . 102, 129, 174, 175, 213-214, 218-219
Fee guidelines . . . 92
Fiction
    ghosted . . . 118-119
    novels . . . 162-168, 168-172, 172,187-188, 203, 235, 242
    stories . . . 125, 140-141, 169, 172,231, 242
First draft . . . 74, 77, 116
First rights . . . 126, 132, 137
Flyers . . . 93, 95, 98, 102, 179
For Dummies . . . 119
Foreign markets . . . 125, 127, 168
Form . . . 62
Forthcoming Books . . . 151, 242
Frame of reference . . . 71-72
Free verse . . . 141
Freelance fee schedule . . . 92
Freewriting . . . 8, 64-65, 75, 77
Fulfillment . . . 179, 181
Fundraising . . . 110

Gags . . . 144
Games . . . 51, 144, 172, see "Interactivesoftware"
Getting clients . . . 93-99
Getting paid . . . 100-101, 117
Getting started . . . 87-92
Ghostwriting . . . 109, 118-122, 234
Goals . . . 6, 37, 38, 77, 99, 195, 196, 197, 199-208, see "Purpose-Audience-Strategy"
Golden Books . . . 169
Government writing . . . 110-111, 113, 243
Grant proposals . . . 120-121 243
Grants for writers . . . 243-244
Grantsmanship Center . . . 121
Grapes of Wrath . . . 43
Greeting cards . . . 142-143
Grosset & Dunlap . . . 169
Gutenberg, Johan . . . 59

Harry Potter . . . 169
Hemingway . . . 37, 40, 69, 81
Herman, Jeff . . . 150, 166-167,242
Hero's journey . . . 4, 162
Hillenbrand, Laura . . . 74, 127
Hippaglobium . . . 61
Histories . . . 110, 120, 149
Holt, Robert . . . 183
Hook . . . 128, 150, 163
Humor . . . 135, 142-144
Humor and Cartoon Market . . . 144

IABC . . . 112
IRS . . . 88-89, 222
ISBN . . . 177-178
ITA . . . 112
Iambic pentameter . . . 62
Ideas, getting . . . 64-70
In Search of Excellence . . . 173
Infomercials . . . 112
Inner critic . . . 54, 56-57, 61, 67, 77, 131
Inner kingdom . . . 33-35
Inner writer . . . 14, 34, 53, 61
Inspiration . . . 38, 47, 54, 67, 79
Inspiration cycle . . . 67
Instructions . . . 118
Interactive software . . . 114, 172
Internet . . . 93, 185-188, see "e-writing"

Job shopping . . . 117
Journal, Learning . . . 68
Journal, Writer's . . . 5, 36, 42
Journalism . . . 19, 136-140
Journalize . . . 68
Jung, Carl . . . 33

Kill fee . . . 127
King . . . 33, 199
King Features . . . 140
King, Stephen . . . 40, 203

Lant, Jeffrey . . . 179-180
Lay down, The . . . 166
Lean writing . . . 131
Learning journal . . . 68
Left brain . . . 48, 54-56, 57, 61, 62, 64, 68
Legalities . . . 87-89, 126, 152, 167,

174, 178, 184, see "Contracts"
Lennon, John . . . 60
Letter of agreement . . . 100
Letterhead . . . 90, 94-95, 128
Licensed books . . . 171
Listservs . . . 245-246
Literary Marketplace, The . . . 119,150, 167, 178, 242
Logs . . . 48-50, 222-224
London, Jack . . . 38
Lover . . . 33-34, 38, 200
Lyrics . . . 141, 142

Magazines . . . 123-136, 140-142
Magician . . . 33, 199
Mailing lists . . . 104, 174, 175, 178, 179, 181, 184
Manuals . . . 111, 117-118
Manuscript guidelines . . . 125
Marketing collateral . . . 93, 102, 105,106, 110, 122, 189
Marketing principles . . . 209-219
Marketing research . . . 123, 210
Maslow, Abraham . . . 81
Medical writing . . . 113-114
Meditation . . . 7, 44, 52-53, 64
Michelangelo . . . 62
Middle readers . . . 170
Milestones . . . 203-205, 208
Military writing . . . 113
Mind mapping . . . 65-66
Mini-movie . . . 30-35
Mission statement . . . 20-23, 53, 95, 195, 220, 247
Motion efficiency . . . 238
Motion picture rights . . . 126
Movies . . . 145-148, 235
Multi-level marketing . . . 112, 118
Multiply profits . . . 122, 124-125,127, 179, 234
Muse . . . 37-38, 159
Muse and Lover . . . 38
Museheimer's Disease . . . 37-38
Music . . . 38, 68
Mysteries . . . 134, 166

National Newspaper Association . . . 139
Networking . . . 91, 95-96, 97, 109,119, 189, 221, 245, 246

New Yorker, The . . . 141
Newsletters
    business . . . 93, 102, 104, 109, 111
    self-published . . . 98, 173, 180, 182-183, 184, 185
    subscription . . . 138, 182-183
Newspapers . . . 136-140
Non-profit organizations . . . 93, 110-111, 113, 120, 121
Novel proposal . . . 163-165
Novels . . . 162-168, 168-172, 172, 187-188, 203, 135, 242

Odyssey . . . 248
On acceptance . . . 127, 231
On publication . . . 127
One Minute Manager . . . 172
One-time rights . . . 126, 137
Option . . . 147
Oprah . . . 151
Organize . . . 47, 74, 90, 118, 247
Orion the Hunter . . . 58
Outline . . . 47, 74, 76, 77, 78, 115, 121, 123, 153, 164, 174, 203

PERT chart . . . 221
POD . . . 178, 184
PQN . . . 178, 184
PSAs . . . 149
Packages . . . 119
Pamphlets . . . 111
Paradox, The Great . . . 61-63
Parameters . . . 70-77, 114, 115, 138, 150, 182
Parents . . . 123
Pareto Principle . . . 204, 236
Perfectionism . . . 36-37
Permissions . . . 152, 177
Persig, Robert . . . 55
Persistence . . . 6, 44
Person 21, 73
Peters, Tom . . . 173
Photographs . . . 107, 124, 125, 152, 230
Picture books . . . 169-170
Pitch . . . 113, 128, 129, 130, 131, 141, 146, 147, 148, 151, 152, 170, 180, 211, 239, 243, 245
Pitch letter . . . 128, 129, 146
Placement letters . . . 108-109

Play writing
    adult . . . 149
    children . . . 171
Poetry . . . 62, 141-142, 142-143, 172, 242
Poetry anthologies . . . 142
Poetry contests . . . 142
Polish . . . 79-82
Political writing . . . 110, 173
Portfolio . . . 94, 113, 236, 238
Positioning 211, 214
Power Cycle . . . 195-196
Premiere Radio Network . . . 144
Press kits . . . 106-107
Press releases . . . 106-108, 188, 192
Print ads . . . see "Advertising"
Priorities 14, 18, 220
Procrastination . . . 30-31, 35-36, 47
Producer . . . 45, 113, 128, 129, 145, 146, 147, 148, 149, 234
Producing . . . 149, 234
Product releases . . . 108
Production values . . . 114-115
Program directors . . . 192
Project plan . . . 216-219
Proofreading . . . 82
Proposals
    business . . . 110, 111, 118, 191, 211
    book . . . 150, 154-162, 165
    educational . . . 172
Psycho . . . 61
Psychographics . . . 212, 216, 228, 230, 238
Public Relations Society ofAmerica . . . 109
Public relations writing . . . 106-109
Publishers . . . 45, 72, 75, 126, 133, 141, 143, 150, 151, 152, 163, 165, 166, 168, 171, 172, 173, 177, 180, 184, 187
Publisher's Marketing Association . . . 185
Publisher's Weekly . . . 122, 151, 172, 242
Purchase order . . . 100, 101, 117
Purpose-Audience-Strategy . . . 70-75,94, 209-213, 222
Puzzles . . . 144

Query . . . 94, 109, 120, 123, 124, 125,

127, 128-136, 139, 141, 142, 144,
145, 146, 147, 150, 163, 167, 172,
209, 211
Quest . . . 4, 21-23, 22, 26, 199-200,
207

Radio ads . . . 106
Radio interviews . . . 159, 160, 189
Radio writing 120, 144, 149
Random House . . . 169
Real audience . . . 72, 211, 212,
214,218-219, 229, 230
Reference group . . . 216
Referrals . . . 96, 118, 122, 136
Reframe . . . 40, 196
Relaxation . . . 7, 44, 47, 48, 51, 52-53,
63, 64, 67, 77, 79
Reporting . . . 19, 136-140
Reports . . . 93, 102, 111, 117-118,
173,180, 191
Reprint rights . . . 126, 132
Research . . . 67, 74, 77, 101, 113, 117,
121, 122, 123, 137, 139, 144, 145,
153, 167
Residuals . . . 117
Restrictions and creativity . . . 61-63
Resumes . . . 121
Revising . . . 78-79
Right brain . . . 54-56, 61, 62, 68
Right word . . . 21, 81, 84
Rights . . . 125-126, 127, 132, 139,
171, 177, 187
Rituals . . . 14, 38, 69, 220
Rock, Brad . . . 138
Rolling Stone . . . 123
Romance . . . 162, 166, 170-171
Romance your service . . . 103
Romeo & Juliet . . . 69
Royalties . . . 117, 142, 149, 152, 165,
169, 170, 171, 187, 188

SASE . . . 130, 131, 139
Safe harbor . . . 7, 30, 44, 52-53, 64, 69
Salenger Films . . . 112
Sales brochures . . . 102-104
Sales letters . . . 98, 104, 105, 175, 176
Sample book proposal . . . 154-162
Sample marketing plans . . . 225-241
Sample queries . . . 132-136
Samuel French . . . 171

Schedule C . . . 88-89
Science fiction . . . 166
Science writing . . . 226
Scientific method . . . 53
Screenwriter's Bible, The . . . 148, 176,
182, 184
Screenwriting . . . 145-148, 235
Scribaphobia 35-36
Script doctors . . . 120
Script format . . . 116
Seabiscuit . . . 74
"Second Effort" . . . 113
Second rights . . . 125, 126, 132
Segmentation . . . 209
Self-defeating attitudes 45-46
Self-promotion . . . 188-192
Self-Publisher's Manual . . . 178, 180
Self-publishing . . . 16, 172-185, 187,
188, 190, 234-235
Self-talk . . . 34, 41-42, 53
Series books . . . 119, 162, 169, 170
Sermons . . . 120
Shakespeare . . . 69
Short fiction . . . 125, 140-141, 169,
172, 231, 242
Short runs . . . 178
Sidebar . . . 124, 214
Simultaneous queries . . . 163
Simultaneous rights . . . 126
Simultaneous submissions . . . 124, 165
Sitcoms . . . 148
Slant . . . 72, 76, 123, 129, 139, 183
Slim jims . . . 102
Soap operas . . . 148
Society for Technical Communication
. . . 118
Song writing . . . 141, 142
Sonnett . . . 62
Spec script . . . 145
Specialty letters . . . 108-109
Speeches . . . 108, 109, 120
Standard Rate and Data . . . 106
Stationery . . . 90, 94-95, 128
Steal . . . 69
Steinbeck, John . . . 43
Stereotypes . . . 170
Stories . . . 125, 140-141, 169, 172,
231, 242
Strategy...see "Purpose-Audience-
Strategy"

Stress reduction . . . 53
Stringer . . . 137
Stuck . . . 47-48, 56, 79
Stuckitis . . . 47-48
Subconscious . . . 53-56, 62, 68, 155
Submission guidelines . . . 121, 124, 125, 130, 141, 143, see "Writer's guidelines"
Subsidiary rights . . . 126
Sweet William Cottage . . . 108-109
Syndication . . . 139, 140

Tale of Two Cities . . . 81
Taylor, J. D 73
Tax deductions . . . 110
Taxes . . . 87-89
Teaching . . . 188-192, see "Educationalwriting"
Technical writing . . . 117-118, 119, 211
Telemarketing scripts . . . 110
Television ads . . . 105, 106
Television rights . . . 126
Television writing . . . 145-148, 235
Testimonials 93, 97, 178, 179
Testing . . . 99, 104, 175-176, 179, 181
Textbooks . . . 172, 187
Therapy . . . 5
Thesis . . . 71, 73, 76
Time . . . 5-6, 39, 48-52, 196-198, 220, 226
Time log . . . 48-49
Traditional writing . . . 16
Transmutation 35, 40, 43
Travel expenses . . . 89
Travel writing . . . 125, 136-137
Trottier's Theory of Evolution . . . 202
Twain, Mark . . . 69

Updates . . . 5, 243
Ultimate viewer . . . 114

Values . . . 10-11, 14, 17-19, 21, 138, 196, 197, 200, 220, 225
Victoria . . . 108
Video games . . . see "Games"
Video scripts . . . 111, 112-117, 184, 234
Viewer . . . 114
Virgo the Virgin . . . 57
Visualize . . . 36, 38, 52, 68

Voice over . . . 115, 116

WGA . . . 145
Waitley, Denis . . . 28
Warrior . . . 28, 32, 33-34, 36, 179, 199-200, 202, 213
Web host . . . 188, 189
Web logs...see "Blogs"
Web site . . . 94, 130, 132, 174, 178, 186, 187, 188, 189-191
Web writing . . . 186-187
What if? . . . 60, 70, 79, 129
White, E. B 38
Word-of-mouth . . . 99, 122
Wordsworth, William . . . 62
Worry . . . 44
Writer's Block . . . see "Blocks"
Writer's Digest 90, 123, 172, 242
Writer's Golden Rule . . . 42
Writer's groups . . . 47, 245-248
Writer's guidelines . . . 72, 108, 121, 123, 124, 130, 131, 127, 141, 143, 233
Writer's journal . . . 5, 36, 42
Writer's Market . . . 90, 123, 231, 242
Writer's notebook . . . 36, 67, 68
Writer's recorder . . . 67, 68
Writing as therapy . . . 5, 14
Writing business . . . 87-91
Writing colonies . . . 244
Writing conferences . . . 69, 167, 189, 197, 244-245, 246
Writing environment . . . 89
Writing franchises . . . 182
Writing mission . . . 20-23, 53, 95, 195, 220
Writing opportunities . . . 249
Writing partners . . . 153
Writing plan . . . 74-77, see Book IV
Writing process . . . 63-82, 114, 121, 123-124, 153
Writing rituals . . . 14, 38, 69, 220

"You" attitude . . . 105
Young adult novels . . . 120-121

Xlibris . . . 187

Zen . . . 55, 56
zines . . . see "e-zines"

Support for Freelance Writers

- **Free *MUSELETTER* and *Bible* Updates**
- **QUERY LETTER EVALUATION**
- **ONLINE COURSES**
- **LINKS TO WRITING RESOURCES and MORE**

www.keepwriting.com

– Everything for the Writer –

~ ~ ~

Another book by Dave Trottier:

THE SCREENWRITER'S BIBLE
A Complete Guide to Writing, Formatting, and Selling Your Script

4th Edition – Expanded and Updated

Available at bookstores everywhere
and www.keepwriting.com